Old Testament

Who's WHO

ILLUSTRATED EDITION

Old Testament

Who's WHO

ILLUSTRATED EDITION

A Comprehensive Guide to the People in the
Old Testament and Pearl of Great Price

Ed J. Pinegar · Richard J. Allen

Front cover images (clockwise from top left): *Moses Parting the Red Sea* by Robert T. Barrett © Intellectual Reserve, Inc.; *Jonah Is Cast Ashore* © Robert T. Barrett; *An Atonement Sacrifice Is Presented to the Priests* © Robert T. Barrett; *Samson and the Philistines* © Robert T. Barrett.; *City of Zion* by Del Parson © Intellectual Reserve, Inc.; *Jacob Blessing Joseph* by Harry Anderson © Intellectual Reserve, Inc. Courtesy of the Church History Museum; *Elijah Contends Against the Priests of Baal* by Jerry Harston © Intellectual Reserve, Inc.; *Daniel Refusing the King's Meat and Wine* by Del Parson © Intellectual Reserve, Inc.; *Where Is Thy Brother?* © Walter Rane. Courtesy of The Stable Gallery, 801-355-6872; *The Lord Fulfilleth All His Words* by Clark Kelley Price © Intellectual Reserve, Inc. Courtesy of the Church History Museum; *Moses and the Brass Serpent* by Judith Mehr © Intellectual Reserve, Inc.

Back cover and spine image: *Moses Ordaining Joshua* by Darrell Thomas © Intellectual Reserve, Inc.

Cover design copyrighted 2009 by Covenant Communications, Inc.

Published by Covenant Communications, Inc.
American Fork, Utah

Copyright © 2009 by Ed J. Pinegar and Richard J. Allen.

Printed in China
First Printing: October 2009

15 14 13 12 11 10 09   10 9 8 7 6 5 4 3 2 1

ISBN 10: 1-59811-850-1
ISBN 13: 978-1-59811-850-6

Preface

For many a mortal, the journey of life is an aimless quest on the seas of doubt. For others, buoyed by the gospel light, there is joy in the passing of time toward a sure and certain goal—the return to the home we seek in the glorious presence of the Father and the Son. If we belong to the latter group, then our ship is our faith in God, our compass is His word, our sails are moved by His Spirit, and our travel companions consist of the loved ones dear to our heart.

The eternal plan of happiness is not a fuzzy and abstract Utopian dream dancing in our fantasy beyond the distant horizon; rather, it is a clear and concise plan of power and action for today—this very hour and all the hours to come until the destination is attained. The voice of the Lord, conveyed through the words of His chosen prophets, calls to us through the pages of holy writ—the panoramic record of the Old and New Testaments, the fulness of the gospel preserved in the Book of Mormon, and the fundamentals of exaltation unfolded through the Doctrine and Covenants and the Pearl of Great Price in our own dispensation.

For some, the Old Testament represents a vast ocean of complexity obscured by the shadows of antiquity, masked by the unfamiliar patterns of distant cultures, and diluted by the claims of unsympathetic interpreters that it represents only legend and myth. Viewed, however, through the lens of gospel truth and illuminated by the light of continuing revelation, the Old Testament emerges for what it truly is—the wellspring document of God's inexorable design for bringing to pass the immortality and eternal life of His faithful children through priesthood blessings, saving ordinances, and the power to endure to the end.

Magnificent in scope and detail, inspiring in thematic content, and riveting in its anecdotal abundance, the Old Testament is the foundational scripture of the divine canon. Above all else in terms of mission and purpose, the Old Testament—augmented by the books of Moses and Abraham from the Pearl of Great Price—constitutes a grand and glorious exposition of the character, qualities, and mission of the Messiah. The thoughtful and prayerful reader cannot ponder the ancient passages of scripture concerning the Savior without being touched spiritually by the profound significance of His love, the mercy of His longsuffering, and the majesty of His divine intercession on behalf of mankind.

Considered separately, any one of the prophets of the Old Testament—whether Adam, Melchizedek, Moses, Isaiah, or any of the rest—presents an inspiring memorial of the truths of the gospel of Jesus Christ. But considered together—as if in a constellation of heavenly lights configured about the central glory of the Father and the Son—the prophets offer a vivid and magnificent array of witnesses to the verity of God's saving principles and ordinances. It is in the blending of their testimonies—just as Nephi stood forth to offer his word, intermingled with that of his brother Jacob and the prophet Isaiah, all three having seen the Lord in person (see 2 Nephi 2:1–4)—that we have irrefutable evidence of the truth of the plan of happiness as confirmed by multiple witnesses and the whisperings of the Spirit.

Across the vast landscape of the Old Testament we see a panoramic view of mixed scenes, encompassing alternately both a wasteland patchwork of man's prideful intemperance and sin as well as fertile pastures of penitence, humility, and covenant devotion. As travelers across this terrain, we labor in grief and sorrow (as did Enoch in Moses 7:20–40) over the accounts of Israel's travail under the burdens of wickedness; but we also rejoice from time to time through our encounters along the way with scenes of grandeur and triumph as the Lord's prophets and disciples, leaders and Saints, men and women both, rise on eagle's wings to the potential of their God-given destiny. Such are the spiritual oases that beckon the anxious traveler seeking the fountains of living water to quench their thirst for truth, truth that is embedded in the sacred chronicles of the Lord's dealings with His children.

As authors and compilers, our purpose in preparing this volume—*Who's Who in the Old Testament: A Comprehensive Guide to the People in the Old Testament and Pearl of Great Price*—is to render more accessible the wealth of wisdom unfolded in the lives of the key individuals who populate the landscape of this sacred volume of scripture. Our primary guide has been the scriptures themselves. Wherever possible, we have included specific scriptural references to bring these personalities to life before our eyes. The Lord said unto Moses: "All things are present with me, for I know them all" (Moses 1:6). Our hope is to make the leading personalities of the Old Testament and Pearl of Great Price seem veritably "present" unto the readers so that they may "know them all." We have added a chronological chart at the end of the work to aid in the task of tracing the milestones of development over the generations covered by the Old Testament.

Of the myriad personalities of the Old Testament—amounting to thousands—we have centered our focus on 423 entries (many with sub-entries of like name) that can be counted as among the most important first- and second-rank individuals included in the text. Our guide for selection, principally, has been the Bible Dictionary included in the King James Version of the Bible published by The Church of Jesus Christ of Latter-day Saints. In some cases we have augmented this array with the addition of other individuals who might be of interest to the readership—especially if these additions carry the same name as an Old Testament figure of renown. Other useful sources were *Encyclopedia of Mormonism*, ed. Daniel H. Ludlow, 4 vols. (New York: Macmillan, 1992), and Bruce R. McConkie's *Mormon Doctrine*, 2nd ed. (Bookcraft, 1966), among others. Online sources were at times helpful for cross-checking facts and perspectives, including *Easton's Bible Dictionary* and *Smith's Bible Dictionary*. In all cases, however, the accent has been on the scriptural text itself, especially as augmented by cross-references from other standard works of scripture (New Testament, Book of Mormon, and Doctrine and Covenants—plus the inspired Joseph Smith Translation of the Bible).

Our objective is centered chiefly on the hope that this material may be helpful to individuals, parents, and teachers who desire to strengthen testimonies of the truthfulness of the gospel of Jesus Christ and magnify the desire to honor covenant obligations with faith and valor. We are grateful to Covenant Communications for their service in bringing this work into circulation. We are grateful to the artists and illustrators who have added a keen visual perspective to the volume. We are especially grateful to our wives, Patricia Pinegar and Carol Lynn Allen, for their encouragement and support during the process of research and writing.

The Authors

TABLE OF CONTENTS

ABBREVIATIONS

DCE   Hoyt W. Brewster, Jr., *Doctrine and Covenants Encyclopedia* (Salt Lake City: Bookcraft, 1996)

FAR   Kent P. Jackson, *From Apostasy to Restoration* (Salt Lake City: Deseret Book Co., 1996)

JD   *Journal of Discourses*, 26 vols. (London: Latter-day Saints' Book Depot, 1854–1886)

MD   Bruce R. McConkie, *Mormon Doctrine*, 2nd ed. (Bookcraft, 1966)

TPJS   Joseph Smith, *Teachings of the Prophet Joseph Smith* (Salt Lake City: Deseret Book, 1976)

WJS   Joseph Smith, *The Words of Joseph Smith: The Contemporary Accounts of the Nauvoo Discourses of the Prophet Joseph*, comp. and ed. Andrew F. Ehat and Lyndon W. Cook, 2nd ed. (Brigham Young University: Religious Studies Center, 1996)

PRONUNCIATION GUIDE

For proper names that may be difficult to pronounce, a general guide using everyday English vowel applications is provided. Note that the use of the letter "y" in these applications always implies a long "i" (as in the vowel sound in words like *try*, *high*, *eye*, or *sky*). An example is the pronunciation of the name *Adonijah* as ad'-uh-ny'-juh. An accented syllable is marked with an apostrophe (') following the syllable. The pronunciations suggested in this volume are not intended to be definitive but to serve only as a general aid based on recommendations adapted from a variety of general sources.

AARON

Next to Moses, Aaron was the most pivotal figure in the Lord's cause to free the Israelites from Egyptian bondage, shape their spiritual preparation, and lead them back to the Holy Land (see Exodus 4:10–16, 27–31; 5:1 to 12:50). Aaron had the administrative keys and powers for the operation of the lesser priesthood—which has been perpetually named in his honor following Sinai—conferred upon him. He and his worthy progeny among the Levites were those designated to perform sacred rites and services on behalf of Israel down through the generations (see Numbers 18:20–23; 1 Chronicles 23:13). As the Apostle Paul confirmed, Aaron's priesthood calling by revelation and installation under the authority of prophetic leadership established the pattern of how divine commissions are conveyed and inaugurated: "And no man taketh this honour unto himself, but he that is called of God, as was Aaron" (Hebrews 5:4).

The first time Aaron is named in the Old Testament, it is in connection with his commission as spokesman for his younger brother Moses, who initially felt inadequate to assume the prophetic mantle (see Exodus 4:10, 14–16). The Psalmist characterized Aaron as "the saint of the LORD" (Psalm 106:16; compare Psalm 77:20; 115:10–12). Bruce R. McConkie stated: "As a possessor of the Melchizedek Priesthood, Aaron held a position of prominence and leadership among the elders. (Ex. 18:12; John Taylor, *Items on Priesthood*, p. 5.)" (*MD*, 9).

HISTORY: Aaron was born in Egypt, the son of Amram and his wife, Jochebed (see Exodus

Aaron assists Moses in the court of Pharaoh

6:20). His remarkable life and ministry lasted 123 years (see Numbers 33:39).

Aaron's life was marked at times by a need to show a spirit of penitence and remorse. While Moses was upon the holy mount receiving the tablets of the covenant, Aaron yielded to the enticings of the people in their desire for idols by preparing for them a golden calf (see Exodus 32:4). On another occasion, both Aaron and his sister Miriam reprimanded Moses for taking an Ethiopian woman to wife. Severe punishments followed both of these mistakes, and both Aaron and Moses, on Aaron's behalf, pleaded with the Lord for forgiveness and the lifting of the punishments. Finally, at the waters of Meribah, both Aaron and Moses offended the Lord by not faithfully following His instructions (see Numbers 20:7–12—see especially footnote 12a). For this indiscretion, they were both excluded from entry into the promised land (see Numbers 20:12, 24).

Despite these lapses, Aaron has been upheld in honor and dignity for the devoted service he performed as a priesthood leader and for his priesthood office. The Prophet Joseph Smith confirmed that John the Baptist "was a descendant of Aaron. . . . and held the keys of the Aaronic Priesthood" (*TPJS*, 272–73). The Aaronic Priesthood was restored in the latter days under the hands of John the Baptist on May 15, 1829 (see D&C 13; compare D&C 68:14–21). Furthermore, the worthiness of priesthood holders in serving in the house of the Lord and honoring the oath and covenant of the priesthood is embraced in the promised title "sons of Moses" and sons "of Aaron" (D&C 84:34).

Abed-nego in the furnace

ABED-NEGO

(Meaning: servant of Nego or Nebo.) Abed-nego (pronounced uh-bed'-nih-go) was a Jewish youth captured along with Daniel and several others (including Hananiah—later called Shadrach—and Mishael—later called Meshach) by the forces of King Nebuchadnezzar and taken to the Babylonian palace on the eve of the conquest of Jerusalem (around 587 BC; see Daniel 1:3–7). His real name was Azariah, but he was given the name *Abed-nego* by the prince of the eunuchs (see Daniel 1:7). *See entry for Shadrach for more details.*

ABEL

Abel was a righteous son of Adam and Eve—and one for whom the "LORD had respect" (Genesis 4:4; see Hebrews 11:4). Abel was born into an environment of gospel instruction, for his parents heeded the voice of the

Lord when "he gave unto them commandments, that they should worship the Lord their God" (Moses 5:5). Through angelic instruction, confirmed by the Holy Ghost, Adam was taught about the Atonement of the Only Begotten Son (see vv. 7–11) and he and his wife "blessed the name of God, and they made all things known unto their sons and their daughters" (v. 12)—including Abel. Abel, "a keeper of sheep" (v. 17), was not the oldest child—he and Cain came into mortality after Eve had already born unto Adam other "sons and daughters" (v. 2). However, Abel is singled out for his devotion and righteousness as one "who walked in holiness before the Lord" (v. 26). He willingly complied with the divine commandment to offer sacrifices: Abel "also brought of the firstlings of his flock, and of the fat thereof. And the Lord had respect unto Abel, and to his offering; But unto Cain, and to his offering, he had not respect" (vv. 20–21), since Cain "loved Satan more than

God" (v. 18). Out of greed and jealousy, Cain murdered his younger brother in cold blood (see Genesis 4:8; Moses 5:32), having been instructed and motivated to that egregious end by Satan himself, "the author of all sin" (Helaman 6:30; see also Moses 5:29–30).

Abel is also mentioned in the other standard works. The first reference in the text of the Doctrine and Covenants occurs in connection with the descent of the priesthood lineage—"And from Enoch to Abel, who was slain by the conspiracy of his brother, who received the priesthood by the commandments of God, by the hand of his father Adam" (D&C 84:16). Abel is mentioned once again as one of the elect personages viewed by President Joseph F. Smith in his vision of the spirit realm: "Abel, the first martyr, was there." (D&C 138:40).

ABIATHAR

(Meaning: father of excellence or abundance.) Abiathar (pronounced uh-by'-uh-thahr), son of Ahimelech in the succession of priestly leadership from Aaron through the line of Eli and Ithamar, was able to elude the murderous campaign of Saul against David and his loyalists (see 1 Samuel 22:20–23) and subsequently served as high priest and counselor in David's circle (see 1 Samuel 23:6, 9; 30:7; 2 Samuel 15:24–36; 1 Chronicles 15:11–12; 27:33–34). Abiathar was loyal to David during the rebellion of David's third son, Absalom (see 2 Samuel 15:1) but supported David's fourth son, Adonijah, as successor, rather than Solomon (see 1 Kings 1:7) and was for this disloyalty suspended in his priestly duties by King Solomon (see 1 Kings 2:26–27; compare 1 Samuel 2:31–35; also Mark 2:25–28).

Abel and Cain

ABIGAIL

(Meaning: father of joy or source of rejoicing.)

1. Abigail, the wife of Nabal and future wife of David, is a memorable example of courage, humility, and selflessness. A "woman of good understanding, and of a beautiful countenance" (1 Samuel 25:3), she persuaded David, fugitive from Saul's murderous campaign against him, to suspend his planned attack on her husband's Carmel estate in response to Nabal's unkind refusal to provide supplies for David's army (see 1 Samuel 25:10–11). When Nabal passed away soon thereafter (see 1 Samuel 25:37–38), David sent for Abigail and she became his wife (1 Samuel 25:42; 27:3; 30:5; 2 Samuel 2:2–3; 1 Chronicles 3:1).

2. Abigail was a sister of David (see 2 Samuel 17:25 and 1 Chronicles 2:16, 17).

ABIHU

(Meaning: he is my father.) Abihu (uh-by'-hoo or uh-by-hyoo), son of Aaron (see Exodus 6:23; compare Numbers 3:2; 26:60; 1 Chronicles 6:3; 24:1), was consecrated to the office of priest along with his three brothers Nadab, Eleazar, and Ithamar (see Exodus 28:1). Abihu and Nadab were among the group of leaders privileged to view the Lord on Mount Sinai (see Exodus 24:1–2, 9–11); however, they both later profaned their office and brought the ultimate judgment of the Lord upon their heads (see Leviticus 10:1–2; compare Numbers 3:4; 26:61; 1 Chronicles 24:2).

ABIMELECH

(Meaning: father-king.)

1. During the time of Abraham, Abimelech (pronounced uh-bim'-uh-lek) was king of Gerar, located in the Western Negev southeast of Gaza and northwest of Beersheba. Following the destruction of Sodom and Gomorrah (see Genesis 19), Abraham journeyed with his wife Sarah southward to Gerar, where he secured from Abimelech permission to sojourn there in peace (see Genesis 20:7, 11–12, 17–18; 21:22–34).

2. Abimelech was king of Gerar during the days of Isaac, son of Abraham. Perhaps the same as Abimelech (1) or perhaps that person's son (see Genesis 26), he assisted Isaac during a sore famine (see Genesis 26:1–5) and allowed him to remain until his Philistine landsmen grew uneasy over Isaac's increasing affluence. Abimelech then ordered him to leave but came to visit him later at Beersheba, where they entered into a covenant of peace much like the one established with Abraham years earlier (see Genesis 26:26–33).

3. Abimelech was the son of Gideon (see Judges 8:31). Following the death of his father, he aspired to and obtained the office of king, murdering his paternal brethren (numbering "threescore and ten"—Judges 9:5) to preserve his power and office. Abimelech ruled with treachery and cunning, generating many enemies in the process and losing his own life while bringing destruction to one of the towns in his realm (see Judges 9:53–56; compare 2 Samuel 11:21.)

4. Abimelech (also rendered Ahimelech) was identified as the father of Abiathar, high priest during the time of David (see 1 Samuel 22:20–23; also 1 Chronicles 18:16; 2 Samuel 8:17—where the names for Abiathar and Abimelech or Ahimelech have apparently been interchanged).

5. Abimelech, referred to in the lead-in to

Psalm 34, is Achish, king of Gath (see 1 Samuel 21:10–15).

ABINADAB

(Meaning: noble father or father of nobleness.)

1. Abinadab was a Levite in whose house at Kirjath-jearim, located a short distance west of Jerusalem, the ark of the covenant was kept after it was retrieved from Philistine hands (see 1 Samuel 7:1–2). David removed the ark from the house of Abinadab and brought it forth to be eventually returned to Jerusalem (see 2 Samuel 6:1–4; 1 Chronicles 13:7).

2. Abinadab was the second of the eight sons of Jesse (see 1 Samuel 16:8). Abinadab participated in King Saul's campaign against the Philistines (see 1 Samuel 17:3).

3. Abinadab was the son of Saul killed by the Philistines in the battle of Gilboa (see 1 Samuel 31:2; 1 Chronicles 10:2).

4. Abinadab was the father of one of king Solomon's twelve officers (1 Kings 4:7, 11).

ABISHAG

(Meaning: father of error.) Abishag (pronounced ab'-uh-shag) was David's nurse during his final senior years (see 1 Kings 1:1–4, 15; compare 1 Kings 2:13–25).

ABNER

(Meaning: father of light.) Abner was the commander over the army of King Saul (see 1 Samuel 14:50; 17:55; 20:25; 26:5) and cousin of the king (see 1 Samuel 14:51). It was he who introduced David to Saul following the defeat of Goliath (see 1 Samuel 17:55–58),

though he later participated with Saul in his murderous designs against David (see 1 Samuel 26:5, 9–10, 15–16) and supported Ish-bosheth, son of Saul, as king over Israel (2 Samuel 2:8–9). When Ish-bosheth was defeated and perished in battle (see 2 Samuel 4:7), Abner made gestures of support toward the courteous David (see 2 Samuel 3:12, 18, 21), but Joab, David's army commander, whose brother Asahel had earlier been slain by Abner, took action on his own to end the life of Abner (see 2 Samuel 3:27; compare 1 Kings 2:5, 32; 2 Samuel 3:36–38; compare 1 Kings 2:5, 32; 1 Chronicles 26:28; 27:21).

ABRAHAM/ABRAM

(Meaning: father of a multitude.) Abraham, the ancient prophet with whom the Lord established His ongoing and eternal covenant, was born more than two millennia before the coming of Christ. He was known as Abram (meaning "exalted father") until he was ninety-nine (see Genesis 17:5, 24). For many, the most memorable aspect of Abraham's life might well be his consummate obedience, demonstrated by his willingness to sacrifice his own son as the Lord commanded (see Genesis 22). However, what is most significant about Abraham is his central role regarding the archetypal covenant the Lord made with him and his seed to bless the lives of all the sons and daughters of God, that they might become, as the resurrected Lord said, "the children of the prophets" and "of the covenant" (3 Nephi 20:25–27; compare the Lord's teachings concerning Abraham in Matthew 3:9; 8:11; Luke 16:22; John 8:56.)

The Lord prepared Abraham carefully for his service in His kingdom (even though his fathers had turned from the ways of the Lord),

Abraham pleads with God

he being a righteous man by nature, having a desire to obtain the blessings of heaven, receive more knowledge, and be a "greater follower of righteousness" (Abraham 1:2; compare also verse 4). We recall how anxious Abraham and Sarah were to have a child together, and how incredulous both were when the Lord promised them in their old age that Isaac would be born as the channel for carrying on the covenant promise (see Genesis 17:15–22). The Lord kept His promise, and Sarah bore a child that would enable Abraham to become the covenant father of many nations. As the Lord declared: "I will make of thee a great nation, and I will bless thee above measure, and make thy name great among all nations, and thou shalt be a blessing unto thy seed after thee, that in their hands they shall bear this ministry and Priesthood unto all nations" (Abraham 2:9; see also verses 10–11; compare Genesis 12:1–3).

HISTORY. Some of the key milestones in the life of Abraham include the attempt by the idolatrous Egyptian priests to sacrifice him as sanctioned by his father, Terah; the bestowal of covenant promises upon Abraham by the Lord; his sojourn in Eygpt; his meeting with Melchizedek; and his willingness to sacrifice his only son, Isaac, at the request of the Father. From modern-day revelation, we gain further insight into the exemplary character of Abraham—father of Isaac, grandfather of Jacob, great-grandfather of Joseph, and the foundational figure in the institution of the Abrahamic covenant of the Lord to spread the blessings of the gospel of salvation and the priesthood of God to the world (see Abraham 2:9–11).

The Lord declared the exaltation of Abraham, Isaac, and Jacob, who "did none other things than that which they were commanded; and because they did none other things than that which they were commanded, they have entered into their exaltation, according to the promises, and sit upon thrones, and are not angels but are gods" (D&C 132:37). Those who live up to the oath and covenant of the priesthood "become the sons of Moses and of Aaron and the seed of Abraham, and the church and kingdom, and the elect of God" (D&C 84:34). The Lord holds up Abraham as a model of obedience for the Saints to follow: "Therefore, they must needs be chastened and tried, even as Abraham, who was commanded to offer up his only son. For all those who will not endure chastening, but deny me, cannot be sanctified" (D&C 101:4–5). In terms of the ordinances of the new and everlasting covenant, the Lord has commanded: "Go ye, therefore, and do the works of Abraham; enter ye into my law and ye shall be saved" (D&C 132:32). Joseph Smith saw Father Abraham in his vision of the future world of glory (see D&C 137:5). The Lord revealed to Joseph Smith details of a future glorious sacrament meeting when all the faithful prophets of old would convene again, including "Joseph and Jacob, and Isaac, and Abraham, your fathers, by whom the promises remain" (D&C 27:10).

We can be grateful for the heritage of Abraham, "the father of the faithful" (D&C 138:41), and for his unsurpassed example of obedience and honor. In following the example of Abraham, we can make obedience a governing pattern in our lives, love God with all our heart, and make correct choices based on eternal principles. By so doing, we can verily become "the seed of Abraham" (D&C 84:34) on our eternal journey as sons and daughters of God.

ABSALOM

(Meaning: father of peace.) Absalom (pronounced ab'-suh-lum) was the third son of David (see 2 Samuel 3:3). The relationship of father and son in this case is among the most poignant in the scriptures, for Absalom, being rebellious and proud, reflected in his demeanor the very opposite of his name, while David remained full of love for his mutinous son to the very end (see 2 Samuel 13:39; compare 2 Samuel 13:37–38; 14:28, 33). In the wake of his having taken over the throne by insurrection (see 2 Samuel 15–17), Absalom was slain by the army commander, Joab (contrary to David's instructions—see 2 Samuel 18:9, 14–15), causing his father to declare in anguish: "O my son Absalom, my son, my son Absalom! would God I had died for thee, O Absalom, my son, my son!" (2 Samuel 18:33; compare 2 Samuel 19:1, 4).

Absalom

Achan sneaks away with his stolen spoils

ACHAN

Achan (pronounced ay'-can) was a member of the tribe of Judah in the days of Joshua. In the battle of Jericho the Lord guided Joshua and his hosts to take the city and destroy it, with the reservation that all the goods seized were to be consecrated for the treasury of the Lord (see Joshua 6:19). When it was later discovered that Achan had secretly made off with certain items of spoil (see Joshua 7:21), he was stoned to death for acting willfully against a divine commandment (see Joshua 7:25; also Joshua 22:20).

ACHISH

Achish (pronounced ay'-kish), Philistine king of Gath during the days of David's flight from King Saul, extended to David the opportunity to sojourn in that part of the realm (see 1 Samuel 21:10–15; 27:6) and later join with him in a battlefield alliance (see 1 Samuel 29:3–5). When the Philistine confreres of

Achish objected, David went forth on his own to continue his quest to become the king of Israel. *Note that Achish is referred to as Abimelech in the heading to Psalm 34; see also the references to Achish in 1 Kings 2:39–40.*

ADAM

(Meaning: man or many.) From holy writ we know that Adam was the first man: "And the first man of all men have I called Adam, which is many" (Moses 1:34; compare Genesis 1:27; D&C 84:16). Abraham referred to Adam as the "first father" (Abraham 1:3; compare D&C 107:40–53), meaning the head of the descending lineage of priesthood authority in the succession of dispensations upon the earth. Modern revelation speaks of "Michael, or Adam, the father of all, the prince of all, the ancient of days" (D&C 27:11). The last of these titles, "ancient of days," is expounded by Daniel in various passages associated with the final period of the world (see Daniel 7:9, 13, 22; compare D&C 116:1; 138:38).

The name *Michael* is generally used to refer to Adam in his premortal or post-mortal state. Michael is also identified by the title "archangel": "Michael, the prince, the archangel" (D&C 107:54; compare D&C 128:21; Jude 1:9). The name *Michael* in Hebrew means "one who is like God." Indeed, "Michael, mine archangel" (D&C 29:26) will have the assignment to accomplish the final defeat of Satan and his hosts at the end of the millennial period (see D&C 88:112–115)— just as he defeated Lucifer (Satan) and his followers in the premortal realm (see Revelation 12:7–8). At Adam-ondi-Ahman—where Adam, three years prior to his death, rendered his final blessing unto his posterity—the Lord appeared and said to him, "I have set thee to be at the head; a multitude of nations shall come of thee, and thou art a prince over them forever" (D&C 107:55). The title of *prince* in this context opens the view to the extraordinary authority and responsibility conferred upon Adam (or Michael) in terms of the plan of salvation: "Who hath appointed Michael your prince, and established his feet, and set him upon high, and given unto him the keys of salvation under the counsel and direction of the Holy One." (D&C 78:16).

Thus Adam is a figure of supernal importance in the work and glory of God, beginning in the premortal realm, continuing throughout mortality, and extending into the eternities. Daniel was given a vision of the future gathering involving Adam in his capacity as one holding the keys of salvation, being commissioned to meet the "Son of man" upon His return (Daniel 7:13–14). This consummating assembly is also spoken of in the Doctrine and Covenants (see D&C 27:5–13) and marks the defining moment in time when Adam will receive from those holding priesthood stewardships and keys an accounting of these keys over which he (Adam) presides, prior to conveying them back to Jesus Christ, the millennial King (see *TPJS*, 158; compare D&C 137:5; 138:38, 40).

Adam has a pervasive presence throughout the holy record of God. He is mentioned either by name or by the title "ancient of days" numerous times in all of the standard works. These passages comprise a remarkable account of this exemplary leader in the program of Heavenly Father and His Son Jesus Christ.

Through the wise use of their agency by Adam and Eve, mankind experienced the Fall,

Adam and Eve

enabling their posterity to come to know the gospel of Jesus Christ. We can honor their examples and follow in the pathway of righteousness with our own choices.

Adonijah

(Meaning: the Lord [Jehovah] is my Lord.)

1. Adonijah (pronounced ad'-uh-ny'-juh) was the fourth son of David (see 2 Samuel 3:2–4; 2 Chronicles 3:1–2) who, with the help of his allies, usurped the throne from his aging father (see 1 Kings 1:5–9). When the prophet Nathan disclosed to Bathsheba, mother of Solomon, what had happened, she agreed to go to David to seek redress (see 1 Kings 1:17–18). David immediately arranged for Solomon to be enthroned (1 Kings 1:35, 39–43), and the new king put Adonijah to death as a usurper and schemer.

2. Adonijah was a Levite sent out by Jehoshaphat, king of Judah, to give instructions to the people out of the book of the law of the Lord (see 2 Chronicles 17:8), sometime between 926 and 873 BC.

3. Adonijah was one of the leading individuals mentioned as participating in the covenant of the Lord along with Nehemiah, governor of Judaea, around 444 BC (see Nehemiah 10:16).

Adoniram

(Meaning: my Lord is exalted; sometimes shortened to Adoram.) Adoniram (pronounced ah-doh'-nee-rahm) was an officer "over the tribute" (1 Kings 4:6; 2 Samuel 20:24) or "over the levy" (1 Kings 5:14) during the reigns of kings David, Solomon, and Rehoboam. This office oversaw the forced labor for public works, a campaign that caused the people to rebel and stone Adoniram (Adoram) to death (see 1 Kings 12:18–20; compare 2 Chronicles 10:18, where Adoram is referred to as Hadoram).

Adoni-zedek

(Meaning: Lord of righteousness.) Adoni-zedek (pronounced ah-doh'-nee-zee'-dek) was king of Jerusalem prior to the influx of Israel into Canaan (see Joshua 10:1). He was one of five Amorite kings who went to war against the city of Gibeon after it had made peace with the forces of Israel (see Joshua 10:3–5), and he was then defeated and executed by Joshua (see Joshua 10:3–5, 22–27).

Adoram (see Adoniram)

Adrammelech

(Meaning: splendor of the king, or fire-king.)

1. Adrammelech was the name of an idol evidently representing the sun (see 2 Kings 17:31). This idol was worshipped by the colonists coming into Samaria at the time of the Assyrian conquest of Israel and the leading away of the ten tribes from 722 to 721 BC.

2. Adrammelech was the son of Sennacherib, king of Assyria (see 2 Kings 19:36–37; Isaiah 37:37–38). Sennacherib reigned from around 705 to 681 BC.

Agag

(Possible meaning: flame; the name was probably a general designation for the Amalekite kings, similar to "Pharaoh" among the Egyptians.)

1. Agag was a king of the Amalekites referred to by Balaam at the time of the Exodus (see Numbers 24:7).

2. Agag was king of the Amalekites when Saul was purging the country of the enemies of Israel (sometime after 1095 BC). The Lord had commanded Saul to completely destroy the Amalekites and all their possessions (see 1 Samuel 15:1–3, 8–9). When Saul, in his devastating attack, spared Agag and retained much spoil (see 1 Samuel 15:8–9), Samuel the prophet declared the displeasure of the Lord and the rejection of Saul as king (see 1 Samuel 15:22–23, 33).

AHAB

(Meaning: father's brother.)

1. Ahab was king of northern Israel from about 869 to 850 BC. He is distinguished by his unparalleled wickedness (see 1 Kings 16:30–31). Complicit with Ahab in his perversion of righteousness was Jezebel, the Phoenician princess from Sidon (or Zidon, the Mediterranean port city), who brought with her the worship of the god Baal and cultivated it with fanatic zeal. It was during the reign of Ahab that the prophet Elijah invoked the Lord's judgment upon the priests of Baal (see 1 Kings 18:17–21), resulting in their utter destruction and that of the associated system of worship (see 1 Kings 18:39–40; 19:1). Thereafter, Ahab focused on preserving his political station by overcoming the forces of Ben-hadad, king of Syria, with whom he then formed an alliance to oppose Assyria (see 1 Kings 20:34). Ahab turned to Jehoshaphat, king of Judah, to take joint action against Syria (see 2 Chronicles 18:3), and in the course of that campaign, Ahab was killed, real-

King Ahab and Elijah in the Vineyard of Naboth

izing the doom that the Lord had pronounced upon his head (see 1 Kings 21:17–24; 22:35; 2 Chronicles 18:33–34).

2. Ahab, a false prophet at the time of Jeremiah (see Jeremiah 29:21).

AHASUERUS

1. Ahasuerus (pronounced uh-haz'-yoo-ee'-ruhs or ah-haz'-uh-ee'-ruhs) was the father of Darius the Mede (see Daniel 9:1–2).

2. Ahasuerus was an additional Persian king (see Ezra 4:6). This Ahasuerus could possibly be the son and successor of Cyrus (from around 529 BC). In 537 BC Cyrus promulgated the decree to allow the Israelites to return to Jerusalem and rebuild the temple.

3. Ahasuerus, the king discussed in the book of Esther, became Esther's husband (see Esther 2:17). He is usually identified with Xerxes, king of Persia, whose rule began around 486 BC.

King Ahasuerus and Esther

AHAZ

(Meaning: possessor.) Ahaz was king of Judah in the 730s and 720s B.C. To the towering spiritual strength of Isaiah, his contemporary, Ahaz provides a dramatic contrast, for Ahaz was given over to a life of idolatry and evil. Ahaz is to Isaiah what Ahab was to Elijah over a century earlier: a king representing the depth of depravity, just as the Lord's prophet represented the sublime summit of righteousness and honor. Ahaz was the son and successor of Jotham, king of Judah (see 2 Kings 16; Isaiah 7–9; 2 Chronicles 28). Beginning at age twenty, Ahaz ruled in wickedness, corrupting the temple rites and subjecting his own son to a fire walk "according to the abominations of

the heathen" (2 Kings 16:3; 2 Chronicles 28:3).

During his days, Ahaz and his nation were vexed by the aggression of the alliance between Syria (under King Rezin) and the northern kingdom of Israel (under King Pekah). The Lord commanded Isaiah to speak with Ahaz and counsel him to be comforted in the view that these aggressors would soon be silenced (see Isaiah 7:4–5, 7–9). As a sign from the Lord, Isaiah prophesied to Ahaz regarding the birth of Immanuel to a virgin (see Isaiah 7:1–15; compare Hosea 1 and Micah 1 for additional prophecies given in those days).

But Ahaz could not lift his view to such wonders and instead buried himself in the political turmoils of the day, cultivating a protective alliance with Tiglath-pileser, king of Assyria. This initiative did not have wholesome consequences for the people of Judah (see 2 Kings 16:7–16; compare Isaiah 14:24–28). To his dying day, Ahaz did not relinquish his misguided and evil ways (see 2 Chronicles 28:27).

AHAZIAH

(Meaning: the Lord upholds, or the Lord sustains.)

1. Ahaziah (pronounced ah-hah-zy'-uh) was king of Israel, succeeding his father, Ahab. Ahaziah continued the depraved practices of Ahab and furthered the idolatrous culture of his mother, Jezebel (see 1 Kings 22:51–53; 2 Kings 1:2; 3:4–7; 2 Chronicles 20:35–37). Ahaziah died as a result of injuries sustained when he fell through the roof of his palace, his death being portended by the prophet Elijah (see 2 Kings 1:2–4, 17).

2. Ahaziah, son of Jehoram and Athaliah, was a king of Judah at the time of the ministry of the prophet Elisha (during the first part of the 800s BC), reigning but a single year in wickedness (see 2 Kings 8:26–27). Ahaziah and his uncle, Jehoram—son of Ahab, brother to a different Ahaziah, and king of Israel—were slain by Jehu—whom Elisha, under inspiration of the Lord, had anointed as the new king of Israel—and his men (see 2 Kings 9:27; compare 2 Chronicles 22:9).

AHIJAH

(Meaning: brother or friend of Jehovah.)

1. Ahijah (pronounced uh-hy'-juh) was a prophet from the town of Shiloh (north of Jerusalem, in the land of Ephraim) who lived during the days of Jeroboam, the servant of Solomon who was to ascend the throne of Israel. Ahijah delivered to Jeroboam the extraordinary word of the Lord concerning the impending division of the tribes of Israel (see 1 Kings 11:29–38.)

In addition, Ahijah prophesied the death of Jeroboam's son and the demise of his family (see 1 Kings 14:1–18; 15:29; 2 Chronicles 9:29).

2. The name *Ahijah* is also used in connection with many other individuals in the Old Testament (see 1 Samuel 14:3, 18 [Ahiah]; 1 Kings 4:3 [Ahiah]; 1 Chronicles 2:25; 8:7 [Ahiah]; 11:36; 26:20).

AHIMAAZ

(Meaning: brother of anger.)

1. Ahimaaz (pronounced uh-him'-uh-az) was the father of Ahinoam, the wife of Saul (see 1 Samuel 14:50).

2. Ahimaaz was the son of Zadok, the high priest (see 2 Samuel 15:27, 36). Ahimaaz was supportive of David's cause during the rebellion of David's son Absalom (see 2 Samuel 17:17–21; 2 Samuel 18:19–29; see also 1 Chronicles 6:8–9, 53).

3. Ahimaaz was one of the officers in Solomon's court and the husband of Basmath, one of Solomon's daughters (see 1 Kings 4:15).

AHIMELECH

(Meaning: brother king.)

1. Ahimelech (pronounced ah-him'-uh-lek) was the priest who gave to David the sword of Goliath and the hallowed bread when David was a fugitive escaping the assaults of King Saul (see 1 Samuel 21:1–6). For his services to David, Abimelech and his fellow priests at

David Spares Saul

Nob were slain by Saul (see 1 Samuel 22:9–20; 23:6; Psalm 52, heading; compare Mark 2:25–28, where Christ referred to this event using the name of Abiathar, surviving son of Abimelech—see 1 Samuel 22:20–23).

2. Ahimelech was also identified as the son of Abiathar (see 2 Samuel 8:17; 1 Chronicles 24:3, 6, 31). It is possible that the names of Ahimelech and Abiathar were transposed in these passages.

3. Ahimelech was the name of a Hittite in David's camp (see 1 Samuel 26:6).

AHINOAM

(Meaning: brother of grace or brother of pleasantness.)

1. Ahinoam (pronounced uh-hin'-oh-uhm) was the daughter of Ahimaaz and wife of Saul (see 1 Samuel 14:50).

2. Ahinoam, from the town of Jezreel, was the wife of David and the mother of his firstborn son, Amnon (see 1 Samuel 25:43; 27:3; 30:5; 2 Samuel 2:2; 3:2; 1 Chronicles 3:1).

AHITHOPHEL

(Meaning: brother of folly.) Ahithophel (pronounced uh-hith'-oh-fel), one of David's counselors, was party to the failed conspiracy of Absalom, David's son. Disgraced, Ahithophel hanged himself (see 2 Samuel 15:12, 31, 34; 2 Samuel 16:15–17:23). He may also have been the grandfather of Bathsheba (see 2 Samuel 11:3; 23:34; 1 Chronicles 27:33–34).

AHOLIAB

(Meaning: the tent of the father.) Aholiab (pronounced uh-hoh'-lee-ab) was one of the craftsmen given to Moses by the Lord to help prepare the Tabernacle (see Exodus 31:6–7; 35:34; 36:1–2; 38:23).

AMALEK

(Meaning: dweller in a valley.) Amalek (pronounced am'-uh-lek) was the son of Eliphaz and grandson of Esau (see Genesis 36:12; 1 Chronicles 1:36). He was the head of one of the territorial tribes, the Amalekites.

AMALEKITES

The Amalekites (pronounced uh-mal'-uh-kites) were an ancient Arab tribe that existed at the time of Abraham (see Genesis 14:7) and continued on to the time of Moses and beyond. The Amalekites were constantly at war with the Hebrews in connection with the Exodus and the return to the Holy Land (see

Exodus 17:8–16; Numbers 13:29; 14:25, 43, 45; Judges 6:3, 33; 7:12; 10:12). The power of the Amalekites was eventually broken by Saul and David (see 1 Samuel 15; 27:8; 2 Samuel 8:12; 1 Chronicles 4:43).

AMASA

(Meaning: burden.) Amasa (pronounced ah-may'-suh) was appointed captain of the army by Absalom, the insurgent son of David (see 2 Samuel 17:25). After Joab had slain Absalom contrary to David's instructions, David wanted to elevate Amasa to Joab's position as captain of the army (see 2 Samuel 19:13), but Joab slew Amasa (see 2 Samuel 20:9–10; 1 Kings 2:5, 32).

AMASAI

(Meaning: burden bearer.)

1. Amasai (pronounced am'-uh-sy) was a Levite listed among the descendants of Kohath (see 1 Chronicles 6:25).

2. Amasai (perhaps the same as 1) was listed among the singers at the time of David (1 Chronicles 6:35).

3. Amasai was the chief among the captains of David, pledging his loyalty to the king under the inspiration of the Spirit (see 1 Chronicles 12:18).

4. Amasai was one of the musicians who performed with a trumpet before the ark of God during the reign of David (see 1 Chronicles 15:24).

5. Amasai was a Levite and father of Mahath, the latter being one of those who assisted in the cleansing of the temple during the time of Hezekiah (see 2 Chronicles 29:12).

AMAZIAH

(Meaning: strong is the Lord.)

1. Amaziah (pronounced am'-uh-zy'-uh) was the father of Joshah, one of the Simeonite chiefs during the time of Hezekiah (see 1 Chronicles 4:34).

2. Amaziah was a Levite, the son of Hilkiah (see 1 Chronicles 6:45).

3. Amaziah was the son and successor of Joash, king of Judah (see 2 Kings 12:21; 13:12). During his tenure the servants who had taken his father's life were slain, and the Edomites were conquered because Amaziah heeded a man of God who laid out a winning strategy for him to follow (see 2 Chronicles 25). Regretfully, Amaziah appropriated some of the idolatrous ways of the Edomites and incurred the anger of the Lord (see 2 Chronicles 25:15). Thereafter Judah was defeated by Israel, and, Amaziah was in time slain in a conspiracy against him (see 2 Chronicles 25:27–28; compare also 2 Kings 12:21; 13:12; 14:1–23; 15:1, 3; 2 Chronicles 24:27 to 25:4.)

4. Amaziah was a priest of Beth-el who murmured against the prophecies of Amos (see Amos 7:10–17).

AMMON/AMMONITES

The name *Ammon* in the Old Testament is usually mentioned in the expression "children of Ammon," meaning the tribal people of that name who were descended from Lot, the nephew of Abraham. Benammi was the son of Lot by his younger daughter, the child being conceived by an incestuous union unbeknownst to the sedated and sleeping Lot: "And the younger [daughter], she also bare a son, and called his name Benammi: the same is the father of the children of Ammon unto this day" (Genesis 19:38; see also Deuteronomy 2:19).

The "children of Ammon" were generally at odds with the Israelites. It was against the Ammonites that David's army was fighting when he became involved with Bathsheba and orchestrated the death of her husband, Uriah (2 Samuel 12:7–9). Later, Solomon took an Ammonitess as one of his wives (see 1 Kings 14:31; 2 Chronicles 12:13) and offended the Lord by choosing to adopt the idolatrous practices of Ammonite worship (see 1 Kings 11:5–7). Eventually the Ammonites came under the yoke of Assyria and Chaldea, according to the judgments of the Lord (see Zephaniah 2:8–11; compare Amos 1; 2 Kings 24:2; Ezekiel 25).

AMORITES

In general, this designation seems to apply to a fair-skinned, blue-eyed people who inhabited the land of Canaan prior to the arrival of the Semitic peoples, including the Israelites and related tribes like the Ammonites and Edomites (see Numbers 13:29; compare Genesis 14:7; Deuteronomy 1:7, 20). At the direction of the Lord, Joshua defeated five of the Amoritish kings in battle (see Joshua 10).

AMOS

(Meaning: burden.) The prophet Amos is perhaps best remembered for his declaration, "Surely the Lord GOD will do nothing, but he revealeth his secret unto his servants the prophets" (Amos 3:7; the JST renders it "until he revealeth"). Amos was one of the twelve prophets of the Old Testament with shorter books (though by no means reflecting messages

Amos

of lesser import). He was a shepherd from a community south of Jerusalem (see Amos 7:14–17), but his ministry was in the northern kingdom of Israel. Amos prophesied during the reign of Uzziah, king of Judah (who died around 740 BC, about the time of the commencement of Isaiah's ministry) and that of Jeroboam II, king of Israel (who died around 750 BC). Amos, in keeping with his prophetic calling, discerned the evils around him and invoked the spirit of divine exhortation to lift the people from their shackles of sin and motivate them to rise to their godly potential (see, for example, Amos 5:4, 14, 21–27; 6:1). He viewed the end from the beginning through the power of revelation and warned the people of impending destruction and dire spiritual famine if they would not repent, yet he promised them that the Lord would eventually bring about the restoration of His work and gather the faithful together again in light and truth (see Amos 8:11–12 and 9:14–15).

AMOZ

(Meaning: strong.) Amoz is identified in the Old Testament as the father of Isaiah (see 2 Kings 19:2, 20; 2 Kings 20:1; 2 Chronicles 26:22; 32:20, 32; Isaiah 1:1; 2:1; 13:1; 20:2; 37:2, 21; 38:1). Little else is known about him. His name was rendered "Amos" in earlier editions of the Book of Mormon (see 2 Nephi 12:1; 23:1).

AMRAM

(Meaning: exalted people.)

1. Amram (pronounced am'-ram) and his wife Jochebed were the parents of Moses, Aaron, and Miriam (see Numbers 3:17–19; 26:59; 1 Chronicles 6:2–3, 18). Amram was a Levite by descent.

2. Amram was an Edomite mentioned in 1 Chronicles 1:41 (referred to as Hemdan in Genesis 36:26).

3. Amram was a Jew who had married a foreign wife (see Ezra 10:34).

ANAK/ANAKIM(S)

(Meaning: strong-necked or long-necked.) The Anak or Anakim(s) were a long-standing race of large-statured people who lived primarily near the city of Hebron (south from Jerusalem), but also in other hilly areas. At the command of the Lord, Joshua came against them and destroyed them (see Joshua 11:19–23; 14:12–15; Numbers 13:32–33; Deuteronomy 1:28; 2:10–11; 9:1–2).

ANCIENT OF DAYS (SEE ADAM)

ANGELS

Angels are ministering servants of the Lord. Some of the most celebrated angelic events in scripture include the intercession by the angel of God as Abraham was about to sacrifice his son, Isaac (Genesis 22:10–12); the rescue of Daniel in the den of lions (Daniel 6:22); the angelic instruction to Adam concerning sacrifice as a similitude of the Atonement of Jesus Christ (Moses 5:6–8); and the preservation of Abraham by the angel of Jehovah at the moment of heathen sacrifice (Abraham 1:15–16; 2:13).

ANOINTED

As a noun, the term "Anointed" is one of the many sacred titles of the Son of God. The word "Christ" derives from a Greek word

An angel administers to Elijah

17

meaning "anointed"; the word "Messiah" comes from a Hebrew and Aramaic term of the same meaning. (See the reference of the Psalmist to "his anointed" in Psalm 2:2, 6–7; compare Isaiah 61:1–2.)

APHARSACHITES/APHARSATHCHITES/ APHARSITES

These are the names applied to certain groups of Assyrian colonists who had settled in Samaria, north of Jerusalem (see Ezra 4:9; 5:6; 6:6), and failed in their attempt to thwart the rebuilding of Jerusalem and the temple following the Babylonian conquest (see Ezra 4:11–14; 5:6–17; 6:11–12). The temple was completed in 516 BC.

ARABIA/ARABIANS

Arabia, the vast territory to the east of the Holy Land bounded by the Red Sea on the west, the Indian Ocean on the south, and the Persian Gulf and Euphrates River on the east, was occupied by a variety of peoples over the generations: the Joktanites in the south (a trading people descended from Joktan, the son of Eber, who was a great-grandson of Shem—see Genesis 10:26–31); the Ishmaelites in the central region (descendants of Abraham through Ishmael—see Genesis 21:14–21; 25:13–14); and the Midianites and various other wandering tribes in the north (tracing their descent from Abraham and Keturah—see Genesis 25:1–4). Contacts with the Arabian peoples were of a diverse nature throughout Israelite history (see, for example, Judges 6–7; 1 Kings 9:26–28; 10:1–15; 2 Chronicles 9:1–14; 17:10–12; 21:16–17; Isaiah 21:13–17; Jeremiah 25:23–27; 49:28–33; Nehemiah 2:19; 4:7–13; 6; compare Galatians 1:17).

ARAM/ARAMAEANS

The Aramaeans (pronounced air'-uh-mee'-uhns) were a major branch of the Semitic race stemming from Aram, son of Shem, according to Genesis 10:22—or, the son of Kemuel and grandson of Nahor (Abraham's older brother—see Genesis 11:22–25)—according to Genesis 22:21. In general, the Aramaeans are referred to as Syrians in the King James Version of the Bible (see 2 Samuel 8, 10; 1 Kings 20, 22; 2 Kings 5–9, 13, 16, 24; 1 Chronicles 18–19, 22, 24; also Isaiah 9:12; Jeremiah 35:11; Amos 9:7). Originally the Aramaeans were situated between the Tigris and Euphrates rivers (Mesopotamia), but they eventually crossed westward over the Euphrates and toward the Holy Land (2 Samuel 8:5–6; compare 2 Samuel 10:6–19; see also 1 Kings 20, 22; 2 Kings 5; 7:6; 13:3, 5; 18:26). Jesus Christ spoke a form of Aramaic during His mortal ministry.

ARBA

(Meaning: four.) Arba was the father of Anak (see Joshua 15:3), the latter being the ancestor of a race of giants. Arba was the founder of the city of Kirjath-arba ("city of Arba"), known among the Israelites as Hebron, located about twenty miles south of Jerusalem, west of the Dead Sea (see Genesis 13:18; 23:2, 17–20; 35:27; Joshua 14:14–15; 21:11; 2 Samuel 2:1–4, 11; 5:5). It was in Hebron that David was anointed king of Israel (see 2 Samuel 5:3).

ARCHEVITES

The Archevites (mentioned in Ezra 4:9) were settlers in Samaria (an area about thirty miles north of Jerusalem) who—along with eight other confederate groups—unsuccessfully attempted to thwart the rebuilding of Jerusalem and the temple following the Babylonian conquest (see Ezra 4:11–14; 6:11–12).

ARTAXERXES

Artaxerxes (pronounced ahr' tuh-zurk'-seez) was the son of Xerxes and king of Persia around 465 to 425 BC. Artaxerxes was called *Longimanus* ("long-handed"). At first he hindered the Jews from restoring Jerusalem because the enemies of the Jewish state had raised warnings of sedition against and loss of revenues to the king (see Ezra 4:7–23). Later, however, he permitted the rebuilding of the temple to go forward (see Ezra 6:14; 7:1–28) and eventually appointed Nehemiah as governor of Judea and permitted him to rebuild the

Artaxerxes

walls of the city of Jerusalem (see Nehemiah 2:1–10; 5:14; 13:6).

ASA

(Meaning: healer or physician.)

1. Asa was king of Judah from around 956 to 916 BC, his heart being "perfect with the LORD all his days" (1 Kings 15:14). He strengthened Israel's defenses and held off enemy aggression (see 2 Chronicles 14; 16:7–10). Inspired by the words of the prophet Azariah, Asa took comprehensive action to cleanse the land of idolatry and cause the people to renew their vows to Jehovah (see 2 Chronicles 15:2–4, 7, 12, 15). Asa died in the forty-first year of his reign (see 2 Chronicles 16:13) and was succeeded by his son, Jehoshaphat (see 2 Chronicles 17:1).

2. Asa was a Levite listed among the inhabitants of Judah after the return from Babylon (see 1 Chronicles 9:16).

ASAHEL

(Meaning: God hath made.)

1. Asahel, son of David's sister Zeruiah, was a leader in David's army (see 1 Chronicles 27:7) who was known for his remarkable swiftness (see 2 Samuel 2:18). He was slain by Abner, who had been commander under Saul and later supported Ish-bosheth, son of Saul, rather than David (see 2 Samuel 2:18–32). Asahel was considered one of David's thirty heroes (see 2 Samuel 23:24; 1 Chronicles 11:26).

2. Asahel was one of the Levites during the reign of Jehoshaphat who was sent throughout the cities of Judah to instruct the people (see 2 Chronicles 17:9).

3. Asahel was a Levite during the reign of king Hezekiah who provided service with tithes and offerings (see 2 Chronicles 31:13).

4. Asahel was a priest during the time of Ezra (see Ezra 10:15).

ASAPH

(Meaning: gatherer or convener of the people.)

1. Asaph (pronounced ay'-saf) was a prominent musician in the court of David and the leader of the choir (see for example 1 Chronicles 6:39; 15:15–17, 19; 16:5, 37). Asaph established a family or guild of singers called the "sons of Asaph" (1 Chronicles 25:1, 2; 26:1; see also 2 Chronicles 20:14; 29:13; 35:15; Ezra 3:10; Nehemiah 11:22) or the "children of Asaph" (Ezra 2:41; Nehemiah 7:44). Asaph is mentioned in the titles to a number of the Psalms (see Psalms 50, 73–83). In one passage he is identified as "the seer" (2 Chronicles 29:30).

2. Asaph was a "recorder" in the days of king Hezekiah (2 Kings 18:18, 37).

3. Asaph was the "keeper of the king's forest" (Nehemiah 2:8). Nehemiah requested of Artaxerxes a letter to Asaph in order to obtain timber for rebuilding the walls and gates of Jerusalem.

ASENATH

(Meaning: gift of the sun-god.) Asenath (pronounced as'-un-nath) was the wife of Joseph and the mother of his sons, Ephraim and Manasseh. Her father was Potipherah, priest of On (see Genesis 46:20; Genesis 41:45, 50).

ASHER

(Meaning: happy.) Asher was a son of Jacob and Zilpah, handmaid of Leah (see Genesis 30:13). Jacob's blessing upon Asher included these words: "Out of Asher his bread shall be fat, and he shall yield royal dainties" (Genesis 49:20; compare the blessing of Moses upon the tribe of Asher—Deuteronomy 33:24–25; see also Joshua 19:24–31). The prophetess Anna (Luke 2:36) was of this tribe.

ASHTAROTH/ASHTORETH

Ashtaroth (pronounced ash'-tuh-roth) is the plural form of the name *Ashtoreth* (pronounced ash'-tuh-reth), the principal female goddess of the Phoenicians. The principal male god was Baal (plural Baalim). During the days of Joshua, the Israelites served the Lord according to the covenant (see Judges 2:7), but after the passing of Joshua, the children of Israel began to adopt the gods of the surrounding cultures, including Ashtaroth (see Judges 2:11–13). This idolatry continued from time to time as the Israelites struggled to find the pathway of righteousness (see Judges 10:6). The prophet Samuel persuaded the people to abandon such evil and return to the Lord (see 1 Samuel 7:3–4), but they all too soon forgot their promise (1 Samuel 12:10; 31:10). In his old age, Solomon turned his heart toward Ashtoreth, among other pagan gods (see 1 Kings 11:4–5, 33), but later Josiah the reformer destroyed the "high places" Solomon had erected in honor of Ashtoreth (see 2 Kings 23:13).

ASSYRIA/ASSYRIANS

Countless tribes and cultures interacted with Israel over the generations—often with aggressive designs. At the highest level of stature and power were the three grand empires of Egypt, Assyria, and Babylonia—each with its own hour of predominance. In terms of the rise of Assyrian power, there were two major events that had special impact on the Israelites: 1) the invasion of Shalmaneser into the northern kingdom (around 721–722 BC) and the dispersion of the ten tribes northward into Assyria and beyond (see 2 Kings 17; 1 Nephi 22:4; 3 Nephi 16:1–3; 17:4; 21:26); and 2) the defeat of Sennacherib and his hosts through divine intervention during the siege of Jerusalem around 699 BC (see 2 Kings 19:7, 35–37).

ATHALIAH

Athaliah (pronounced ath'-uh-ly'-uh) was, according to the reference in 2 Kings 8:18, the daughter of Ahab (king of Israel in the days of Elijah) and Jezebel (Ahab's Phoenician wife; see also 2 Kings 8:26). As the wife of Jehoram, son and successor to Jehoshaphat, king of Judah (see 2 Kings 8:18, 26), she was complicit in the wickedness of that dynasty by promoting the worship of Baal in the southern kingdom (see 2 Chronicles 21:6; 22:2–4; 24:7). Following the eight-year reign of Jehoram (ending around 885 BC) and the one-year reign of his son and successor Ahaziah (see 2 Kings 8:25–26), Athaliah assumed control over the throne but was later slain during an insurrection led by the priest Jehoiada to restore the worship of the true God of Israel (see 2 Kings 11:12–21; 2 Chronicles 22:10–12; 23:15).

AZARIAH

(Meaning: Jehovah has helped.)

1. Azariah (also called Uzziah—see 2 Chronicles 26:1–7) was the son and successor of Amaziah, king of Judah (see 2 Kings 14:21–22). The fifty-two-year reign of Azariah (pronounced az'-uh-ry'-uh) commenced when he was but sixteen years old (see 2 Kings 15:1–2): "And he did that which was right in the sight of the Lord." (2 Kings 15:3–4).

2. Azariah was a prophet, son of Oded, whose message given to Asa, king of Judah, inspired the king to restore righteous worship among the people and renew their covenant vows to the Lord (see 2 Chronicles 15:2–4, 7, 12). The result was grand: "And all Judah rejoiced at the oath: for they had sworn with all their heart, and sought him with their whole desire; and he was found of them: and the Lord gave them rest round about" (2 Chronicles 15:15).

3. Azariah was the original name of Abednego, one of the companions of Daniel taken captive by Nebuchadnezzar (see Daniel 1:7; 4:1–30). *See also Abed-nego.*

4. Azariah was the name of many additional individuals in the Old Testament (see 1 Kings 4:2, 5; 1 Chronicles 2:8, 38–39; 3:12; 6:9–14, 36; 9:11; 2 Chronicles 21:2; 22:6; 23:1; 26:16–21; 28:12; 29:12; 31:10, 13; Ezra 7:1–3; Nehemiah 3:23–24; 7:7; 8:7; 10:2; 12:33; Jeremiah 43:2).

B

BAAL/BAALIM

(Meaning: lord, possessor.) Baal (pronounced bayl or bah-al; plural Baalim) was the supreme male god in the Phoenician pagan culture (see 1 Kings 16:31). The female counterpart was Ashtoreth (plural Ashtaroth). From the summit of Sinai, the Lord forbade all such forms of idolatry with the commandment, "Thou shalt have no other gods before me" (Exodus 20:3).

Centuries before Sinai, Jehovah rescued Abraham from the sacrificial knife of conspiring priests serving pagan gods in Ur of the Chaldees (see Abraham 1:15–17). Over the ensuing centuries, the purging of idol worship from among the ranks of the seed of Abraham continued unabated. Yet after the passing of Joshua, the Israelites "forsook the LORD, and served Baal and Ashtaroth" (Judges 2:13; compare Judges 3:7; 10:6). Gideon followed the commandment of the Lord to throw down the altars of Baal (see Judges 6), but after the death of Gideon (renamed Jerubbaal—"he who strives against Baal"), "the children of Israel turned again, and went a whoring after Baalim, and made Baal-berith their god. And

the children of Israel remembered not the LORD their God, who had delivered them out of the hands of all their enemies on every side" (Judges 8:33–34). The prophet Samuel persuaded the people to abandon such idolatry and return to the Lord (see 1 Samuel 7:3–4), but they all too soon forgot their promise (see 1 Samuel 12:10). Solomon, in his later tenure, encouraged the practice of idol worship and built sanctuaries in high places to honor false gods (see 1 Kings 11:6–11). Later, Josiah the reformer destroyed the pagan sanctuaries Solomon had erected (see 2 Kings 23:11; 2 Chronicles 34:4).

The most significant confrontation between the forces of covenant righteousness and the benighted forces of Baal took place during the tenure of the prophet Elijah. Jezebel, the wife of King Ahab, had introduced Baal worship—with all of its immoral and licentious practices—among the people of northern Israel (see 1 Kings 16:30–31). During the days of famine, Elijah challenged Ahab and his priests to an ultimate test of identifying the true God—whether they could invoke their god to intervene and ignite the sacrificial

Elijah contending with the priests of Baal

offering upon the altar of Baal, or whether the Lord of heaven should show forth His power upon the altar to be set up by Elijah. The result was a remarkable event showing the power of the one true God (see 1 Kings 18:26–29, 36–40).

Thus the Lord intervened with power to prevent idolatry from creeping into the patterns of life among His children and to prevent the damage to their spiritual well-being that such pagan worship would occasion. Nonetheless, even in the days of Jeremiah the worship of Baal persisted (see Jeremiah 7:9; 9:14; 11:13, 17; 19:5; 23:13, 27; 32:29, 35; compare also Hosea 2:8, 13, 17).

In the various manifestations of Baal worship among different cultures over the generations, the name went through an evolutionary transition, showing up in multiple combinations, such as Baal-peor ("lord of the opening"—see Numbers 25:1–5; Deuteronomy 4:3; Psalm 106:28; Hosea 9:10; 11:2; 13:1; Zephaniah 1:4), Baal-berith ("lord of the covenant"—Judges 8:29, 33; 9:4), and the more familiar Baal-zebub ("lord of the flies"—2 Kings 1:2–6, 16).

BAAL-ZEBUB

(Meaning: lord of the flies.) This is a variant appellation belonging to the family of terms relating to the pagan god Baal. Baal-zebub was worshipped in the Philistine city of Ekron (see 2 Kings 1:1–6). *See also the entries for Baal and Beelzebub.*

BAASHA

(Meaning: bravery.) Baasha became king of Israel around the middle of the tenth century

BC and reigned twenty-three years in wickedness. According to the prophecy of the prophet Ahijah (see 1 Kings 14:1–18), Baasha's destruction of the house of Jeroboam was a consequence of its evil ways (see 1 Kings 15:16–22, 27–34; 2 Chronicles 16:1–6; Jeremiah 41:9). Baasha and his circle were the next to experience the judgment of the Lord as prophesied by the prophet Jehu (see 1 Kings 16:2–3; 13).

BABYLONIA

Babylonia was one of the great empires—along with Egypt and Assyria—that defined the broad geographical and cultural environment in which the people of Israel emerged as a chosen nation (see Deuteronomy 7:6). The two Mesopotamian cultures of Assyria and Babylonia—emergent between the Tigris and Euphrates rivers—were constant rivals, Assyria lying to the north and Babylonia to the south. A key milestone of the interaction between Babylonia and Israel was the captivity of Judah by the forces of Nebuchadnezzar (who reigned around 604–561 BC—see 2 Kings 24:14–16; 25:1, 8, 22; 1 Chronicles 6:15; 2 Chronicles 36; 1 Nephi 1:13; 10:3; Omni 1:15), and the subsequent changes made by Cyrus of Persia, victor over the Babylonians, who permitted the rebuilding of the temple at Jerusalem and the return of the captive people (see 2 Chronicles 36:22, 23; Ezra 1; 3:7; 4:3; 5:13, 17; 6:3; Isaiah 44:28; 45:1; Jeremiah 29:10).

BALAAM

Balaam (pronounced bay'-lum) was a prophet figure who lived in Pethor, a city by the Euphrates (see Deuteronomy 23:4; Numbers 22:5). When the hosts of Israel were encamped on the plains of Moab, Israel was perceived as a distinct threat to the Moabites and their confederate associates, the Midianites. The king of the Moabites, Balak, took action to hire Balaam—who apparently had the reputation of divine influence—to curse Israel "that [he] may drive them out of the land" (Numbers 22:6). Because Balak's delegation came "with the rewards of divination in their hand" (Numbers 22:7), Balaam agreed to approach the Lord on the Moabites' behalf. But the message from heaven was not to their liking, for the Lord told Balaam, "Thou shalt not go with them; thou shalt not curse the people: for they are blessed" (Numbers 22:12). Still, Balak insisted, so Balaam supplicated the Lord again and received permission to go, provided he would do according to the Lord's command. Thus Balaam went, though "God's anger was kindled because he went" (Numbers 22:22).

It was then that the famous event took place manifesting that Balaam's means of transportation (his donkey) had more spiritual discernment than Balaam himself. Seeing the angel of the Lord blocking the way, the donkey repeatedly held back, despite Balaam's cruel prodding. Then the Lord opened Balaam's eyes, causing him to repent of his spiritual short-sightedness (see Numbers 22:27–35). Thereafter, Balak enjoined Balaam three times to view the hosts of Israel and perform the cursing that he had paid for. But each time the answer came back in almost rhapsodic affirmation that Israel was to be blessed by the Lord rather than cursed (see Numbers 23:19–24; 24:4–9, 17–19).

Balak and Balaam then went their separate ways, but the Israelites continued to have intimate contact with the Moabites and began to assimilate their pagan practices and immoral ways. Thus the Lord commanded Moses to strike out against the indigenous peoples and eliminate their evil influence. The result was decisive: "And they slew the kings of Midian, beside the rest of them that were slain; . . . Balaam also the son of Beor they slew with the sword" (Numbers 31:8).

BALAK

(Meaning: empty, spoiler.) During the time of the Exodus, Balak, king of the Moabites, hired the prophet Balaam to curse the Israelites encamped on the plains of Moab near Jericho. *See Balaam.*

BARAK

(Meaning: lightning.) Barak, the son of Abinoam, of the tribe of Naphtali, was commissioned by the prophetess Deborah, judge of Israel, to wage battle against the encroaching Canaanites under the command of Sisera. Barak agreed to gather the forces and attack, provided Deborah would consent to accompany him. She did so, and that day the Canaanites, with their much larger force, were annihilated along with their king, Jabin (see Judges 4:23–24). Thereafter Deborah and Barak joined in singing a glorious anthem of praise to the Lord (see Judges 5).

BARUCH

(Meaning: blessed.)

1. Baruch, son of Neriah from the tribe of Judah (see Jeremiah 43:3; 51:59), served as scribe for the prophet Jeremiah, recording the prophet's words of inspiration as they were given and then reading them before the people

Baruch

as a warning to repent (see Jeremiah 36:4–8). Jehoiakim, king of Judah, took offense at the prophecies of Jeremiah concerning the impending destruction of Judah at the hands of the Babylonians, and he burned the written text (see Jeremiah 36:22–23). Jeremiah simply had Baruch write down the word of the Lord once again—manifesting that the word of the Lord cannot be annulled or destroyed (see Jeremiah 36:27–32). Baruch accompanied Jeremiah to Egypt (see Jeremiah 43:2–6). For Baruch's faithful service, Jeremiah promised him that his life would be preserved (see Jeremiah 45).

2. Baruch was among the associates of Nehemiah (see Nehemiah 3:20; 10:6; 11:5).

BATHSHEBA

(Meaning: daughter of the oath.) Bathsheba was the wife of Uriah the Hittite, a warrior in

David and Bathsheba

David's army. At the time of Israel's successful battle against the Ammonites, David remained in Jerusalem. Having observed Bathsheba from the roof of his residence, David desired and pursued her, resulting in the conception of a child (see 2 Samuel 11:2–5). He then attempted to cover up his sin by sending for Uriah to return home to his wife, Bathsheba. But out of solemn duty to his military commission, Uriah demurred to go in unto Bathsheba (see 2 Samuel 11:11). Thereupon David compounded his own guilt by arranging through Joab, his commander, to send Uriah to the front lines, where his death was assured. Uriah did indeed perish (see 2 Samuel 11:21), and David took Bathsheba to wife.

The first child of David and Bathsheba did not survive (see 2 Samuel 12:18–19), but as David's wife, Bathsheba subsequently bore four more sons: Solomon, Shimea, Shobab, and Nathan. In David's old age, his son Adonijah (born of Haggith—see 2 Samuel 3:4) "exalted himself, saying, I will be king" (1 Kings 1:5) and conspired with Joab, commander of David's military forces, and Abiathar, the priest, to take over the throne. Nathan came to Bathsheba and disclosed what was happening,

counseling her to go before David to seek redress. Bathsheba did as Nathan suggested and petitioned her husband in Solomon's behalf (see 1 Kings 1:17–18). These things being confirmed by Nathan, the aging David gave the command that Solomon should be brought forth and anointed king (1 Kings 1:35, 39–43).

As for Bathsheba, we know that she suffered because of the death of her first husband: "And when the wife of Uriah heard that Uriah her husband was dead, she mourned for her husband" (2 Samuel 11:26). We know that she was loyal to her new husband, David, and exceedingly committed to the rise and success of her son Solomon. She was also remembered in Matthew's statement about her place in the lineage of Jesus Christ: "And Jesse begat David the king; and David the king begat Solomon of her that had been the wife of Urias" (Matthew 1:6). Bathsheba is the only other woman mentioned or alluded to in this fourteen-generation review besides Ruth and Mary (see Matthew 1:5, 16).

BEELZEBUB

The New Testament name Beelzebub (pronounced bee-el'-zuh-bub) is generally the equivalent to the Old Testament Baal-zebub ("lord of the flies")—a linguistic extension of the name *Baal*—but may also be used to refer to Satan (see 2 Kings 1:1–6; Matthew 12:24–30; Mark 3:25–30; Luke 11:14–26).

BELIAL

(Meaning: without usefulness, good for nothing.) Belial is a term used in the Old Testament as an epithet signifying worthless, as in: "children of Belial" (Deuteronomy 13:13; Judges 20:13; 1 Samuel 10:27), "sons of

Belial" (Judges 19:22; 1 Samuel 2:12; 2 Samuel 23:6; 1 Kings 21:10), "son of Belial" (1 Samuel 25:17); "daughter of Belial" (1 Samuel 1:16), "man of Belial" (1 Samuel 25:25; 2 Samuel 16:7; 20:1); and "men of Belial" (1 Samuel 30:22; 1 Kings 21:13).

BELSHAZZAR

Belshazzar is identified in the book of Daniel as the king of Babylon and son and successor to Nebuchadnezzar (see Daniel 5:11, 18, 22). From recent archaeological discoveries it appears that Belshazzar may in actuality have been the son of Nabonidus (the last king of Babylon) and therefore the grandson of Nebuchadnezzar—making him prince-regent of the empire, rather than king. During the feast of Belshazzar Daniel interpreted the mysterious inscription on the wall announcing his imminent defeat by the Darius the Mede: "Thou art weighed in the balances, and art found wanting" (Daniel 5:27; see also Daniel 5:30–31).

BELTESHAZZAR

Belteshazzar was the name given to Daniel by the officers in the court of the Babylonian king, Nebuchadnezzar (see Daniel 1:6–7; Daniel 2:26; 4:8, 9, 18, 19; 5:12; 10:1). The name *Belteshazzar* was also maintained for Daniel after the Persians took over the Babylonian empire (see Daniel 10:1). *See the entry for Daniel.*

BENAIAH

(Meaning: the Lord hath built.)

1. Benaiah (pronounced buh-ny'-uh), son of Jehoiada, was one of the leading officers in

David's guard (see 2 Samuel 23:20–23; 1 Chronicles 11:22–25; 18:14–17; 27:5–6). When Adonijah attempted to usurp the throne of his aging father, Benaiah, loyal to David, slew the upstart and was later elevated to commander of the royal forces during the reign of King Solomon (see 1 Kings 1:8, 11–37; 1 Kings 2:24–25, 34–35; 1 Kings 4:4).

2. Benaiah was also the name of another of David's fighters (see 2 Samuel 23:30; 1 Chronicles 11:31; 27:14).

3. Benaiah was also the name of several other figures in the Old Testament (see 1 Chronicles 15:18, 20, 24; 16:5, 6; 2 Chronicles 31:13; Ezra 10:25, 30, 35, 43).

BEN-HADAD

(Meaning: son or worshipper of Hadad.)

1. Ben-hadad (pronounced ben-hay'-dad) was a king of Damascus who formed an alliance with Asa to conquer much of northern Israel (see 1 Kings 15:16–24; 2 Chronicles 16:1–10).

2. Ben-hadad, the son of the previous king (1), waged war against Ahab, king of Israel, but was defeated (see 1 Kings 20:1–34). When Ahab spared his life contrary to the Lord's direction, the prophet of the Lord declared, "Thus saith the Lord, Because thou hast let go out of thy hand a man whom I appointed to utter destruction, therefore thy life shall go for his life, and thy people for his people" (1 Kings 20:42). When Ben-hadad later became infirm, he sent his officer Hazael to hear counsel from the prophet Elisha concerning his recovery. Elisha predicted that Ben-hadad would die and that Hazael would secure the throne to inflict great harm upon Israel (see 2 Kings 8:7–15). Such occurred as prophesied.

Ahab also perished in due course of time according to the judgment of God (see 1 Kings 22:35; 2 Chronicles 18:33–34).

3. Ben-hadad was the son and successor of Hazael, mentioned above (see 2 Kings 13:3, 24). This Ben-hadad was defeated three times by Joash (or Jehoash), king of Israel (see 2 Kings 13:25; Jeremiah 49:27; Amos 1:4).

BENJAMIN

(Meaning: son of my right hand.)

1. Benjamin, son of Jacob and Rachel (and full brother to Joseph), was born during a journey between Bethel and Bethlehem. His mother named him Ben-oni before dying in childbirth (see Genesis 35:18), but Jacob called him Benjamin. Later, when a serious famine came over the land, Jacob sent his ten oldest sons to Egypt to obtain grain—Joseph having been

Joseph's brothers present his coat to Jacob

lost through the misdeeds of his brethren (see Genesis 37) and Benjamin being too young to travel. The story of the sons' encounters with the governor of Egypt—their brother Joseph in disguise—is one of the most well-known accounts of the Old Testament (see Genesis 42–45).

Jacob's final blessing upon the head of Benjamin included the following words: "Benjamin shall ravin as a wolf: in the morning he shall devour the prey, and at night he shall divide the spoil" (Genesis 49:27). Benjamin and his posterity were indeed aggressive in standing against the enemies of Israel and developed a reputation as skillful archers and slingers (see 1 Chronicles 8:40; 12:2). Moses bestowed the following blessing upon the tribe of Benjamin: "The beloved of the LORD shall dwell in safety by him; and the LORD shall cover him all the day long, and he shall dwell between his shoulders" (Deuteronomy 33:12). Following the return from Babylonian captivity, the tribes of Benjamin and Judah comprised the main body of the Jewish nation (see Ezra 1:5; 10:9). The most famous of the descendants of Benjamin were King Saul (see 1 Samuel 9:1) and the Apostle Paul (see Romans 11:1).

2. Other individuals with the name *Benjamin* are mentioned in 1 Chronicles 7:10, Ezra 10:32, Nehemiah 3:23, and Nehemiah 12:34.

BEN-ONI

(Meaning: son of my sorrow.) Ben-oni was the name given by Rachel to her son, later named Benjamin by his father, Jacob (see Genesis 35:18). *See also Benjamin.*

BETHUEL

(Meaning: man of God or house of God.) Nahor, brother of Abraham, had eight sons by his wife Milcah, of which Bethuel (pronounced buh-thoo'-uhl or buh-thyoo-uhl) was the youngest (see Genesis 22:22). Bethuel was the father of Rebekah, future wife of Isaac (see Genesis 22:23; 24:15, 24, 47, 50–51; 25:20). It was to the household of Bethuel that Isaac later sent his son Jacob to seek a wife among the daughters of Laban (see Genesis 28:1–5).

BEZALEEL

(Meaning: in the shadow of God, or under God's protective care.)

1. Bezaleel (pronounced bi-zahl'-ee-el) was one of the skilled craftsmen given by the Lord to Moses, along with Aholiab, to help prepare the Tabernacle under inspiration of the Spirit of God (see Exodus 31:1–5; 35:30–35; 36:1–2; 37; 38:22; 1 Chronicles 2:20; 2 Chronicles 1:5).

2. Bezaleel was a Levite at the time of Ezra who is listed among those who selected wives from non-Israelite cultures (see Ezra 10:30).

BILHAH

(Meaning: bashful, wavering.) Bilhah was a maidservant of Laban whom he gave to his daughter Rachel when she became Jacob's wife (see Genesis 29:29; 46:25). When Rachel was at first not able to bear children, she gave Bilhah unto Jacob to wife (see Genesis 30:1–5). Bilhah bore two sons, Dan and Naphtali (see Genesis 30:5–8; 35:25). *See also Reuben*.

Boaz notices Ruth in his fields

BOAZ

(Meaning: in him is might, or splendor.) Boaz was a prosperous farmer in Bethlehem and a relative of the Elimelech family. When this family moved to Moab to seek relief during a severe famine, the man of the house passed away, leaving his wife, Naomi, and her two sons (Chilion and Mahlon) to fare for themselves. The two sons each married a Moabite woman and then, tragically, also passed away (see Ruth 1:1–5). When Naomi decided to return alone to Bethlehem, hearing "how that the LORD had visited his people in giving them bread" (Ruth 1:6), one of her two daughters-in-law, Ruth, the widow of Mahlon, desired to remain with her (see Ruth 1:16). Naomi consented, and when they returned to Bethlehem, Ruth went forth to glean in the fields of their kinsman, Boaz. Boaz admired Ruth for her noble character (see Ruth 2:11–12) and was generous and protective of her (see Ruth 2:16), causing Naomi to catch the vision of their future union. And indeed, Boaz, as a near kinsman, stepped into the role of benefactor and husband according to the legal custom of the people (see Deuteronomy 25:5–10; compare Ruth 3:11–13). When the nearest male relative of Elimelech (Naomi's deceased husband) declined the opportunity to redeem the family estate (see Ruth 4:6), Boaz, as the next in line, was legally able to take charge of the situation and receive Ruth as his wife (see Ruth 4:9–10, 13).

Boaz and Ruth were soon favored with a son: "And the women her neighbours gave it a name, saying, There is a son born to Naomi; and they called his name Obed: he is the father of Jesse, the father of David" (Ruth 4:17). Thus the marriage of Boaz and Ruth provided a direct link to the future descendant of David, Jesus Christ. (Boaz is rendered *Booz* in the New Testament passage detailing this lineage—see Matthew 1:5.)

(Boaz, for an unknown reason, was also the name of one of the two great pillars in the temple of Solomon, the other being Jachin—see 1 Kings 7:21; 2 Chronicles 3:17.)

C

CAIN

Cain was a son of Adam and Eve. He was not the firstborn, since both he and his younger brother Abel came into mortality after Eve had already born unto Adam other "sons and daughters" (Moses 5:2). Cain was born into an environment of gospel instruction from his parents, who heeded the voice of the Lord when "he gave unto them commandments, that they should worship the Lord their God, and should offer the firstlings of their flocks, for an offering unto the Lord" (v. 5). Adam and his wife "blessed the name of God, and they made all things known unto their sons and their daughters" (v. 12)—including Cain. However, unlike Abel, "who walked in holiness before the Lord" (v. 26), Cain followed a path of selfishness and evil. In terms of compliance with the divine commandment to offer sacrifices, Abel "brought of the firstlings of his flock, and of the fat thereof. And the Lord had respect unto Abel, and to his offering; But unto Cain, and to his offering, he had not respect" (vv. 20–21)—since he "loved Satan more than God" (v. 18) and declared in arrogance: "Who is the Lord that I should know him?" (v. 16).

When the Lord rejected his offering, Cain became angry. The Lord did not reject Cain as a person, but did warn him, "If thou doest well, thou shalt be accepted. And if thou doest not well, sin lieth at the door, and Satan desireth

Cain murders Abel

31

to have thee; and except thou shalt hearken unto my commandments, I will deliver thee up, and it shall be unto thee according to his desire. And thou shalt rule over him" (v. 23; see also vv. 24–25).

Despite this divine counsel and the chance to rise from his abyss, Cain chose not to repent (vv. 26–27). Out of greed and jealousy, Cain murdered his younger brother (see Genesis 4:8; Moses 5:32), having been instructed by Satan himself, "the author of all sin" (Helaman 6:30; see also Moses 5:29–30). The moment of Cain's accountability before the Lord for this atrocity is chilling in its consequences (see Genesis 4:9–13; compare Moses 5:33–41).

Because of his actions, Cain became the prime example of evil and Satanic conspiracy—the opposite of the love at the core of the gospel plan (see 1 John 3:11–12). The evil in Cain's actions was rooted in his relationship with his demonic mentor, who taught him to cultivate secret combinations of murder and evil (see Moses 5:29–30): "And Cain said: Truly I am Mahan, the master of this great secret, that I may murder and get gain. Wherefore Cain was called Master Mahan, and he gloried in his wickedness" (Moses 5:31). Cain was therefore cast out of God's presence (see Genesis 4:16; Moses 5:39, 41) and established a culture and lineage of his own—one that preserved and applied the cloak-and-dagger strategies inspired of Satan (see Moses 5:49, 51).

CAINAN

Cainan was the son of Enos and the great-grandson of Adam and Eve (see Genesis 5:9–14; Moses 6:17–19). He was the father of Mahalaleel. Cainan's lifespan extended 910 years. He is mentioned twice in the Doctrine and Covenants: once in connection with the descent of the priesthood lineage (see D&C 107:45), and again as a participant in the assembly of elect individuals gathered together by Adam to receive his benedictory blessing (see D&C 107:53).

CALEB

1. Caleb was one of the twelve princes, or heads of the tribes of Israel, whom Moses sent by command of the Lord to spy out the land of Canaan (see Numbers 13:1–3). When these scouts returned, they brought Moses a mixed report: the land was rich "with milk and honey" but was already inhabited by many strong peoples, including the Canaanites (see Numbers 13:27–29).

Despite the odds against them, Caleb entreated Moses to let them go up against the Canaanites, "for we are well able to overcome it" (Numbers 13:30). Still, his companions resisted, saying, "We be not able to go up against the people; for they are stronger than we" (Numbers 13:31). Thus Israel shrank in fear and lamented the situation facing them in Canaan—even wanting at that moment to return to Egypt.

But Caleb and Joshua, seeing Israel's divine destiny, stood forth in strength and enjoined the people to obey the Lord and have faith in His power to deliver the land of milk and honey into their hands (see Numbers 14:6–10; compare Deuteronomy 1:22–36). When the Israelites persisted in their murmurings, the anger of the Lord was kindled against them for their lack of faith. It took the earnest supplication of Moses to dissuade the Lord from sending destruction upon the people in that very hour. Though the murmurers were pardoned, those twenty years of age and older at that time were denied entry into the promised land at the conclusion of the sojourn in the wilderness (see Numbers 14:29). Those of faith and courage—like Caleb and Joshua—would, however, enter therein (see Numbers 14:24, 30). As for the other scouts who returned a report of fear to the people, they perished according to the judgment of God (see Numbers 14:36–38; see also Numbers 25:65; 32:12).

Caleb, of the tribe of Judah, received an inheritance in the promised land and, at the age of eighty-five, left behind a legacy of faith and courage when he passed away (see Joshua 14:6–14; 15:13–18; 21:12; Numbers 34:19; Judges 1:12–15, 20; 1 Chronicles 4:15; 6:56).

2. Caleb was a priesthood leader mentioned twice in the Doctrine and Covenants in connection with the lineage of the priesthood at the time of Moses, the latter having received the priesthood from his father-in-law, Jethro: "And Jethro received it under the hand of Caleb; And Caleb received it under the hand of Elihu" (D&C 84:7–8). The Caleb in these references is not likely the Caleb sent to scout out the land of Canaan (1, above).

3. Caleb was one of the three sons of Hezron of the tribe of Judah as listed among the posterity of Israel (see 1 Chronicles 2:18–19, 42–49; see also 1 Chronicles 2:50).

CANAAN/CANAANITE

(Meaning: low, humbled.)

1. Canaan was the fourth son of Ham, son of Noah (see Genesis 9:18; Genesis 10:6). In a few instances, the word Canaanite has specific reference to those of the lineage of Canaan, son of Ham (see Genesis 10:15–20).

Noah cursing Canaan

2. Canaan/Canaanite is also used in connection with the non-Israelite peoples who inhabited the lowland area toward the Mediterranean coast of Palestine, west of the Jordan River (see Genesis 24:3). Since these peoples (especially the Phoenicians) were accomplished merchants and traders, the word *Canaanite* came to mean people in these professions and shows up in some English translations as "merchant" or "merchants" (see for example Isaiah 23:8; Ezekiel 17:4; Hosea 12:7).

CHAMBERLAIN

This title designates a private and confidential officer of an eastern king (see 2 Kings 23:11; Esther 2:3, 14, 15; Acts 12:20; Romans 16:23). In some cases the word is also given the translation "eunuch."

CHEDORLAOMER

Chedorlaomer (pronounced "ked-or-lay-o'-mer" or "ked-or-lay'-o-mer") was a king of Elam who, in league with three princes of Babylon, defeated the kings of Sodom, Gomorrah, and several other cities in that region who had revolted from their agreement to be subservient to Chedorlaomer (see Genesis 14:1–12). Learning that the victors had abducted his nephew Lot along with their spoil, Abraham went out with 318 of his own men and rescued Lot (and the others taken captive) by battling the forces of Chedorlaomer (see Genesis 14:14–17).

CHERUB/CHERUBIM

A cherub (Hebrew plural cherubim) is an angel of some particular order and rank among the hierarchy of the hosts of heaven. When Adam and Eve were driven from the Garden

A cherub guards the tree of life

of Eden because of their transgression, cherubim were deployed to guard the pathway to the tree of life (see Moses 4:31; compare Genesis 3:24 concerning "cherubims"; see also Alma 12:21–37; 42:2–3). The figure of the cherub was used in Old Testament times as a symbolic accoutrement associated with the sacred structure of the ark of the covenant and other features of the Tabernacle and later with the décor of the temple (see, for example, Exodus 25:18–22; compare also the various references in 2 Samuel 22:11; Psalms 18:10; 80:1; 99:1; Isaiah 37:16; Ezekiel 10–11; D&C 77:4).

CHEMOSH

Chemosh was a god worshipped by the Moabites (see Numbers 21:29) and the Ammonites (see Judges 11:24). Solomon, in his later years of idolatry, built a sanctuary to Chemosh on Mount Olivet (see 1 Kings 11:7–8); such pagan sanctuaries were later destroyed in the reform movement of Josiah (see 2 Kings 23:13; compare Jeremiah 48:7, 13, 46).

CHILEAB

Chileab was David's son by Abigail (see 2 Samuel 3:3), also referred to as Daniel (see 1 Chronicles 3:1).

CHITTIM (OR KITTIM)

Chittim was the son of Javan, who was the son of Japheth, the son of Noah (see Genesis 10:4; 1 Chronicles 1:7). The name *Chittim* was later appropriated for an island country, probably the Cyprus of today (see Numbers 24:24; Isaiah 23:1, 12; Jeremiah 2:10; Ezekiel 27:6; Daniel 11:30).

CHRIST (SEE JESUS CHRIST)

COMFORTER (SEE HOLY GHOST)

CUSH

Cush was a son of Ham, the son of Noah (see Genesis 10:6; 1 Chronicles 1:8). Cush was also the father of the warrior Nimrod (see Genesis 10:8; 1 Chronicles 1:10). The name *Cush* then came to be applied to a people living in eastern Africa, south of Egypt, and in the southern part of Arabia (see Ezekiel 29:10). Cush was also the name of a country (see Isaiah 11:11)—apparently Ethiopia (Psalm 68:31; Ezekiel 30:4–6; 38:5).

CYRUS

(Meaning: the sun.) Cyrus the Great was the king of Persia who took over Babylonia and defeated the Chaldean dynasty that had been elevated to power by Nebuchadnezzar. The last king of this dynasty was Nabonidus, whose son Belshazzar was apparently prince-regent when the kingdom fell (see the entry for Belshazzar). Cyrus issued a decree in 537 BC allowing the Jewish people to return from captivity in Babylon to rebuild the temple at Jerusalem (see 2 Chronicles 36:22–23; Ezra 1; 3:7; Isaiah 44:28; 45:1). Daniel was well received in the court of Cyrus (see Daniel 1:21; 6:28; 10:1).

DAN

(Meaning: judge.) Dan was the son of Jacob and Bilhah, Rachel's maid (see Genesis 30:5–6), and full brother to Naphtali (see Genesis 30:8; 35:25; compare Genesis 46:23–24). For the final blessing bestowed by Jacob upon Dan, see Genesis 49:16–17, and for Moses' blessing upon the tribe of Dan, see Deuteronomy 33:22 (compare Joshua 19:40–48). Samson was of the Danite lineage (see Judges 13:2, 24).

DANIEL

(Meaning: God is judge.)

1. Daniel was the second son of David by Abigail (see 1 Chronicles 3:1). Daniel was also called Chileab (see 2 Samuel 3:3).

2. Daniel was one of the Lord's great prophets of the Old Testament and the author of the book that bears his name. The book of Daniel is one of the major prophetic books of the Old Testament, along with Isaiah, Jeremiah, and Ezekiel. It stems from the time of the Babylonian conquest of Jerusalem.

Daniel, apparently of royal heritage (see Daniel 1:3), was taken captive to the court of the Babylonian king Nebuchadnezzar (reigned around 604–562 BC) shortly before the turn of the sixth century BC. It was a period of foment and transition leading to the ultimate destruction of Jerusalem around 587 BC. Daniel was renamed Belteshazzar by an officer of the royal court (see Daniel 1:6–7). He prophesied during his captivity, around the same time Jeremiah and Ezekiel were prophesying. He was a contemporary of Nephi, son of Lehi in the Book of Mormon.

The book of Daniel confirms by prophetic pronouncements that the Lord is in charge of the destiny of humankind, and that righteousness will ultimately prevail over the forces of worldly pride and power. Through obedience to the commandments of God, the faithful will receive magnificent blessings of wisdom and light and will inherit a place in the triumphant kingdom of the Lord, which will roll forth until it fills the entire world. Daniel is a prominent example of *apocalyptic* writing (from the Greek word meaning "revealed" or "uncovered"), as in the Apocalypse

Daniel in the lions' den

or Revelation of John, where similar great and symbolic visions of the ultimate consummation of God's work are presented. Highlights from Daniel's life include his interpretations of King Nebuchadnezzar's many dreams and the prophecies accompanying those dreams (see Daniel 2:35, 44–45; 4:25); his loyalty to his covenants (see Daniel 1:15–17); his association with Shadrach, Meshach, and Abednego and their fiery furnace experience (see Daniel 3); his service and leadership in Darius' kingdom, his defiance of Darius' decree to not worship the Lord, and his subsequent stint in the lions' den; and the resultant decree by Darius that all might worship Daniel's God freely (see 3:26).

The nobility and valor of Daniel and his captive associates can be expressed in three overarching themes: 1) uncompromising commitment to God, 2) the spirit of revelation, and 3) the power of sincere prayer.

DARIUS

1. Darius is identified in the book of Daniel as the king of Babylon after the death of Belshazzar (see Daniel 5:30–31). Darius reportedly made Daniel the leading president among three presidents overseeing the realm (see Daniel 6:1–3). When Daniel's associates in government conspired against him by inducing Darius to issue a death decree against those (like Daniel) who prayed to God (see Daniel 6:4–9), Daniel resolved to pray only in

secret within his private quarters. But these prayers were discovered by his eavesdropping enemies and reported to Darius, who was forced by his own decree to consign Daniel to the lions' den. Daniel's miraculous protection in the lions' den overjoyed the king, who then cast the conspirators into the lions' den and issued a new proclamation that all should "tremble and fear before the God of Daniel: for he is the living God, and stedfast for ever, and his kingdom that which shall not be destroyed, and his dominion shall be even unto the end" (Daniel 6:26; see also Daniel 9:1; 11:1).

It has not been possible for historians to relate the Darius in these references to any of the kings of Babylon in the secular records. Belshazzar, identified in these passages as the "king of the Chaldeans" (Daniel 5:30) and the son of Nebuchadnezzar (see Daniel 5:2, 18, 22), was, according to recent archaeological discoveries, most probably the son of Nabonidus (the last king of Babylon) and therefore the grandson of Nebuchadnezzar.

2. Darius is also mentioned in the book of Ezra as the Persian king who renewed the decree of Cyrus permitting the rebuilding of the temple at Jerusalem following the Babylonian captivity (see Ezra 6:12–15; compare also Ezra 4:5, 24; 5:5–7; 6:1, 12–15; Haggai 1:1, 15; 2:10; Zechariah 1:1, 7; 7:1).

3. Another Darius is also mentioned in Nehemiah 12:22 as "Darius the Persian," possibly the last king of Persia, who was defeated by Alexander the Great in 330 BC.

DAUGHTER OF PHARAOH

The daughter of Pharaoh was the one who discovered the babe Moses hidden in an ark of bulrushes on the bank of the river and had compassion on him. She named the infant Moses and raised him as her own son (see Exodus 2:6–10).

We know little more about this daughter of the pharaoh, except that she performed a supremely important task in preserving the life of Moses, thus enabling him to rise to the station of liberator of his people and prophet of the Lord.

DAVID

(Meaning: beloved.) David was the celebrated king of Judah and Israel who united the tribes as one great nation and ensured that the government was based on the law of God. He is also one of the most tragic figures in the Old Testament because of his transgression with Bathsheba and Uriah, though his union with Bathsheba brought forth Solomon, who was an ancestor of Jesus Christ.

1 Samuel chronicles David's life and his associations with King Saul. We hear of his early anointing, as the youngest son of Jesse, to become king of Israel (see 16) and of his victory over Philistine giant Goliath and how Saul subsequently puts David in charge of his armies (see 18:5–29), but then fears David's popularity and potential. We read of Saul's murderous conspiracies on David and David's escape and rise to prominence among the people, along with Saul's ultimate demise.

2 Samuel continues the history of David by providing a detailed portrait of David as king of Israel—his towering strengths of leadership and magnanimity as well as his devastating weakness in succumbing to carnal temptation.

We can remember David with five themes that serve to define his life: 1) his courage in the strength of the Lord (as demonstrated in his battle against Goliath); 2) his leadership in

David writing the Psalms

establishing a unified kingdom grounded in righteous principles; 3) his experience with sorrow and repentance; 4) his magnanimity and forgiveness of his enemies; and 5) his mastery of the poetic word of inspiration (as in the Psalms). The Psalms were written during David's reign and many—though not all—of the Psalms in the Old Testament collection are ascribed to David personally.

DEBORAH

(Meaning: a bee.)

1. Deborah was a nurse who accompanied her mistress, Rebekah, on her journey to the household of Abraham to become Isaac's wife (see Genesis 24:59). Many years later Deborah passed away at Bethel (see Genesis 35:8).

2. Deborah the prophetess was a celebrated leader who served as judge over Israel and unified the people in strength to defeat their enemies (see Judges 4:4–5). Note that the term *prophetess* should not be construed as the equivalent of the prophet who leads our Church today; rather, *prophetess* in this setting refers to a female leader who has spiritual strength or insight. Deborah commissioned Barak, son of Abinoam, to wage battle against the encroaching Canaanites under the command of Sisera. Barak agreed to gather the forces and attack, provided Deborah would consent to accompany him. She did, saying: "Up; for this is the day in which the Lord hath delivered Sisera into thine hand: is not the Lord gone out before thee?" (Judges 4:14). That day the Canaanites, with their much

larger force, were annihilated, along with their king, Jabin (see Judges 4:23–24). Thereafter Deborah and Barak joined in singing a glorious anthem of praise to the Lord (see Judges 5:7, 11–12).

DEHAVITES

The Dehavites (mentioned in Ezra 4:9) were settlers in Samaria (an area about thirty miles north of Jerusalem) who—along with eight other confederate groups—attempted, without success, to prevent the rebuilding of Jerusalem and the temple following the Babylonian conquest (see Ezra 4:11–14). The temple was completed in 516 BC in accordance with the decree of the Persian king Cyrus issued in 537 BC (see 2 Chronicles 36:22–23; Ezra 1; 3:7; Isaiah 44:28; 45:1) and confirmed by Darius (see Ezra 5:6–17; 6:11–12).

DELILAH

(Meaning: weak, languishing.) Delilah was a woman from the valley of Sorek whom Samson loved (see Judges 16:4). The Philistines bribed her to discover the secret of Samson's astounding strength, but, as Samson provided her with false information each time she tried, her efforts were futile (see vv. 5–15). She persisted, asking him daily until "his soul was vexed unto death" (v. 16), and he explained that if his head was shaved he would become weak. When Samson slept, Delilah had a man shave Samson's head, then she woke him and sent him out to meet the Philistines, who put out Samson's eyes and imprisoned him at Gaza (see vv. 17–21). Later—after Samson's hair had grown long once again (see v. 22)—the Philistines assembled a vast throng of people to celebrate their

Samson and Delilah

victory and to make sport of Samson. Calling one last time upon the Lord, he pulled down the pillars of the house, destroying himself and all three thousand of the celebrants who were therein (see vv. 28–30).

DEVIL (SEE SATAN)

DINAH

(Meaning: judged and vindicated.) Dinah was the daughter of Jacob and Leah (see Genesis 30:21). Shechem, the son of Hamor the Hivite, fell in love with Dinah and defiled her (see 34:1–4). Angered over this act, the sons of Jacob pretended to accept the peace overtures of Hamor by requiring the males of the Hivites to be circumcised in exchange for the hand of Dinah and assurance of cooperation and intermarriage with the Israelites. When Hamor and Shechem had agreed to the arrangement and carried out the requirement, two of the sons of Jacob, Simeon and Levi, fell upon the Hivite community, killed all of the males, "and took Dinah out of Shechem's house, and went out" (34:26). They then raided the city and took all the survivors captive. When Jacob learned of their actions, he was greatly distressed (see 34:30). He then gathered his people together and moved away to Beth-el at the command of God (see 35:1–5). Dinah later journeyed to Egypt with Jacob's family circle (see 46:8, 15).

DINAITES

The Dinaites (mentioned in Ezra 4:9) were settlers in Samaria (an area about thirty miles north of Jerusalem). *See the entry for Dehavites for details.*

EBED-MELECH

(Meaning: king's servant.) Ebed-melech (pronounced ee'-bid-mell'-ik or ee'-bid-mell'uhk), an Ethiopian eunuch at the court of King Zedekiah of Judah, took compassion on the prophet Jeremiah, who was imprisoned for

Jeremiah imprisoned in a dungeon

prophesying the impending destruction of Jerusalem, and interceded on his behalf (see Jeremiah 38:9–10).

The Lord commanded Jeremiah to give a special blessing of liberty to Ebed-melech for his honor and courage (see Jeremiah 39:16–18).

EBER

1. Eber was the great-grandson of Shem, the son of Noah (see Genesis 10:21–25; compare 1 Chronicles 1:17–19, 25). Eber is regarded as the founding ancestor of the Hebrew people (see Genesis 11:14–17; Numbers 24:24; he is called *Heber* in Luke 3:35).

2. Eber is also the name of two other individuals mentioned in the Old Testament (see 1 Chronicles 8:12; Nehemiah 12:20).

EDOM/EDOMITES

(Meaning: red.) Edom is another name for Esau, the older twin brother of Jacob. Esau sold his birthright to Jacob for a serving of "pottage" (Genesis 25:29). The descendants of Esau (or Edom) were known as Edomites (see

Genesis 36:1, 8, 16–17, 19–21, 31–32, 43; Exodus 15:15; Numbers 20:14; 1 Chronicles 1:35–43), a people living in the mountainous country of Edom (southeast of the Dead Sea)—also called Mount Seir (see Genesis 38:8–9; Deuteronomy 1:2; 2:1, 5; Joshua 24:4; Ezekiel 35:3, 7) and later Idumea (see Isaiah 34:5–6; Ezekiel 35:15; 36:5). The Edomites refused passage to the Israelites during the Exodus (see Numbers 20:18–21) and were later defeated by Saul and David (see 1 Samuel 14:47; 2 Samuel 8:14).

EGYPT/EGYPTIANS (SEE EGYPTUS/DAUGHTER OF EGYPTUS AND PHARAOH)

EGYPTUS/DAUGHTER OF EGYPTUS

There is a woman identified in the book of Abraham as "the daughter of Ham, and the daughter of Egyptus, which in the Chaldean signifies Egypt, which signifies that which is forbidden" (Abraham 1:23). According to the record, this woman (also named Egyptus) discovered the land of Egypt and was the mother of the first pharaoh (see Abraham 1:25).

EHUD

(Meaning: united, strong.)

1. Ehud, a Benjamite, was a deliverer raised up by the Lord to liberate the Israelites, who had fallen under oppression at the hands of the Moabites (see Judges 3:12–15).

The stratagy of Ehud was to gain audience with Eglon, king of the Moabites, in the pretense of presenting a gift. When they were alone, Ehud said to the king, "I have a message from God unto thee" (v. 20). He then drew forth his concealed dagger and took the king's life. Thereafter Ehud snuck away from the royal dwelling place and mobilized Israel with a trumpet. In the ensuing battle, the Moabites were destroyed (see vv. 26–30).

2. Ehud was the great-grandson of Benjamin, son of Jacob (see 1 Chronicles 7:10; 8:6).

ELAM/ELAMITES

1. Elam was the son of Shem (see Genesis 10:22) and the progenitor of the original inhabitants of the area known as Elam (see Genesis 14:1, 9). Concerning prophecies about Elam, see Isaiah 11:11; 21:2; 22:6; Jeremiah 25:25; 49:34–39; and Ezekiel 32:24.

2. The Elamites (mentioned in Ezra 4:9) were settlers in Samaria, an area about thirty miles north of Jerusalem. *See the entry for Dehavites for details.*

3. Elam was the name of a number of others mentioned in Old Testament genealogies.

ELDAD AND MEDAD

(Eldad means "whom God has loved"; Medad means love.) Eldad and Medad were two of the seventy elders called to give assistance to Moses during his sojourn in the wilderness (see Numbers 11:25–26.)

It was reported to Moses by a young man that these two were prophesying, even though they failed to go to the Tabernacle as appointed. When Joshua asked Moses to forbid them from prophesying, he responded with the pronouncement, "And Moses said unto him, Enviest thou for my sake? would God that all the LORD's people were prophets, and that the LORD would put his spirit upon them!" (Numbers 11:29–30).

Moses ordaining Joshua as an elder

ELDER(S)

The term *elders*, as used in the Old Testament, can refer to tribal members with seniority and experience (as in Genesis 50:7 or Ruth 4:2), or to those who are ordained to a specific calling (as in Exodus 24:9–10 or Numbers 11:16). In the operation of the priesthood in the latter days, the word *elder* or *elders* can apply specifically to those who are members of quorums of elders, or, in general, to all holders of the Melchizedek Priesthood, including Apostles and seventies (see D&C 20:38–39; compare D&C 124:139 and D&C 46:2).

ELEAZAR

(Meaning: God hath helped.)

1. Eleazar (pronounced el'-ee-ay'-zuhr) was the third son of Aaron (see Exodus 6:23; compare Numbers 3:2; 26:60; 1 Chronicles 6:3; 24:1). Eleazar and his three brothers—Nadab, Abihu, and Ithamar—were consecrated to the office of priest (see Exodus 28:1). However, despite the glorious blessings accorded them in being able to view the Lord on Mount Sinai (see Exodus 24:1–2, 9–11), Abihu and Nadab profaned their office with "strange fire before the Lord" (Leviticus 10:1) and brought the judgment of the Lord upon their heads so that they perished (see Numbers 3:4; 26:61; 1 Chronicles 24:2). Thereafter Eleazar and Ithamar were the chief assistants to Aaron, with Eleazar having seniority (see Leviticus 10:12, 16). When Aaron died, Moses elevated Eleazar to take Aaron's place (see Numbers 20:28; see also Numbers 26:63; 27:19–21; 31:12, 29; Deuteronomy 10:6; Joshua 14:1;

19:51; 24:33). According to the Bible Dictionary, "All the high priests until the Maccabaean period were descended from Eleazar, with the exception of those from Eli to Abiathar, inclusive, who belonged to the family of Ithamar."

2. Eleazar was the son of Abinadab and the one who oversaw the security of the ark of the covenant at Kirjath-jearam (see 1 Samuel 7:1–2).

3. Eleazar is listed as "one of the three mighty men of David" (2 Samuel 23:9).

4. Eleazar is the name of various other individuals in the Old Testament (see Ezra 8:33; 10:25; Nehemiah 12:42; 1 Chronicles 23:21–22; 24:28; see also Matthew 1:15 concerning the genealogy of Jesus Christ).

EL ELYON

(Meaning: the most high God.) *El Elyon* is the Hebrew expression for Deity rendered as follows in the passage where it occurs for the first time in the Old Testament: "And Melchizedek king of Salem brought forth bread and wine: and he was the priest of the most high God" (Genesis 14:18; see also vv. 19 and 22). The expression "the most high God" occurs rather frequently thereafter in the Old Testament, New Testament, Book of Mormon, and Doctrine and Covenants (see, for example, D&C 39:19).

ELI

(Meaning: ascending.) Eli was a high priest and judge in Israel during the days of Samuel the prophet. Eli was of the lineage of Ithamar, the youngest surviving son of Aaron (see Exodus 6:23; 24:1–2, 9–11; 28:1; Numbers 3:2, 4; 26:60–61; 1 Chronicles 6:3). The priestly

Hannah presenting Samuel to Eli

office remained with Eli's family and the lineage of Ithamar until Abiathar was removed from office by Solomon because of his conflicting loyalty to Solomon's brother, Adonijah, who aspired to the throne (see 1 Kings 1:7; 2:26–27). At that point, the office was conveyed by Solomon to Zadok of the family of Eleazar (see 1 Kings 2:35).

Eli's history is recorded in 1 Samuel 1–4. It was Eli who pronounced a blessing upon Hannah, wife of Elkanah, when she was grieving over her lack of a son (see 1 Samuel 1:17). When she was blessed with a son, whom she named Samuel (see v. 20), Hannah followed through with her pledge to dedicate him to the service of the Lord. Eli once again offered his blessing (see 2:20).

Despite his piety and compassion, Eli was to encounter the judgment of God for his indulgence and passivity concerning his sons, Hophni and Phinehas, both priests. These two sons selfishly misused the offerings brought before the Lord by the people (see 1 Samuel 2:12–17) and were guilty of gross immorality with the women who came before the Tabernacle (see v. 22). In response, Eli confronted them (see vv. 23–25), but his words were not such as to induce them to repent. Therefore, the Lord sent a man of God to reproach Eli for failing to discipline his sons effectively (see vv. 30–31, 34–35). Soon thereafter, the Lord confirmed His word by speaking to the young Samuel during the night in the household of Eli (see 1 Samuel 3:11–14).

In due time the Philistines fell upon Israel and exacted a great slaughter. The ark of the covenant, which had been taken from its resting place in Shiloh as a means to deter the enemy, was then stolen by the Philistines, and "the two sons of Eli, Hophni and Phinehas, were slain" (1 Samuel 4:11). When a messenger reported these calamities to the anxious Eli, waiting on the sidelines, "he fell from off the seat backward by the side of the gate, and his neck brake, and he died: for he was an old man, and heavy" (1 Samuel 4:18). Thus ended the forty-year tenure of Eli, who had attained the age of ninety-eight.

ELIAKIM

(Meaning: God raiseth up.)

1. Eliakim, son of Hilkiah, was the master of king Hezekiah's household at the time Sennacherib, king of Assyria, invaded Judah and took over her defended cities. Hezekiah sent Eliakim (pronounced ee-ly'-uh-kim) and other representatives to the walls of the city to hear the arrogant demands of the Assyrian chief of princes, Rab-shakeh, spoken in the Hebrew language from the midst of the hosts of the Assyrian warriors (see 2 Kings 18:28–30; compare 2 Kings 19:9; 2 Chronicles 32:9–20;

Isaiah 36:4–20; 37:2–13). Having been reassured by the prophet Isaiah (see 2 Kings 19:6–7), Hezekiah prayed before the Lord for the deliverance of the people—something that happened within the hour through the intervention of heaven (see 2 Kings 19:32–36; compare 2 Chronicles 32:21–22; Isaiah 36–37; also see 2 Kings 19:37; 2 Chronicles 32:21; Isaiah 37:38).

Eliakim, the messenger of the royal crown in this episode of history, was also used by Isaiah as a symbol for the Great King who would in due time be raised up to secure the eternal well-being of Israel as Deliverer and Savior (see Isaiah 22:20–25.)

2. Eliakim was the original name of Jehoiakim, the second son of Josiah, whom the Egyptians set up as king of Judah (see 2 Kings 23:34).

3. Eliakim was a priest during the time of Nehemiah, who assisted in the dedicatory service for the rebuilt wall of Jerusalem (see Nehemiah 12:41).

ELIAS

The name *Elias* does not occur in the Old Testament (King James Version). However, Elias is the Greek form of the name of the Old Testament prophet Elijah as it is rendered in the New Testament (see, for example, Matthew 17:1–4; Luke 4:25–26; James 5:17). From modern scripture we learn that Elias is both an individual prophet (as in D&C 110:12) as well as a title meaning "forerunner" (see D&C 27:7) and also Savior (see JST John 1:28).

ELIEZER

(Meaning: God is help.)

1. Eliezer (pronounced el-ih-ee'-zer) is the

man whom Abram (later named Abraham) identified as "steward of my house" (Genesis 15:2). He is apparently the same steward who later acted as emissary in the quest to obtain a wife for Isaac as recorded in Genesis 24. This devoted man in the circle of Abraham—"his eldest servant of his house, that ruled over all that he had" (Genesis 24:2)—was commissioned to go to the city of Nahor in the region of Padan-aram in Mesopotamia, where Abraham's kin were located (see Genesis 25:20) and arrange for Rebekah, daughter of Bethuel, to be betrothed to Isaac (see Genesis 24:11–15, 58–61; 25:24–26).

2. Eliezer was a son of Moses and Zipporah (see Exodus 18:4; compare 1 Chronicles 23:15, 17; 26:25).

3. Eliezer was a prophet who rebuked Jehoshaphat, king of Judah, for his alliance with Ahaziah, wicked king of Israel (see 2 Chronicles 20:35–37).

4. Eliezer was the name of a variety of other individuals in the Old Testament (see 1 Chronicles 7:8; 15:24; 27:16; Ezra 8:16; 10:18, 23, 31).

Elihu

(Meaning: God is he.)

1. Elihu (pronounced ee-ly'-hyoo) is a figure in the book of Job who takes issue with the three friends of Job and counsels with Job to follow a higher perspective: "But there is a spirit in man: and the inspiration of the Almighty giveth them understanding" (Job 32:8). Elihu also counsels that "God is greater than man" (Job 33:12), is the source of life and light (see Job 33:30), is all-knowing (see Job 34:21), and that men are to repent and trust in Him (see Job 34:31; 35:14; 36:5–7).

2. Elihu was a forebear of Elkanah, the husband of Hannah, who was the mother of the prophet Samuel (see 1 Samuel 1:1). This Elihu is called *Eliab* in 1 Chronicles 6:27 and Eliel in 1 Chronicles 6:34.

3. Elihu is the name of several others mentioned in the Old Testament (see 1 Chronicles 12:20; 26:7; 27:18).

4. Elihu (not mentioned in the Old Testament) was a priesthood leader mentioned twice in the Doctrine and Covenants in connection with the lineage of the Melchizedek Priesthood leading up to the time of Moses: "And Caleb received it under the hand of Elihu; And Elihu under the hand of Jeremy" (D&C 84:8–9). More details concerning the life and character of this Elihu are not known at this time.

Elijah

(Meaning: Jehovah is my God.) Elijah the Tishbite is a singularly imposing figure in a long line of extraordinary prophets. He commenced his ministry around 926 BC among the northern tribes of Israel. His influence was felt with compelling force among the people of his day, was called forth again on the Mount of Transfiguration (see Matthew 17:1–11), and touches countless lives today through the restored keys of the sealing power of the priesthood placed in his charge (see D&C 110:13–16).

The history of the prophet Elijah is recounted in 1 Kings 17 through 2 Kings 2 (compare also 2 Chronicles 21:12–15). Elijah's ministry provides an illustration of many themes and doctrines of the gospel of salvation, particularly: the triumph of divine power over idolatry, as in the defeat of the priests of Baal (see especially 1 Kings 18:37–40; compare 2 Nephi 9:20; D&C 88:41); the humility accompanying the fast, as in the exemplary supplication of Elijah during his forty-day fast; and the orderly succession of priesthood leadership upon Elisha (see 2 Kings 2:11–13).

The prophet Elijah occupied a central position in the design of God as the one holding the "keys of the power of turning the hearts of the fathers to the children, and the hearts of the children to the fathers, that the whole earth may not be smitten with a curse" (D&C 27:9; see also 3 Nephi 24–25, which contains the only reference to the ancient prophet Elijah in the Book of Mormon). God sent this prophet on April 3, 1836, to the Kirtland Temple to restore these sacred keys to Joseph Smith as an essential priesthood power in the dispensation of the fulness of times (see D&C 110:14–16; compare also Malachi 4:5–6; 3 Nephi 25:5). The hearts of the children have indeed been turned to their fathers so that the work of the sacred temples of God can proceed in this, the final dispensation prior to the Second Coming.

Elijah restored more than the sealing powers alone, as the Prophet Joseph Smith emphasized:

> Elijah was the last prophet that held the keys of this priesthood, and who will, before the last dispensation, restore the authority and delive[r] the Keys of this priesthood in order that all the ordinances may be attended to in righteousness. . . .
>
> And I will send Elijah the Prophet before the great and terrible day of the Lord &c &c.
>
> Why send Elijah [:] because he holds the Keys of the Authority to administer in *all the ordinances of the priesthood* [italics added] and without the authority is given the ordinances could not be administered in righteousness. (*WJS*, 43.)

ELISHA

(Meaning: God shall save, or God of salvation.) Elisha was the companion and student of Elijah for several years and ultimately became his successor as prophet in the northern kingdom of Israel. His calling came by divine command to Elijah at the same time the prophet was directed to anoint Jehu as king (see 1 Kings 19:16, 19, 21).

Elijah ascending into heaven

Elisha dividing the waters with the mantle of Elijah

The story of Elisha is conveyed for the most part in 2 Kings. Highlights of Elisha's life include his dividing the waters of the Jordan (see 2:11–13); his performance of mighty miracles, including raising the dead (see 4–5); and his protection against Syria with chariots of fire (see 6–7).

The ministry of Elisha lasted more than half a century, concurrent with the reigns of Jehoram, Jehu, Jehoahaz, and Joash. Elisha showed humble dependence on the Lord, and the mighty miracles he was able to perform in the spirit of service and devotion to the Lord's cause exemplified his righteousness as well as the faith of the people for whom they were performed.

ELISHAH

Elishah was the oldest of the four sons of Javan (see Genesis 10:4; 1 Chronicles 1:7). The expression "isles of Elishah" mentioned in Ezekiel 27:7 apparently has reference to Greece, possibly the area where the descendants of Elishah settled.

ELISHEBA

Elisheba (pronounced ih-lish'-ih-buh or ih-ly'-shuh-buh) was the wife of Aaron: "And Aaron took him Elisheba, daughter of Amminadab, sister of Naashon, to wife; and she bare him Nadab, and Abihu, Eleazar, and Ithamar" (Exodus 6:23).

ELKANAH

Elkanah (pronounced el-kay'-nah or el'-kay-nuh) was a devout Ephraimite who lived in the central mountainous district of Israel (see 1 Samuel 1:1–3). He had two wives, Peninnah and Hannah. His wife Hannah, whom he loved dearly, was blessed of the Lord to have a son who became the prophet Samuel. *See Hannah.*

ELKENAH

Elkenah was an ancient god worshipped by the idolatrous people in Ur of Chaldees in the days of Abraham. In the words of Abraham:

> My fathers having turned from their righteousness, and from the holy commandments which the Lord their God had given unto them, unto the worshiping of the gods of the heathen, utterly refused to hearken to my voice;
>
> For their hearts were set to do evil, and were wholly turned to the god of Elkenah . . . and the god of Pharaoh, king of Egypt;
>
> Therefore they turned their hearts to the sacrifice of the heathen in offering up their

children unto these dumb idols, and hearkened not unto my voice, but endeavored to take away my life by the hand of the priest of Elkenah. The priest of Elkenah was also the priest of Pharaoh. (Abraham 1:5–7; see also Abraham 1:13, 17, 20, 29; 2:13; 3:20; Facsimile 1: figures 3, 4, and 5.)

EMIMS

(Meaning: terrible men.) The Emims were a race of people of large stature who resided east of the Jordan River during the days of Abraham (see Deuteronomy 2:10). The Emims were among the peoples defeated at the time by Chedorlaomer, king of Elam (see Genesis 14:5).

EMMANUEL

(Meaning: God with us.) This alternate spelling for *Immanuel*, referring to the Son of God, occurs only one time in the scriptures (see Matthew 1:23). *See Immanuel.*

ENOCH

Enoch was an early descendant of Adam whose father was named Jacob, and who begat many daughters and sons, including Methuselah. At the age of twenty-five Enoch was ordained to the priesthood by Adam and was blessed by him again at age sixty-five (see D&C 107:48). Enoch was present at the event where Adam pronounced his benedictory blessing on his posterity (see v. 53). The details of this event were recorded by Enoch in a record that is to come forth in the due time of the Lord (see v. 57). Enoch was 430 years old when he was translated (see v. 49; vv. 48–49 explain the discrepancy between this number and the 365 quoted in Genesis 5:23).

The Apostle Paul gives us additional insight: "By faith Enoch was translated that he should not see death; and was not found, because God had translated him: for before his translation he had this testimony, that he pleased God" (Hebrews 11:5).

From the light shed on Enoch in the Pearl of Great Price, we begin to grasp the extraordinary dignity and importance of this prophet. Enoch was instructed by his father, Jared, "in all the ways of God" (Moses 6:21), and eventually was called by God to his prophetic office: "And he heard a voice from heaven, saying: Enoch, my son, prophesy unto this people, and say unto them—Repent, for thus saith the Lord: I am angry with this people, and my fierce anger is kindled against them; for their hearts have waxed hard, and their ears are dull of hearing, and their eyes cannot see afar off" (Moses 6:27; compare also vv. 32–34).

Enoch was ardent and devoted in his calling, crying with a loud voice for the people to repent. Word was circulated that a seer was prophesying and indeed "a wild man hath come among us" (Moses 6:38). The people feared him, and no one dared lay a hand on him, for he "walked with God" (Moses 6:39). In Moses 6–7 we see that Enoch taught the people the word of God concerning the Fall, the results of succumbing to the temptations of Satan, and Jesus Christ's mission of redemption and salvation. He admonished them to repent and be baptized and teach repentance to their children. So strong was his faith and so miraculous his power of speech that many heeded his word and followed in the paths of righteousness: "And the

Lord called his people ZION, because they were of one heart and one mind, and dwelt in righteousness; and there was no poor among them. And Enoch continued his preaching in righteousness unto the people of God. And it came to pass in his days, that he built a city that was called the City of Holiness, even ZION" (Moses 7:18–19).

The spirit pervasive in the city of Enoch was the spirit of truth and grace centered in the Holy One of Israel, Jesus Christ—whom Enoch was privileged to see in the unfolding visions with which the Lord blessed him as the prophet/leader of his dispensation.

Before Zion was taken up into heaven, Enoch saw this grand occurrence in a vision from the Lord. But he also saw the remaining peoples of the earth, and how the Lord wept at their continuing wickedness. He observed the resulting sorrow and weeping of the Lord. When Enoch inquired of the Lord concerning such sorrow, the Lord explained to him as follows: "Wherefore should not the heavens weep, seeing these shall suffer?" (Moses 7:37). Enoch also became saddened and wept over the wickedness of his brethren and the great flood in the time of Noah, not being comforted until he saw in vision the future coming of the Lord, at which point "his soul rejoiced" (Moses 7:47).

Enoch was then shown the mighty events that will transpire in the future: the gathering of the Lord's elect, the preparation of a Holy City "called Zion, a New Jerusalem" (Moses 7:62), and the return of the city of Enoch at the Second Coming to join with the congregations of Saints caught up in the cloud to meet the returning Savior and King (see JST Genesis 9:21–25; D&C 45:12), who would usher in a thousand years of peace and reign personally among His people. The conclusion

Enoch and the city of Zion

of the extraordinary story of Enoch's ministry is summarized in this verse: "And Enoch and all his people walked with God, and he dwelt in the midst of Zion; and it came to pass that Zion was not, for God received it up into his own bosom; and from thence went forth the saying, ZION IS FLED" (Moses 7:69). And thus we see that it is possible to become a Zion people: "Therefore, verily, thus saith the Lord, let Zion rejoice, for this is Zion—THE PURE IN HEART" (D&C 97:21).

From the Doctrine and Covenants we find confirming evidence concerning these sacred truths. Enoch and his city were indeed translated, as the Savior declared, "into mine own bosom" (D&C 38:4). The greatness of Enoch is confirmed in the passage that speaks of those who inherit the celestial realm of glory as "priests of the Most High, after the order of Melchizedek, which was after the order of Enoch, which was after the order of the

Only Begotten Son" (D&C 76:57). Such celestial beings are spoken of as those who "have come to an innumerable company of angels, to the general assembly and church of Enoch, and of the Firstborn" (D&C 76:67). Enoch will return at the Second Coming (see D&C 133:54) and be "in the presence of the Lamb" (D&C 133:55) along with all of the elect prophets of God.

A number of apocryphal writings claiming the authorship of Enoch have been preserved, some of them having been discovered only in recent times. The relevance of such pseudepigraphical writings concerning Enoch—and how they confirm the authenticity of modern-day scripture—is explored in detail by Hugh Nibley in his book *Enoch the Prophet* (Salt Lake City: Deseret Book and Provo, Utah: FARMS, 1986).

Enos

(Meaning: mortal man.) Enos was the son of Seth and grandson of Adam and Eve (see Genesis 4:25–26; Luke 3:38; called Enosh in 1 Corinthians 1:1). The Old Testament gives scant information about the life of Enos beyond the fact that he had sons and daughters (including Cainan) and lived 905 years (see Genesis 5:6–11).

The Pearl of Great Price indicates that Enos was a prophet like his father: "Seth . . . prophesied in all his days, and taught his son Enos in the ways of God; wherefore Enos prophesied also" (Moses 6:13; see also vv. 17–18). From the Doctrine and Covenants we learn that "Enos was ordained at the age of one hundred and thirty-four years and four months, by the hand of Adam" (107:44), and that he was a participant in the assembly of elect individuals gathered together by Adam

to receive his benedictory blessing (see 107:53).

Ephraim

(Meaning: fruitful.) Ephraim was the younger of the two sons born to Joseph and Asenath (see Genesis 41:50–52; compare Genesis 46:20). Though younger than Manasseh, Ephraim would be the one to receive the birthright. When the aged Israel (Jacob) was about to give a blessing to Joseph's sons, he placed his hands in such a way as to favor Ephraim (see Genesis 48:17–20).

Since Joseph received the birthright ahead of his older brother Reuben (because of the latter's transgression), Ephraim (with the primary blessing in the family of Joseph) was given the birthright in Israel (see 1 Chronicles 5:1–2; Jeremiah 31:9). In terms of an inheritance in the promised land, Joseph received

Jacob blesses Ephraim and Manasseh

two portions of prime, fertile regions, one for each of his two sons (see Joshua 14:4; 16–17).

The tribe of Ephraim had a colorful history marked at times by an envious nature concerning the other tribes (see Judges 8:1; 12:1; 2 Samuel 19:41–43). Isaiah prophesied of a time when such feelings would be supplanted by the harmony of a new era of gospel illumination: "The envy also of Ephraim shall depart, and the adversaries of Judah shall be cut off: Ephraim shall not envy Judah, and Judah shall not vex Ephraim" (Isaiah 11:13).

Latter-day scripture sheds further light on the position of Ephraim in the designs of the Almighty. Ephraim is mentioned a number of times in the Doctrine and Covenants: once in connection with the Book of Mormon—the "stick of Ephraim" (D&C 27:5; compare Ezekiel 37:15–17)—and once in connection with the "rod" that should come forth "out of the stem of Jesse" (see Isaiah 11:1): "Behold, thus saith the Lord: It [the rod] is a servant in the hands of Christ, who is partly a descendant of Jesse as well as of Ephraim, or of the house of Joseph, on whom there is laid much power" (D&C 113:4). The term *rod* very likely refers to the Prophet Joseph Smith. To Ephraim is given the primary responsibility for conveying the truths of the gospel of Jesus Christ to all the world under provisions of the Abrahamic covenant (see Genesis 17; 22:15–18; Deuteronomy 33:13–17; Abraham 2:9–11). In the Doctrine and Covenants Ephraim is also mentioned in connection with the return of the ten tribes and the glorious blessings to be poured out upon Israel at that time (see D&C 133:34). In contrast, "For, verily I say that the rebellious are not of the blood of Ephraim, wherefore they shall be plucked out" (64:36).

ESAIAS

Esaias is the Greek equivalent of *Isaiah* (as used in Matthew 3:3, Luke 4:17, and multiple other references in the New Testament). The name *Esaias* is not used in the Old Testament but occurs several times in the Doctrine and Covenants in connection with an ancient prophet of that name who lived during the time of Abraham and was a key figure in the descent of the priesthood lineage (see D&C 84:11–13; see also D&C 76:100).

ESARHADDON

Esarhaddon (or Esar-haddon) succeeded his father, Sennacherib, king of Assyria, when the latter was murdered by two other sons (see 2 Kings 19:37; Isaiah 37:38). Esarhaddon (680–668 BC) was one of the most powerful kings of Assyria. He rebuilt Babylon; achieved major conquests against Egypt, Syria, and Arabia; and made the land of Judah a tributary domain under King Manasseh.

ESAU

(Meaning: hairy.) Esau was the older of two twin sons born to Isaac and Rebekah. Jacob, though born second, "took hold on Esau's heel" at birth (Genesis 25:26). As the boys grew up, Rebekah favored Jacob, but Isaac favored Esau, who "was a cunning hunter, a man of the field" (Genesis 25:27; see Genesis 25:24–28). One day Jacob bargained with his brother, trading Esau's birthright for a bowl of Jacob's "pottage" with lentils (see Genesis 25:29–34; compare Hebrews 12:16–17). Thus the younger son came into possession of the birthright, upon which Esau had put so little value.

Contrary to the wishes of his parents, Esau married non-Israelite women (see Genesis

Esau reconciles with Jacob

26:34–35; compare Genesis 28:9; 36:2). Later, when Isaac was old and frail, he desired to pronounce a blessing upon the head of his first-born, Esau. But Rebekah counseled Jacob to manage the circumstances in such a way that he, rather than Esau, received the primary blessing, much to Esau's dismay (see 27:38–44). Incensed, Esau desired to kill Jacob, but Rebekah determined to send Jacob to stay with her relatives until Esau's anger cooled.

Eventually Esau and Jacob reconciled (see Genesis 33). Nonetheless, their descendants constituted two rival nations, the Israelites and the Edomites (from "edom," meaning red). *See the entry for Edom/Edomites.*

ESTHER

(Meaning: star.) The story of Esther is one of great courage and faith. The events in the book of Esther occurred some half-century following the return from Babylon of many of the Jewish captives (as authorized by the decree of Cyrus in 537 BC).

The book of Esther presents the historical context and the religious/moral foundation for the establishment of the Jewish feast of Purim. *Purim* is the Hebrew word for "lot"—a reference to the plan of Haman, chief officer at the court of the king of Persia (Ahasuerus—most likely Xerxes), to cast lots for determining a good omen for the timing of his plan for putting all the Jews in captivity to death (see Esther 3:7; 9:24). The story unfolds as follows.

King Ahasuerus had decided to divorce his wife Vashti when she refused to display her beauty before the people and the princes (see Esther 1). Mordecai, a Jew who worked at the palace, presented his beautiful cousin Esther (whom he had raised as his own daughter) as a potential successor. Esther gained the king's favor and became his queen, and even called his attention to a plot against his life (see chapter 2). Unfortunately, when Mordecai

Esther accuses Haman

54

refused to bow down to Haman, the chief officer of the court, Haman developed his insidious plan to exterminate all the Jews (see chapter 3). The king had not been aware that Esther was Jewish, but she courageously decided to come before him to plead the cause of her people: "Go," she advised Mordecai, "gather together all the Jews that are present in Shushan, and fast ye for me, and neither eat nor drink three days, night or day: I also and my maidens will fast likewise; and so will I go in unto the king, which is not according to the law: and if I perish, I perish" (Esther 4:16).

Through her courage, Esther causes the decree to be reversed, thus saving the Jewish people from extinction. The king orders Haman hanged on the very gallows that was secretly intended for hanging Mordecai, who is subsequently elevated into Haman's position at court (see chapters 5–8); Haman's family is dispatched forthwith; the Feast of Purim is instituted; the Jews enjoy greater stature and security; and Mordecai is raised in honor to a position next only to Ahasuerus (see chapters 9–10).

Courage of the type embodied in the life of Esther is an expression of faith, for it requires putting aside fear and doubt and moving forward in the strength of the Lord. "And who knoweth whether thou art come to the kingdom for such a time as this?" said Mordecai to Esther (Esther 4:14), implying that she may have been called of God as a deliverer for her people. In the same way, our own acts of courage may be the fulfillment of a destined role of leadership that is part of our calling.

EUNUCH

(Meaning: bed-keeper.) Eunuchs were a class of men deprived of their masculinity and employed to watch over the harems of eastern rulers or to occupy other positions of trust. Here is one example from among many in the Book of Daniel: "And the king spake unto Ashpenaz the master of his eunuchs, that he should bring certain of the children of Israel [i.e., Daniel and his associates], and of the king's seed, and of the princes" (Daniel 1:3).

EVE

(Meaning: the mother of all living.) Eve was the first woman of humankind and the divine "help meet" given to Adam (Genesis 2:18; Abraham 5:14, 21). From the latter-day vision of President Joseph F. Smith concerning the work of salvation in the spirit world, we have the most satisfying one-word attribute used to summarize the character and person of Eve: *glorious*—"Among the great and mighty ones who were assembled in this vast congregation

Eve kneels with Adam at the altar

of the righteous were Father Adam, the Ancient of Days and father of all, And our glorious Mother Eve, with many of her faithful daughters who had lived through the ages and worshiped the true and living God" (D&C 138:38–39).

From various scriptural accounts, we know that, like Adam, she was created in the image of God (see Moses 6:9). She used her God-given agency, in wisdom, in the best interests of her children for generations (see Moses 3:17, 4:6–13). She was partner to Adam, joining him in fervent prayer (see 5:4–10), and with him, taught her children to follow God (see 5:12, 16, 6:5–6). After learning of the great plan of salvation from the Lord, Eve articulated her profound insight: "Were it not for our transgression we never should have had seed, and never should have known good and evil, and the joy of our redemption, and the eternal life which God giveth unto all the obedient" (Moses 5:11).

EVIL-MERODACH

Evil-merodach (pronounced ee'-vuhl-mer'-uh-dahk) was the son of King Nebuchadnezzar of Babylon and his successor on the throne (see 2 Kings 25:27). He is remembered for having liberated and shown kindness to King Jehoiachin of Judah, who had been held captive in Babylon for some thirty-seven years (see Jeremiah 52:31, 33). The reign of Evil-merodach was rather short (561–559 BC), as he was assassinated by his brother-in-law, Neriglissar, who took over his place on the throne.

EZEKIEL

(Meaning: God will strengthen.) Ezekiel, one of the Lord's great prophets of the Old

Ezekiel

Testament, was a priest of the lineage of Zadok and a younger contemporary of Lehi, Jeremiah, and Daniel. Like King Jehoiachin of Judah, he was carried away to Babylon by the forces of Nebuchadnezzar. He prophesied during the period 592–570 BC. The book of Ezekiel is one of the major prophetic books of the Old Testament, along with Isaiah, Jeremiah, and Daniel.

Ezekiel was granted extraordinary visions that establish the principles of the gospel pertaining to the House of Israel, then as now: the consequences of apostasy and idolatry are destruction and scattering; the consequences of repentance and remembering the covenants are peace, unity, and the blessing of being heirs with the Good Shepherd, to partake eternally of His everlasting glory in the kingdom of God.

The forty-eight chapters of Ezekiel comprise three main sections: prophecies of God's judgment against Jerusalem and the nations in proximity (chapters 1–24); prophecies concerning the gathering and restoration (chapters 25–39); and visions of the temple of the Lord, its reconstruction, and its sacred function (chapters 40–48).

Especially significant among Ezekiel's visionary messages is the prophecy of the coming together of the scriptural record of Judah and that of Joseph: "Moreover, thou son of man, take thee one stick, and write upon it, For Judah, and for the children of Israel his companions: then take another stick, and write upon it, For Joseph, the stick of Ephraim, and for all the House of Israel his companions: And join them one to another into one stick; and they shall become one in thine hand" (Ezekiel 37:16–17).

This miraculous event was accomplished through the coming forth and publication of the Book of Mormon, "Proving to the world that the holy scriptures are true, and that God does inspire men and call them to his holy work in this age and generation, as well as in generations of old; Thereby showing that he is the same God yesterday, today, and forever. Amen" (D&C 20:11–12; see also D&C 27:5; 42:12; compare Isaiah 29).

Ezekiel is mentioned as one of the noble and elect prophets witnessed by President Joseph F. Smith in his vision of the work of salvation in the spirit realm: "Moreover, Ezekiel, who was shown in vision the great valley of dry bones, which were to be clothed upon with flesh, to come forth again in the resurrection of the dead, living souls" (D&C 138:43; compare Ezekiel 37:1–14).

EZIAS

Ezias was an ancient prophet who, though not mentioned in the Old Testament, was included among those listed in the Book of Mormon by Nephi, son of Helaman, as having testified of the gospel of Jesus Christ and contributed to the sacred canon of scripture (see Helaman 8:19–20).

EZRA

Ezra was a noted priest and scribe who accompanied a portion of the people of Judah back to their land after the Babylonian captivity (see Ezra 7–10; Nehemiah 8, 12). The book of Ezra covers the period of time from the decree of Cyrus authorizing the Jews to return to Palestine (537 BC) down to the personal ministry of Ezra and the repatriation of many more of the Jewish people around 459 BC.

The book of Ezra extols the process of recovery, rebuilding, repentance, and reform—based on faith and devotion to the statutes of the Lord. The book celebrates the loving-kindness of the Lord in remembering His covenant people as they transcend the adversities and challenges of life and return to His pathways. The two key sections of the book of Ezra are 1) a historical summary as a backdrop to the ministry of Ezra (chapters 1–6) and 2) the mission and service of Ezra (chapters 7–10).

Modern scripture refers back to the campaign of repatriation of the Jewish people, and particularly to the principle of being worthy to be counted among the Lord's favored people. Thus a passage in D&C 85:11–12 cites Ezra 2:61–62, where those whose names were not included in the "book of the law" received no inheritance among the faithful.

Ezra was diligent in his efforts to educate his people so they could make righteous choices. In Nehemiah 8:4–6, 8, we see that Ezra taught the law of Moses to the people and helped them to understand it.

FATHER IN HEAVEN

Our Father in Heaven—as presented in holy writ and confirmed to the devout and faithful through the Holy Ghost—is the Supreme Lord and God of all creation, the eternal Source of light and truth, the benevolent and ever-loving Father of our spirits (see Hebrews 12:9; 1 John 4:7–8), the Author of the glorious gospel plan of happiness (see Abraham 3:23, 27), the merciful Grantor of agency unto His children, and the Benefactor of all mankind through the gift of His Only Begotten Son: "For God so loved the world, that he gave his only begotten Son, that whosoever believeth in him should not perish, but have everlasting life" (John 3:16). It is to our Father in Heaven that we pray, in the name of Jesus Christ, as directed by Jesus Christ Himself (see Matthew 6:9; Luke 11:10–13; 2 Nephi 32:9; 3 Nephi 18:19–23; 19:6–7; 20:31; D&C 20:77, 79).

In the latter days He has assured the Saints concerning the harmony and oneness of the Godhead: "Which Father, Son, and Holy Ghost are one God, infinite and eternal, without end. Amen" (D&C 20:28). The sacred unity of purpose reflected among the three members of the Godhead makes the term "God" or "Lord" in the scriptures often interchangeable in regard to the Father and the Son. But there are distinctions among the individual Beings of the Godhead. Through the Prophet Joseph Smith was revealed this verity: "The Father has a body of flesh and bones as tangible as man's; the Son also; but the Holy Ghost has not a body of flesh and bones, but is a personage of Spirit. Were it not so, the Holy Ghost could not dwell in us" (D&C 130:22). Moreover, as Joseph Smith also confirmed, the Father has preeminence: "Everlasting covenant was made between three personages before the organization of this earth, and relates to their dispensation of things to men on the earth; these personages, according to Abraham's record, are called God the first, the Creator; God the second, the Redeemer; and God the third, the witness or Testator" (*TPJS*, 190). Paul declared: "But to us there is but one God, the Father, of whom are all things, and we in him; and one Lord Jesus Christ, by whom are all things, and we by him" (1 Corinthians 8:6).

Because Jesus Christ is the divine Agent within the expanse of the Father's eternal dominion and infinite design, it is for the most part Jesus Christ who is the One revealed in the holy scriptures. On occasion, the Father makes His presence known, largely as a confirming witness to the mission of the Savior. For example, on the Mount of Transfiguration where Elias and Moses appeared to Peter, James, and John in the presence of the Savior, the Father is presented for what He is: an individual Being of infinite glory who is the supreme God for us all (see Matthew 17:5).

From the very beginning of the Old Testament account, the majestic role of God the Father is confirmed, as in the account of the creation of man. Although only one member of the Godhead is referred to here, we can see that He is conversing with someone else who is complicit in the creation process: "And God said, Let us make man in our image, after our likeness." (Genesis 1:26). The parallel account from the book of Abraham in the Pearl of Great Price is rendered as follows: "And the Gods formed man from the dust of the ground, and took his spirit (that is, the man's spirit), and put it into him; and breathed into his nostrils the breath of life, and man became a living soul" (Abraham 5:7).

Such accounts provide evidence that the Father empowered others to assist Him in the creative process. The word *God* in the Hebrew bible is *Elohim*, a plural term (as in Genesis 1:1–5). The Prophet Joseph Smith explained the significance of this plural reference as follows: "*Eloheim* is from the word *Eloi*, God, in the singular number; and by adding the word *heim*, it renders it Gods. It read first, 'In the beginning the head of the Gods brought forth the Gods,' or, as others have translated it, 'The head of the Gods called the Gods together' " (*TPJS*, 371).

Chief among the Father's agents, as indicated earlier, was the Supreme Mediator Jesus Christ: "And there stood one among them that was like unto God, and he said unto those who were with him: We will go down, for there is space there, and we will take of these materials, and we will make an earth whereon these may dwell; And we will prove them herewith, to see if they will do all things whatsoever the Lord their God shall command them" (Abraham 3:24–25; compare John 1:1–3).

Modern revelation sheds further light on the stature and supremacy of our Father in Heaven and His role in establishing Jesus as His Mediator. Concerning the oath and covenant of the priesthood, the Lord explains a clear connection between Himself and the Father:

> And also all they who receive this priesthood receive me, saith the Lord;
>
> For he that receiveth my servants receiveth me;
>
> And he that receiveth me receiveth my Father;
>
> And he that receiveth my Father receiveth my Father's kingdom; therefore all that my Father hath shall be given unto him.
>
> And this is according to the oath and covenant which belongeth to the priesthood.
>
> Therefore, all those who receive the priesthood, receive this oath and covenant of my Father, which he cannot break, neither can it be moved. (D&C 84:35–40)

G

GABRIEL

(Meaning: man of God.) Gabriel was an angelic messenger who accomplished important priesthood errands for the Lord. We first see him in the Old Testament giving instructions to the prophet Daniel concerning the coming mission of the Messiah (see Daniel 8:15–26, 9:20–23).

It was the same Gabriel who later appeared to Zacharias and informed him that his wife Elisabeth would give birth to a son (see Luke 1:11–20), and to Mary in Nazareth, announcing that she would bring forth the anointed Son of God (Luke 1:26–38). Gabriel is also mentioned once in the Doctrine and Covenants, in connection with the manifestations of various divine messengers during the foundation period of the Restoration (128:21).

From the Prophet Joseph Smith we learn that Gabriel is none other than Noah, the ancient patriarch: "Then to Noah, who is Gabriel: he stands next in authority to Adam in the Priesthood; he was called of God to this office, and was the father of all living in this day, and to him was given the dominion" (*TPJS*, 157).

Gabriel, known as Noah in mortality

GAD

(Meaning: good fortune.)

1. Gad was the son of Jacob by Zilpah, the maid of Leah (see Genesis 30:10–12; 35:26).

Jacob's benedictory blessing on the head of Gad included these words: "Gad, a troop shall overcome him: but he shall overcome at the last" (Genesis 49:19; for Moses' blessing upon the tribe of Gad, see Deuteronomy 33:20–21). The Gadites (also called Gileadites—see Judges 12:4) were skilled in battle (see 1 Chronicles 12:8; see also 1 Chronicles 5:18–22) and in the raising of cattle (see Numbers 32:1–5; Deuteronomy 3:12). The prophet Elijah "was of the inhabitants of Gilead" (1 Kings 17:1). The Gadites, along with the Reubenites and half of the tribe of Manasseh, were carried into captivity by the Assyrians around 721 BC (see 1 Chronicles 5:26; also 2 Kings 10:33).

2. Gad was a prophet who advised David in dealing with his enemies and other matters of the kingdom (see 1 Samuel 22:5; 2 Samuel 24:11–19; 1 Chronicles 21:9–19). Known as "David's seer" (2 Samuel 24:11; 1 Chronicles 21:9), he wrote a record of the acts of David (see 1 Chronicles 29:29) and made arrangements for the music used in the house of the Lord (see 2 Chronicles 29:25).

3. Gad was a priesthood holder mentioned twice in the Doctrine and Covenants (though not in the Old Testament) in connection with the lineage of the priesthood prior to the time of Moses: "And Jeremy [received the priesthood] under the hand of Gad; And Gad under the hand of Esaias; And Esaias received it under the hand of God" (D&C 84:10–12).

GEHAZI

(Meaning: valley of vision.) Gehazi (pronounced gih-hay'-zy) was the servant of the prophet Elisha at the time Naaman the Syrian sought the prophet's healing blessing for his leprous condition. After Naaman had reluctantly consented to dip himself seven times in the Jordan River as instructed by Elisha, the leprosy was dispensed in miraculous fashion. Returning whole to the house of Elisha, Naaman offered to pay Elisha for his services (see 2 Kings 5:15). Elisha refused compensation, and Naaman departed, but Gehazi, Elisha's servant, ignoring the wisdom of his master, followed after Naaman and took advantage of his generosity by accepting for himself gifts of silver and raiment (see 2 Kings 5:26). Upon learning this, Elisha pronounced a severe judgment upon Gehazi for his indiscretion: "The leprosy therefore of Naaman shall cleave unto thee, and unto thy seed for ever. And he went out from his presence a leper as white as snow" (2 Kings 5:27). Gehazi later recounted the great deeds of his master, Elisha, before Joram, king of Judah (see 2 Kings 8:1–6; compare also 2 Kings 4:12, 14, 25, 27, 29, 31, 36).

GENTILES

(Meaning: nations.) The word *Gentiles* as used in the scriptures refers generally to those people who are not of the House of Israel. *Gentiles* can also refer to nations that do not yet have the gospel—even though there may be those of Israelite lineage among them (see Bible Dictionary, 679). The first of multiple occurrences of the word *Gentiles* in the Old Testament comes in reference to the descendants of Japheth (see Genesis 10:1–2, 5).

Isaiah foresaw a future time when the Gentiles would support the cause of Zion (see Isaiah 49:22; compare 1 Nephi 21:23; 2 Nephi 10:9; D&C 19:27; 35:7; 45:28–30; 90:8–9; 109:60; 124:9; Abraham 2:9–11).

GIANTS

The term *giants* refers to individuals of unusually large stature and strength, the most famous being Goliath (see 1 Samuel 17:4). *See also Anak, Anakims; Emims; and Zamzummims.*

GIDEON

(Meaning: warrior.) Gideon was one of the leading figures represented in the book of Judges covering the turbulent period of time commencing with the death of Joshua (around 1477 BC) and extending to the birth of Samuel (around 1125 BC). The judgeship of Gideon commenced around 1263 BC. He was called to deliver Israel from bondage under the Midianites: "And the LORD looked upon him, and said, Go in this thy might, and thou shalt save Israel from the hand of the Midianites: have not I sent thee?" (Judges 6:14). Gideon obeyed the command of the Lord to destroy the altar of Baal and the associated ceremonial grove (see Judges 6:28)—thus earning the alternative name Jerubbaal (meaning he that striveth against Baal—see Judges 6:32; 7:1; 1 Samuel 12:11). He then followed the Lord's instructions and reduced his army, first from 32,000 down to 10,000, and then further down to 300 (see Judges 7:2–8). Using trumpets and lamps, Gideon's little army prevailed over the much larger forces of the Midianites by applying an abundance of strategic know-how (see Judges 7–8). Though triumphant, Gideon refused the kingship: "And Gideon said unto them, I will not rule over you, neither shall my son rule over you: the LORD shall rule over you" (Judges 8:23).

Gideon's army

GIRGASHITES

The Girgashites were one of the indigenous peoples driven out by the influx of the Israelites into the promised land (see Deuteronomy 7:1–2; Genesis 10:16; 15:21; Joshua 3:10; Nehemiah 9:7–8).

GOD (SEE FATHER IN HEAVEN, JESUS CHRIST, AND HOLY GHOST)

GOG

1. Gog was a Reubenite mentioned once in the Old Testament (see 1 Chronicles 5:4).

2. Gog was a ruler over the land and nation of Magog as cited in Ezekiel 38–39. Gog's predicted aggression against Israel and his ultimate defeat is emblematic of the final victory of the forces of God against evil—both at the time of the Second Coming and ultimately at

the end of the millennial period in the so-called battle of Gog and Magog (see Revelation 20:7–9; compare D&C 88:110–116 concerning the final triumph of Michael and his forces against Satan and his minions). (See also Magog.)

GOLIATH

1. Goliath of Gath was the notorious Philistine giant slain by the young David. Goliath's imposing stature (some ten feet tall) and confrontational tone struck fear into the hearts of Saul's warriors, but young David had armor far beyond the efficacy of Goliath's lofty helmet, impenetrable coat of mail, and massive spear—for David was armed with the strength of the Lord. Given permission by King Saul to meet the champion in a decisive one-on-one battle, David encountered Goliath in the valley while two armies watched from opposing mountain slopes. After declaring that the battle was in God's hands, David took his sling and sent a stone missile against Goliath with deadly accuracy. He then decapitated the giant with the latter's own sword and became a legendary icon of the victory of good over evil (see 1 Samuel 17).

The sword of Goliath was preserved as a religious trophy at the city of Nob, and David later retrieved it when, during his flight before the murderous Saul, he visited there with the priest Ahimelech to obtain nourishment (see 1 Samuel 21:6).

2. Goliath was the possible name of another Philistine giant slain by Elhanan (like David, a Bethlehemite) as reported in 2 Samuel 21:19. This same giant is identified as "Lahmi the brother of Goliath" in 1 Chronicles 20:5.

GREEKS

The inhabitants of Greece are identified as descendants of Javan in the Old Testament (see Genesis 10:1–2). The book of Daniel refers to the land "Grecia" (Daniel 8:21; 10:20; 11:2) and the book of Zechariah to the land of "Greece" (Zechariah 9:13).

Goliath contends with David

Habaiah

Habaiah (pronounced hah-by'-uh or hah-by-yah') was the head of one of the priestly families who returned from captivity in Babylon under the oversight of Sheshbazzar (Zerubbabel) after the decree of liberation issued in 537 BC by Cyrus, king of Persia (see Ezra 2:61). Because of a lack of genealogical confirmation, Habaiah and his group were not permitted to serve in priesthood functions (see Nehemiah 7:64).

Habakkuk

Habakkuk (pronounced hah'-buh-kuhk' or huh-back'-uhk) was a prophet of Judah—possibly in the time frame around 600 BC, concurrent with the ministry of Lehi in Jerusalem and contemporary with the work of Jeremiah, Daniel, and Ezekiel. The book of Habakkuk, one of the twelve shorter prophetic books of the Old Testament, confirms that God punishes the wicked through the incursions of the wicked (see Habakkuk 2:8; compare Mormon 4:5) and that the plan of salvation will prevail unto the blessing of all who remember His

commandments (see, for example, Habakkuk 1:12–13; 2:14, 20; 3:10–13).

Hadad

1. Hadad (pronounced hay'-dad) was an individual in the lineage of Esau who served as a king of Edom (see Genesis 36:35–36; compare 1 Chronicles 1:46–47).

2. Hadad was a later king of Edom (see 1 Chronicles 1:50).

3. Hadad was an Edomite of royal heritage who as a youth escaped the campaign of extermination against every male in Edom as conducted by Joab, head of David's army. Hadad fled to Egypt and found favor with the pharaoh, who gave him a sister-in-law in marriage. Hadad returned to Edom after the death of David and Joab to vex the Israelites. (See 1 Kings 11:14–25).

4. Hadad was one of the sons of Ishmael (see 1 Chronicles 1:29–30).

5. Hadad, as learned from archaeological research, was the name of a sun god or storm

god worshipped by the Syrians and Edomites. This name application is not included in the Old Testament.

6. The name *Hadad* also occurs in compound names such as Ben-hadad. *See the entry for Ben-hadad.*

HADORAM (SEE ADONIRAM)

HAGAR

(Meaning: flight.) Hagar was an Egyptian handmaiden to Sarah and was also later the mother of Abraham's son Ishmael (see Genesis 16:1–16; 21:9–21; 25:12; Galatians 4:24 [spelled Agar]). Hagar is also mentioned in the Doctrine and Covenants, each time in connection with the principle of plural marriage (see 132:34, 65).

HAGGAI

Haggai (pronounced hag'-y or hag'-ee-y) was a prophet in Jerusalem who prophesied shortly after the return from the Babylonian exile. The book of Haggai was written around 520 BC. Its purpose was to energize the people to devoted action in building the temple of the Lord (see chapter 1) and to cause them to look forward in hope to the last days, when the Lord will return in glory to reign in peace among the righteous (see chapter 2).

HAM

(Meaning: hot.) Ham was a son of Noah (see Genesis 5:32; 6:10; 7:13; 1 Chronicles 1:4; Moses 8:12). Initially Ham was a righteous man: "And thus Noah found grace in the eyes of the Lord; for Noah was a just man, and perfect in his generation; and he walked with

God, as did also his three sons, Shem, Ham, and Japheth" (Moses 8:27). After the flood, Ham and his progeny were cursed for indiscreet and offensive behavior (see Genesis 9:18–22, 25–27). Ham had four sons: "And the sons of Ham; Cush, and Mizraim, and Phut, and Canaan" (Genesis 10:6; see also 1 Chronicles 1:8). The geographical destinations of these peoples are given in the Bible Dictionary, page 698: "Cush = the dark-skinned race of eastern Africa and southern Arabia. Mizraim = Egyptians. Phut = Libyans. Canaan = inhabitants of Palestine before arrival of the Semitic races."

Modern scripture discloses that Ham's wife and daughter were both named Egyptus and that some of Ham's descendants settled in Egypt (see Abraham 1:21–27). For references to "the land of Ham" (Egypt), see Psalms 105:23, 27; 106:22. *See also Egyptus/Daughter of Egyptus.*

HAMAN

As narrated in the book of Esther, King Ahasuerus of Persia promoted Haman (pronounced hay'-muhn) to a position as chief minister among the princes (see Esther 3:1). However, Mordecai, a Jewish man associated with the court, refused to pay obeisance to Haman. In anger, Haman set up a plan to eliminate all the Jewish people in the kingdom and persuaded the king to authorize it (see vv. 5–15). Esther, the queen (and secretly a Jew herself and the former ward of Mordecai), then intervened in the matter, at great peril to her own life. She arranged for a banquet at which Haman was to be honored. At the banquet the truth came out. Haman's deceit was revealed and he was hanged in consequence, on the very gallows prepared for Mordecai (see 7:3–6, 9–10). *See also Esther and Mordecai.*

HAMOR

Hamor (pronounced hay'-mor) was a Hivite whose son, Shechem, fell in love with Dinah, daughter of Jacob, and defiled her. In response, Levi and Simeon (sons of Jacob) removed Dinah from Shechem's home and initiated a callous campaign of vengeance against the Hivite community, killing all of the males and despoiling the city (see Genesis 34)—resulting in the relocation of Jacob and his people to Beth-el at the command of God (see Genesis 34:30; 35:1–5).

HANANIAH

Hananiah (pronounced han'-uh-ny'-uh) was the court name given to Shadrach, one of Daniel's associates taken into captivity by Nebuchadnezzar of Babylon (see Daniel 1:7). *See Abed-nego, Meshach, and Shadrach.*

HANNAH

(Meaning: grace.) Hannah (pronounced han'-uh) was the wife of Elkanah, a devout Ephraimite who lived in the central mountainous district of Israel (see 1 Samuel 1:1–3). Hannah was barren for some years, a source of sorrow for her, though her husband loved her (in verse 8 he asks her, "Am I not better to thee than ten sons?"). But in the face of torment by Peninnah—Elkanah's other wife, who had children—Hannah wept and fretted to the point that she would not eat. In this state of mind, Hannah prayed one day, near the temple, for a special blessing: "If thou wilt . . . give unto thine handmaid a man child, then I will give him unto the LORD all the days of his

Hannah prays for a son

life." (v. 11). When the priest Eli observed her struggles, he first thought her drunk, but came to understand her burden, and promised her: "Go in peace: and the God of Israel grant thee thy petition that thou hast asked of him" (v. 17). Indeed, the Lord did remember her with a blessing of fruitfulness: "Wherefore it came to pass . . . that she bare a son, and called his name Samuel, saying, Because I have asked him of the LORD" (v. 20). After Samuel was weaned, Hannah brought him to the house of the Lord and said to the priest Eli: "O my lord, as thy soul liveth, my lord, I am the woman that stood by thee here, praying unto the LORD. For this child I prayed; and the LORD hath given me my petition which I asked of him: Therefore also I have lent him to the LORD; as long as he liveth he shall be lent to the LORD" (vv. 1:26–28). Subsequently, Hannah uttered a glorious song of praise unto the Lord for His mercy unto her (see 1 Samuel 2:1–10; contained in verse ten is the first reference to the Messiah as the anointed one in the Old Testament).

As Samuel grew in stature, Hannah lovingly remembered him and "made him a little coat, and brought it to him from year to year, when she came up with her husband to offer the yearly sacrifice" (1 Samuel 2:19). Hannah was also blessed thereafter with five more children: "three sons and two daughters" (1 Samuel 2:21).

HARAN

1. Haran was the son of Terah and the brother of Nahor and Abram (later Abraham). Haran was the father of Lot, Milcah (wife of Nahor), and Iscah (who was, according to Jewish tradition, Sarai [later Sarah], Abraham's wife; see Genesis 11:26–31; Abraham 2:2). Haran passed away during the severe famine in Ur of the Chaldees (see Genesis 11:28; Abraham 2:1) prior to the time that Abram (Abraham) and his entourage left Ur at the command of God and traveled to the place they designated Haran (see Genesis 11:31; Abraham 2:3). Haran the person is pronounced hay'-ran or hair'-uhn; Haran the city is pronounced huh-ran'.

2. Haran was the son of Caleb (see 1 Chronicles 2:46).

3. Haran was a Levite in service during the reign of Solomon (see 1 Chronicles 23:9).

HAVILAH

1. Havilah (pronounced hav'-uh-luh or huh-vil'-uh) was one of the five sons of Cush, who was the son of Ham (see Genesis 10:6–7; 1 Chronicles 1:8–9).

2. Havilah was a son of Joktan (a descendant of Shem, Noah's son) (see Genesis 10:29; 1 Chronicles 1:23).

HAZAEL

Hazael (pronounced hay'-zay-uhl or huh-zay'-uhl) was king of Syria during the tenures of the prophets Elijah and Elisha (see especially 1 Kings 19; 2 Kings 8–10, 12–13; 2 Chronicles 22). During the days of wicked King Ahab, the Lord commanded Elijah to anoint Hazael king of Syria, Jehu king of Israel, and Elisha as prophet (see 1 Kings 19:15–16) in preparation for the judgments of heaven that descended upon the Israelites for their fixation on Baal (see 2 Kings 8:28–29; 9:14–15; 2 Chronicles 22:5–6; 2 Kings 10:32; 12:18; 13:3, 22–25).

HEATHEN(S)

The word *heathen* is used in the text of the Old Testament (the plural form is not used in the scriptures) to distinguish the other nations of the earth from the Lord's covenant people (see, for example, Deuteronomy 4:27; 2 Samuel 22:50; 2 Kings 17:15; 1 Chronicles 16:24). According to the commission of the Abrahamic covenant (see Genesis 17:1–7; Abraham 2:8–11), the gospel is to be preached to all nations—including the heathen nations. The blessings of the priesthood are to be extended to all who will receive them in faith and devotion (see D&C 45:54; 75:22; 90:10; 2 Nephi 26:33).

HEBREWS

Abraham was identified as a Hebrew (see Genesis 14:13), as was Joseph in Egypt (see Genesis 39:14, 17; 40:15; 41:12) and all of the Israelites during their sojourn in that country (see Exodus 1:15–19; 2:6–7, 11, 13). The Lord identified Himself as the God of the Hebrews when He called Moses into service (see Exodus 3:18; 5:3; 7:16; 9:1, 13; 10:3). Following the Exodus and the transition into the promised land, the covenant people were referred to as Hebrews, in contrast with the indigenous peoples (see 1 Samuel 4:6, 9; 13:3, 7, 19; 14:11, 21; 29:3). The word *Hebrew* may derive from an original word meaning to "cross" or "go beyond" (as on the other side of a river) or from a name such as Eber (or Heber), one of the ancestors of Abraham (see Genesis 10:21–25).

HEPHZIBAH

(Meaning: my delight is in her.) Hephzibah (pronounced hef'-zih-buh) was the wife of King Hezekiah and the mother of King Manasseh (2 Kings 21:1). Isaiah also used the term *Hephzibah* symbolically in connection with Jerusalem in the last days (see Isaiah 62:4).

HETH

Heth was a descendant of Ham (see Genesis 10:6, 15; 1 Chronicles 1:13). Heth was the progenitor of the Hittites (see Genesis 10:15; 23). Abraham purchased from Ephron the Hittite the land for burying his wife Sarah (see Genesis 23:20; 49:30–33; see also Genesis 27:46).

HEZEKIAH

(Meaning: whom Jehovah has strengthened.)

1. Hezekiah, king of Judah, was one of the greatest reformers in a long tradition of kings and a refreshing breeze among the contrasting winds of instability arising from enthroned unrighteousness. The story of his tenure (around 726 to 697 BC) is presented in 2 Kings 18–21, 2 Chronicles 29–33, and Isaiah 36–39. His reign is, in part, concurrent with the ministry of the prophet Isaiah (around 740–701 BC), who served him as a religious and political counselor. When Hezekiah succeeded his father, Ahaz (see 2 Kings 16:20), he inaugurated an era of honorable and righteous service (see 2 Kings 18:4–8; compare 2 Chronicles 29).

When Sennacherib of Assyria staged a massive invasion (the second within a short while) and besieged the city of Jerusalem, Hezekiah—who had allied himself meanwhile with Egypt (see Isaiah 36:6–9)—sent out Eliakim, his chief of staff, to negotiate with the spokesman for the enemy host, Rab-shakeh, who issued venomous threats against the city and its king (see 2 Kings 18:29–32). Hezekiah

Hezekiah is healed and his life is prolonged

sent Eliakim and his companions to confer with Isaiah concerning the matter (see 2 Kings 18:6–7).

When the Assyrian hosts persisted in their arrogant threats, Hezekiah went before the Lord to plead on behalf of the people for deliverance from the enemy (see 2 Kings 19:15–19). Through Isaiah came the word of the Lord to Hezekiah with assurances of delivery (see 2 Kings 19:32–35).

Whether by a pestilence that broke out among the Assyrian host or by some other divinely appointed means, the enemy was thwarted, and Sennacherib withdrew his forces and returned to Nineveh, where some time later two of his sons murdered him, fulfilling Isaiah's prophecy (see 2 Kings 19:36–37).

Later, Hezekiah contracted a serious ailment that caused him to inquire of Isaiah if he should survive. When Isaiah brought to him the word of the Lord that his life was about to end, Hezekiah supplicated the Lord for deliverance from the lethal illness. The Lord blessed him with yet fifteen years of life but revealed through Isaiah that future captivity awaited Judah: "Behold, the days come, that all that is in thine house, and that which thy fathers have laid up in store unto this day, shall be carried into Babylon: nothing shall be left, saith the LORD" (2 Kings 20:17).

2. Hezekiah, son of Neariah, is mentioned as one in the lineage of the royal family of Judah (see 1 Chronicles 3:23).

3. Hezekiah, son of Ater, is mentioned in Ezra 2:16 and Nehemiah 7:21.

4. A version of the name rendered as *Hizkijah* is mentioned in Nehemiah 10:17 and as *Hizkiah* in Zephaniah 1:1.

HIEL

Hiel (pronounced hy'-el or hy'-uhl) was a man during the days of king Ahab who set out to rebuild the ancient city of Jericho, destroyed by Joshua many centuries earlier—with the express warning that no one should attempt to rebuild it (see Joshua 6:26). As it turned out, the sons of Hiel perished in the attempt at reconstruction (see 1 Kings 16:34).

HIGH PRIEST

The office of high priest in the Melchizedek Priesthood has been a cardinal position in the governance of the kingdom of God from the beginning. The ancient patriarchs, beginning with Adam, were high priests (see D&C 107:54; Abraham 1:2). When the preparatory priesthood (Aaronic or Levitical) was instituted during the post-Sinai days of Moses, the presiding officer was designated as a "high priest" (see 2 Kings 22:8; Nehemiah 3:1; Haggai 1:1). During times "when Melchizedek Priesthood was on the earth—as in the days of Elijah" such presiding "high priests" may have held the higher priesthood (see *MD*, 355–356). Melchizedek, during the days of Abraham, was a high priest of such valor and honor that his name was appropriated in the designation for the high priesthood (see D&C 107:1–4; compare also D&C 84:14–18; Alma 13:14–18; JST, Genesis 14:25–40; Hebrews 5:4–6; 9:11).

HILKIAH

(Meaning: portion of Jehovah.)

1. Hilkiah (pronounced hill-ky'-uh) was the high priest during the reign of King Josiah to whom the campaign of repairing and purifying the temple was entrusted. While doing so, he

discovered, as he declared, "the book of the law in the house of the Lord" (2 Kings 22:8; compare 2 Chronicles 34:14–15). The king responded earnestly to the message of the book, also called "the book of the covenant" (2 Kings 23:2), by purging the nation of idolatry and directing everyone to turn to the Lord and follow His commandments with full devotion (see 2 Kings 23:3–25).

2. Hilkiah was also the name of various other individuals mentioned in the Old Testament (see 2 Kings 18:18, 26, 37; 1 Chronicles 6:13, 45; 9:11; 26:11; Ezra 7:1; Nehemiah 8:4; 11:11; 12:7, 21; Isaiah 22:20; 36:22; Jeremiah 1:1; 29:3).

HIRAM (OR HURAM)

1. Hiram was the king of Tyre who befriended David as the new king of Israel—"for Hiram was ever a lover of David" (1 Kings 5:1)—and assisted him in building his palace (see 2 Samuel 5:11; 1 Chronicles 14:1). Hiram also assisted Solomon, David's successor, in the construction of the temple (see 1 Kings 5:2–12; 9:11) and in maritime commercial undertakings (1 Kings 9:27; 10:11). The name *Hiram* was also rendered *Huram* (see 2 Chronicles 2:5–12; 8:2, 18; 9:10–21).

2. Hiram was also the name of a workman of Tyre sent to help Solomon (see 1 Kings 7:13–14, 40, 45). He is also called Huram (see 2 Chronicles 2:13; 4:11, 16).

3. Huram was a Benjamite, son of Gera, and grandson of Benjamin (see 1 Chronicles 1–5).

HITTITES

The Hittites were a people descended from Heth (of the line of Ham, son of Noah, through Canaan—see Genesis 10:15). When Moses sent a scouting party to investigate the circumstances in the promised land, the report came back: "The Amalekites dwell in the land of the south: and the Hittites, and the Jebusites, and the Amorites, dwell in the mountains." (Numbers 13:29). The Hittites and associated peoples became the center of focus concerning the need to accommodate the Israelites in the promised land, either by displacing the indigenous peoples or dwelling among them (see Exodus 23:28; 33:2; Deuteronomy 20:17; Joshua 3:10; 12:8; 24:11; 1 Kings 9:20; 11:1; Ezra 9:1; Nehemiah 9:8).

The first mention of a Hittite individual in the scriptures is Ephron the Hittite, from whom Abraham purchased a field and the cave of Machpelah for burying his wife (see Genesis 23:10, 17–20). Esau selected two of his wives from among the Hittites (see Genesis 26:34–35; 36:2). One of the warriors in David's camp was a Hittite by the name of Ahimelech (see 1 Samuel 26:6). Uriah, husband of Bathsheba, was a Hittite (see 2 Samuel 11:3, 6, 17, 21, 24; 2 Samuel 12:9–10; 23:39; 1 Kings 15:5). In general, Israel was censured for her tendency to adopt the ways of non-covenant peoples such as the Hittites—who became emblematic for those who followed a way of life of idolatry, being at variance with gospel ideals (see Ezekiel 16:1–3).

HIVITES

The Hivites were a people descended from Heth (of the line of Ham, son of Noah, through Canaan—see Genesis 10:17). The Hivites were one of the indigenous peoples with whom the Israelites had to deal when they came into the promised land (see Deuteronomy 7:1; Exodus 3:8, 17; 13:5; Joshua

3:10). When Joshua defeated the various tribes in the appointed land, it was only the Hivites who avoided the conflict (see Joshua 11:19), later becoming bondsmen unto the Israelites (see Joshua 9:22–25; compare Joshua 11:19).

HOLY GHOST

The Holy Ghost is the third member of the Godhead, serving in unity and glory with the Father and the Son. Unlike the Father and the Son, who have glorified bodies of flesh and bones, "the Holy Ghost has not a body of flesh and bones, but is a personage of Spirit. Were it not so, the Holy Ghost could not dwell in us" (D&C 130:22).

The term *Holy Ghost* does not occur in the King James Version of the Old Testament. However, the office and function of the Holy Ghost are pervasively represented through the use of terms such as "the spirit," "my spirit," "spirit of God," and similar expressions. In the first verse of the Old Testament we learn: "In

Job is sustained by the Spirit

the beginning God created the heaven and the earth" (Genesis 1:1); then, in the second verse, we learn that the dynamic spirit of generation was at work in that process: "And the Spirit of God moved upon the face of the waters" (Genesis 1:2)—not unlike the later words of Job: "By his spirit he hath garnished the heavens" (Job 26:13).

The book of Job tells us that all are sustained by the Spirit: "All the while my breath is in me, and the spirit of God is in my nostrils" (Job 27:3); "But there is a spirit in man: and the inspiration of the Almighty giveth them understanding" (Job 32:8); "The Spirit of God hath made me, and the breath of the Almighty hath given me life" (Job 33:4).

From the Creation forward, the Holy Spirit, as God's agent of light and truth, is found at work through all the generations of time: guiding, illuminating, warning, counseling, confirming, and blessing the lives of God's children—both prophet-leaders as well as inspired laypersons within the kingdom. Even non-covenant leaders recognized the power of the Spirit: "And pharaoh said unto his servants, Can we find such a one as this is [Joseph], a man in whom the Spirit of God is?" (Genesis 41:38). Aaron was filled with the Spirit—and thus blessed with wisdom to function in the priest's office (see Exodus 28:3). The Lord blessed Bezaleel, the elect temple artisan, with His Spirit: "And I have filled him with the spirit of God, in wisdom, and in understanding, and in knowledge, and in all manner of workmanship" (Exodus 31:3; see also Exodus 35:31). Caleb, the inspired scout dispatched by Moses into the promised land, had the Spirit of the Lord with him to enable him to envision the promise of the land of inheritance (see Numbers 14:24). Even the prophet Balaam, sometimes distracted with earthly interests, had the Spirit of God come upon him (see Numbers 24:12). Joshua was blessed of the Spirit to perform mighty deeds of valor and honor: "And the LORD said unto Moses, Take thee Joshua the son of Nun, a man in whom is the spirit, and lay thine hand upon him" (Numbers 27:18).

The scriptures confirm that many other figures in the Old Testament experienced the operation of the Holy Ghost within their lives: Moses (see Isaiah 63:10–14); Othniel the judge (see Judges 3:10); Gideon the judge (see Judges 6:34); Jephthah, commander of the armies of Israel (see Judges 11:29); Samson (see Judges 13:25; see also Judges 14:6, 19; 15:14); Saul (in his earlier tenure—see 1 Samuel 10:6; see also 1 Samuel 10:10; 11:6; 19:23); David (see 1 Samuel 16:13; compare 2 Samuel 23:2; 1 Chronicles 28:11–12); Elijah (see 1 Kings 18:12; 2 Kings 2:15–16); Amasai, chief of the captains of Israel (see 1 Chronicles 12:18); Azariah, one of the men of Israel (see 2 Chronicles 15:1–2); Jahaziel the Levite (see 2 Chronicles 20:14–15); and Zechariah, a prophet (see 2 Chronicles 24:20).

The Lord worked on the heart of Cyrus, who issued an edict in 537 BC allowing the captive Jewish nation to return to its homeland and thus fulfill the designs of God (see 2 Chronicles 36:22–23). By that same Spirit, the leaders of Judah and Benjamin were inspired to rebuild the temple (see Ezra 1:5)—in conformity with the blessings of Lord unto Israel in the Exodus (Nehemiah 9:20–21, 30). The prophet Haggai also confirmed that the Spirit of the Lord inspired the people to complete this sacred task of temple building (see Haggai 1:13–14; 2:45). Zechariah bore the same witness: "Then he answered and spake unto me, saying, This is the word of the LORD unto Zerubbabel [the temple builder], saying, Not by might, nor by power, but by my spirit, saith the LORD of hosts" (Zechariah 4:6).

Others expressly inspired and guided by the Holy Ghost include Ezekiel (see Ezekiel 2:1–2; 3:12–14, 24; 8:3; 43:5); Daniel (see Daniel 4:8–9, 18); and Micah (Micah 3:8).

The blessings that the Holy Spirit provides are universal—accessible to all who seek the Lord's guidance with humble hearts and willing minds.

We learn from the Old Testament that the blessings of the Spirit are conditioned on faithfulness and virtue: "And the LORD said, My spirit shall not always strive with man" (Genesis 6:3). Saul, for one, learned that lesson painfully: "But the Spirit of the LORD departed from Saul, and an evil spirit from the LORD troubled him" (1 Samuel 16:14; the JST corrects this reference to say "an evil spirit which was not of the Lord"; see also Zechariah 7:12).

Isaiah not only makes it clear that the Spirit of the Lord would bless and sustain the Only Begotten in His mission of redemption (see Isaiah 11:2; 42:1; 48:16–17), but he assures us that the Spirit of the Lord would also be at work in the last days, gathering the Saints, preparing the world for the Second Coming, and inaugurating the millennial reign (see Isaiah 32:15–16; 34:16): "For I will pour water upon him that is thirsty, and floods upon the dry ground: I will pour my spirit upon thy seed, and my blessing upon thine offspring: And they shall spring up as among the grass, as willows by the water courses" (Isaiah 44:3–4).

The prophet Joel foresaw a time when the Spirit of the Lord would again abound among those caught up in the joy and glory of the Restoration of gospel truths:

And it shall come to pass afterward, that I will pour out my spirit upon all flesh; and your sons and your daughters shall prophesy, your old men shall dream dreams, your young men shall see visions:

And also upon the servants and upon the handmaids in those days will I pour out my spirit. (Joel 2:28–29)

Saints who follow God's commandments have the promise "that they may always have his Spirit to be with them" (D&C 20:77; also D&C 20:79). The voice of the Spirit comes, in general, as a still, small voice, as the prophet Elijah confirmed (see 1 Kings 19:9). The book of Job tells us that all are sustained by the Spirit: "The Spirit of God hath made me, and the breath of the Almighty hath given me life" (Job 33:4; compare 3 Nephi 11.)

Although the Old Testament does not use the term "Holy Ghost," the book of Moses does—including the term "the gift of the Holy Ghost." In the record of Moses we witness the Holy Ghost coming into the life of Adam and Eve and their offspring:

And in that day the Holy Ghost fell upon Adam, which beareth record of the Father and the Son, saying: I am the Only Begotten of the Father from the beginning, henceforth and forever, that as thou hast fallen thou mayest be redeemed, and all mankind, even as many as will. . . .

And thus the Gospel began to be preached, from the beginning, being declared by holy angels sent forth from the presence of God, and by his own voice, and by the gift of the Holy Ghost. (Moses 5:9, 58)

God taught Adam, "If thou wilt turn unto me, and hearken unto my voice, and believe, and repent of all thy transgressions, and be baptized, even in water, in the name of mine Only Begotten Son, . . . ye shall receive the gift of the Holy Ghost" (Moses 6:52).

For a better understanding of the Holy Ghost, you may wish to turn to the Doctrine and Covenants, which contains many references to the operation and ministry of the Holy Ghost. It is there, for example, that we discover that the only transgression that would place an individual outside the grasp of redemption from the second death (separation from God) is to commit blasphemy against the Holy Ghost: "Having denied the Holy Spirit after having received it, and having denied the Only Begotten Son of the Father, having crucified him unto themselves and put him to an open shame" (D&C 76:35; see also D&C 132:27).

HOLY ONE OF ISRAEL

The Holy One of Israel—a term used frequently in the Old Testament, particularly by Isaiah—is the Savior, Jesus Christ: "For I am the LORD thy God, the Holy One of Israel, thy Saviour: . . . I, even I, am the LORD; and beside me there is no saviour. . . . Thus saith the LORD, your redeemer, the Holy One of Israel" (Isaiah 43:3, 11, 14; see also Isaiah 47:4; 54:5; compare 2 Nephi 25:29—one of many such references in the Book of Mormon).

The Holy One of Israel with disciples

HOPHNI

Hophni (pronounced hof'-ny) was the first son of Eli (see the entry for Eli).

HOSEA

Hosea (pronounced ho-see'-uh or ho-say'-uh) is the only prophet of the northern kingdom whose writings have been handed down to us as part of the canon. He prophesied in the eighth century BC, probably in the latter reign of Jeroboam II and just prior to the ministry of Isaiah (who prophesied in the time span 740–701 BC). Hosea reflects the universal theme of all the prophets of God: that God is holy and supreme and that happiness and joy can flow to mankind only through obedience to His laws and commandments. Though the people trek through the valley of darkness and misery occasioned by their iniquity and pride, yet will the Lord in His loving-kindness and mercy remember them in His own due time and guide them to emerge eventually into the light of His redemptive love. In short, the theme of Hosea is love.

HOSHEA

(Meaning: salvation.)

1. Hoshea (pronounced hoh-she'-uh) was the original name of Joshua, son of Nun (see Deuteronomy 32:44; also rendered *Oshea* in Numbers 13:8, 16). *See Joshua.*

2. Hoshea, son of Azaziah, was the ruler of the tribe of Ephraim during the time of David (see 1 Chronicles 27:20).

3. Hoshea was the last king of Israel prior to the Assyrian deportation of the ten tribes of Israel beyond the Euphrates River around 721 BC (see 2 Kings 15:30; 17:1–6; 18:1, 9–12; Hosea 10:7; 13:11).

4. Hoshea was one of the leading residents of Jerusalem who signed a covenant to keep God's law following the return from Babylonian captivity (see Nehemiah 10:23).

HULDAH

Huldah was a prophetess consulted by King Josiah concerning the discovery of "the book of the law" hidden for generations in the house of the Lord and uncovered by the high priest Hilkiah (see 2 Kings 22:8; compare 2 Chronicles 34:14–15). Anxious about the message of the book, Josiah asked Huldah for the word of the Lord. She confirmed the impending judgments about to befall the people but prophesied that Josiah would be called home before that time came (see 2 Kings 22:15–20). Josiah proceeded to complete a comprehensive campaign to purge all idolatry from the country, putting the people under covenant to follow the teachings of God (see Josiah). Besides Huldah, Miriam (see Exodus 15:20) and Deborah (see Judges 4:4) are also designated in the Old Testament with the title "prophetess."

HUR

1. Hur was a leading official in Israel who assisted Aaron in supporting the hands of Moses on a hill during the battle in which Joshua prevailed against the Amalekites (see Exodus 17:10–13.)

Hur also assisted Aaron in overseeing the people while Moses was on Mount Sinai (see Exodus 24:14).

2. Hur was the grandfather of Bezaleel, artisan of the tribe of Judah, who assisted in the building and furnishing of the Tabernacle (see Exodus 31:2; 35:30; 38:22).

3. Hur was one of the Midianite kings slain in battle when Moses sent an army of twelve thousand—one thousand warriors from each tribe, under command of Phinehas—to avenge the Israelites of their enemies (see Numbers 31:8).

4. Hur was the father of one of the officers in the court of King Solomon (see 1 Kings 4:8).

5. Hur was the son of Caleb, mentioned in the lineage of the Israelites (see 1 Chronicles 2:19–20, 50; compare 1 Chronicles 4:1, 4).

HURAM (SEE HIRAM)

I AM

I Am is another name for the Lord of the Old Testament. The sublime and eternal implication of the name was expressed to Moses by the Lord Himself: "And Moses said unto God, Behold, when I come unto the children of Israel, and shall say unto them, The God of your fathers hath sent me unto you; and they shall say to me, What is his name? what shall I say unto them? And God said unto Moses, I AM THAT I AM: and he said, Thus shalt thou say unto the children of Israel, I AM hath sent me unto you" (Exodus 3:14). An understanding of this name makes even more powerful the question and answer in 3 Nephi 27:27: "Therefore, what manner of men ought ye to be? Verily I say unto you, even as I am."

IDOL

Idols were representations of personalities or aspects of nature that became the objects of worship among the heathen nations (and at times among the wayward Israelites)—as contrasted with the worship of the true God. The Decalogue opened with the divine injunction:

> Thou shalt have no other gods before me.
>
> Thou shalt not make unto thee any graven image, or any likeness of any thing that is in heaven above, or that is in the earth beneath, or that is in the water under the earth:
>
> Thou shalt not bow down thyself to them, nor serve

Idolatry of the golden calf

them: for I the Lord thy God am a jealous God, visiting the iniquity of the fathers upon the children unto the third and fourth generation of them that hate me. (Exodus 20:3–5)

The Old Testament is replete with references condemning idol worship and any degree of allegiance to the gods idolized by the non-covenant races, such as Ashtoreth, Baal, Baal-zebub (New Testament Beelzebub), Chemosh, Merodach, Molech (Milcom), Nebo, Nisroch, Rimmon, Succoth-Benoth, Tammuz, and the like (see the entries for these names). The book of Abraham in the Pearl of Great Price identifies additional heathen gods adopted and worshipped by those who had fallen away from the true pathway (see Abraham 1:5–6).

Why do the scriptures repeatedly draw attention to the false idols of pagan and apostate worship? Perhaps because we learn by contrast and comparison how idolatry brings about consequences of destruction and misery, while worshipping the true God in faith and trust brings eternal blessings.

IMMANUEL

(Meaning: God with us.) Immanuel is a name for the Son of God: "Therefore the Lord himself shall give you a sign; Behold, a virgin shall conceive, and bear a son, and shall call his name Immanuel" (Isaiah 7:14; compare also Isaiah 8:8; 2 Nephi 17:14; 18:8; D&C 128:22). *See also Emmanuel and Jesus Christ.*

ISAAC

(Meaning: he laugheth.) Isaac was the son of Abraham and Sarah and the heir of the covenant promises of the Lord (see Genesis 15:1–6; 17:15–19; 18:9–15; 21:1–8). Abraham's willingness to sacrifice Isaac by command of the Lord (see Genesis 22; D&C 132:36) was the supreme manifestation of this father's ultimate faith and devotion to God—and an extraordinary symbolic anticipation of the Father's sacrifice of His Only Begotten Son for all mankind. In the case of Isaac, the Lord said: "Take now thy son, thine only son Isaac, whom thou lovest, and get thee into the land of Moriah; and offer him there for a burnt offering" (Genesis 22:2).

Abraham then took Isaac and two other young men on the journey to Moriah, where he was to offer Isaac as a burnt offering. On the third day Abraham and Isaac went forward to worship. Isaac carried the wood as they journeyed. Isaac asked about the sacrifice, and Abraham replied, "My son, God will provide

Jacob receives the blessing from Isaac

himself a lamb for a burnt offering" (v. 8). Abraham then bound Isaac and laid him on the altar, preparing for the ultimate sacrifice.

It was at that point that Isaac must have affirmed the action of his father in obedience to the commandment of God. There is no indication that Isaac attempted to revolt against the deed—any more than Jesus Christ shrank from the ultimate offering of sacrificial Atonement. As Abraham raised his knife—no doubt consumed by the anguish of a loving father—an angel of the Lord forbade him and said, "For now I know that thou fearest [i.e., showest unyielding reverence to] God, seeing thou hast not withheld thy son" (v. 12). A ram was subsequently provided, and the Lord promised Abraham, "In thy seed shall all the nations of the earth be blessed" (v. 18).

Isaac is also mentioned in the Doctrine and Covenants. The Lord revealed to Joseph Smith the details of a future glorious sacrament meeting when all the faithful prophets of old would convene again, including Isaac (see 27:10). Moreover, the Lord declared the exaltation of Abraham, Isaac, and Jacob for their obedience. Other references to Isaac deal with the Lord's law of war (see 98:32), the doctrine of plural marriage (see 132:1), the glorious congregation of the elect of God at the Second Coming (see 133:55), the identity of the Lord as "the God of your fathers, the God of Abraham and of Isaac and of Jacob" (see 136:21), and the presence of Isaac (see 138:41) among "the great and mighty ones who were assembled" in the "congregation of the righteous" (D&C 138:38) in the vision granted to President Joseph F. Smith concerning the work of salvation in the spirit realm.

Isaac is also mentioned in the Book of Mormon, typically in connection with the covenant promises of Abraham, Isaac, and Jacob. The prophet Jacob, younger brother of Nephi, also mentions Isaac in the context of the law of Moses and the obedience of Abraham in being willing to offer up his son as a sacrifice according to the commandment of God (see Jacob 4:5).

The name *Isaac* is itself an emblem of the principle of faith. When word came to Abraham and Sarah that they were about to become the parents of a son in their old age, "Abraham fell upon his face, and laughed, and said in his heart, Shall a child be born unto him that is an hundred years old? and shall Sarah, that is ninety years old, bear?" (Genesis 17:17). His wife's response was the same, for she laughed with disbelief. In response, the Lord said, "Wherefore did Sarah laugh, saying, Shall I of a surety bear a child, which am old? Is any thing too hard for the LORD?" (Genesis 18:13–14).

Isaac married Rebekah and had two sons with her: Esau and Jacob. See the entry for Rebekah for more details on their extraordinary meeting and their life together.

ISAIAH

(Meaning: the Lord is salvation.) Isaiah, son of Amoz, was one of the greatest prophets of the Lord in any dispensation—and the most quoted of all the prophets in holy writ. Jesus said of him, "Great are the words of Isaiah" (3 Nephi 23:1). The Book of Isaiah is one of the major prophetic books of the Old Testament, along with Jeremiah, Lamentations (by Jeremiah), Ezekiel, and Daniel. Isaiah's ministry in Jerusalem was in the time frame 740–701 BC. He was chief advisor to Hezekiah, king of Judah.

In his prophetic and inspired discourse, Isaiah captures with consummate skill the grand and sweeping contours of the Lord's plan for mankind. If blessings of peace and spiritual awakening are to be forthcoming unto Israel, then Israel must obey; the disobedient are to be scattered and chastened until they reform their ways. Nevertheless, in the Lord's due time, He will remember His promises to the faithful and reign as Lord and King in the midst of His children forever. Isaiah is unequalled in his ability to speak as if viewing a panoramic vista encompassing the entire range of the Lord's plan of salvation—from the premortal existence to the meridian of time to the millennial reign. Often Isaiah will span the entire range of man's existence in the space of a verse or two—in breathtaking and inspiring arches of time—always returning to the central theme of the Messiah, the Savior of mankind.

Key sections of the Book of Isaiah include the following: Isaiah gives inspired commentary on the Lord's design for His covenant children and their eventual salvation (chapters 1–5); the Lord calls Isaiah as His prophet (chapter 6); Isaiah continues with his Messianic prophecies and exhortations to Israel (chapters 7–35); Isaiah gives inspired counsel to King Hezekiah on the security and protection of Judah (chapters 36–39); Messianic prophecies and counsel for Israel are concluded (chapters 40–66).

Some of the highlights found throughout the book of Isaiah include poignant explanations of the Lord's roles in the plan of salvation, the events of the Second Coming, the gathering of the ten tribes, the coming forth of the Book of Mormon, the Restoration of the gospel, and the destiny of Israel.

The Book of Mormon and the Doctrine and Covenants shed valuable light on the inspired words of Isaiah. Nephi especially extolls the universal importance of reading and pondering the words of Isaiah, which were included on the brass plates of Laban appropriated for the journey to the promised land (see 1 Nephi 19:23–24; compare Jacob's testimony in 2 Nephi 6:5).

Nephi and Jacob include abundant excerpts from the writings of Isaiah in the scriptural record: see 1 Nephi 20–21 (Isaiah 48–49); 2 Nephi 7–8 (Isaiah 50–51 and 52:1–2); 2 Nephi 12–24 (Isaiah 2–14); and 2 Nephi 27 (Isaiah 29). Throughout, Nephi (and to a lesser extent, Jacob) gives commentary and exposition on the words of Isaiah, rendering them lucid and clear—because, as Nephi says, "The words of Isaiah are not plain unto you, nevertheless they are plain unto all those that are filled with the spirit of prophecy" (2 Nephi 25:4). For further excerpts from Isaiah, see also Mosiah 14 (Isaiah 53), Mosiah 15 (portions of Isaiah 52), and 3 Nephi 22 (Isaiah 54).

Isaiah

Isaiah is also mentioned in the Doctrine and Covenants in connection with interpretations of passages in Isaiah 11 and 52 (see D&C 113:1, 3, 7), in connection with the vision of the spirit realm granted unto President Joseph F. Smith (see 138:42), and concerning the degrees of glory (see 76:100).

ISH-BOSHETH

(Meaning: man of humiliation or shame.) Ish-bosheth was the youngest of the four sons of Saul. When Saul and his three other sons perished in the battle of Gilboa (see 1 Samuel 31:6), Ish-bosheth became king of Israel (see 2 Samuel 2:8–12), while David became king of Judah (see 2 Samuel 2:4). The two-year reign of Ish-bosheth ended when he was murdered by two of his captains (see 2 Samuel 3:22–27; 4:1–8, 9–10).

ISHMAEL

(Meaning: God heareth.)

1. Ishmael was the oldest son of Abram (soon thereafter renamed Abraham), being born of Hagar, the Egyptian handmaid of Sarai (soon thereafter renamed Sarah)—see Genesis 16; 17:15–26; compare 1 Chronicles 1:28–31. On the weaning of Isaac, a separation occurred in the household of Abraham:

> And Sarah saw the son of Hagar the Egyptian, which she had born unto Abraham, mocking.
>
> Wherefore she said unto Abraham, Cast out this bond-woman and her son: for the son of this bondwoman shall not be heir with my son, even with Isaac.
>
> And the thing was very grievous in Abraham's sight because of his son.
>
> And God said unto Abraham, Let it not be grievous in thy sight because of the lad, and because of thy bond-woman; in all that Sarah hath said unto thee, hearken unto her voice; for in Isaac shall thy seed be called.
>
> And also of the son of the bondwoman will I make a nation, because he is thy seed. (Genesis 21:9–13)

Upon the passing of Abraham, Isaac and Ishmael came together again to bury their father (see Genesis 25:9). Ishmael passed away at age 137 (see Genesis 25:17–18). His descendants seem to have become a wandering people who intermingled with the nations of Canaan. Thus Joseph was sold by his brethren into the hands of "Ishmeelites" who took him to Egypt (see Genesis 37:25–28; 39:1).

2. Ishmael was the son of Nethaniah "of the seed royal" (2 Kings 25:25) at the time of the Babylonian captivity. Ishmael conspired against Gedaliah, the appointed governor over the remainder of the Jewish people in Jerusalem, and put him and his officers to death, causing a great disturbance in the land. Eventually Ishmael went over among the Ammonites (see 2 Kings 25:26; Jeremiah 40–41).

3. Ishmael was also the name of several other individuals mentioned in the Old Testament (see 1 Chronicles 9:44; 2 Chronicles 19:11; 2 Chronicles 23:1; Ezra 10:22).

The Israelites crossing Jordan

ISHMAELITES (SEE ISHMAEL)

ISRAEL

(Meaning: one who prevails with God, or let God prevail.) During the time of his conflict with his twin brother, Esau, Jacob experienced an event in which he wrestled all night with a messenger from God, who told him that "as a prince [he had] power with God and with men, and [had] prevailed" (Genesis 32:28). Thereafter, Israel was the name applied to Jacob and (as Israel or Israelites) to his posterity (see Genesis 49:28; compare Genesis 49:7, 16, 24; Exodus 3:13–16; 19:5–6; 20:22; Deuteronomy 14:2—and frequently throughout the Old Testament and the Book of Mormon). In due course, after the kingdom was separated into two divisions, the northern part came to be designated *Israel* and the southern part *Judah*.

In a general sense, the term *Israel* is applied to all those who are true believers in Christ, as Paul explained: "BRETHREN, my heart's desire and prayer to God for Israel is, that they might be saved" (Romans 10:1; compare Romans 11:7; Galatians 6:16; Ephesians 2:12; 1 Peter 2:9). Similarly, the Doctrine and Covenants uses the term *Israel* to denote all of those belonging to the covenant people of God, literally or through adoption, according to their obedience to gospel principles. An example, from the words of the "new song" revealed for the last days: "The Lord hath brought again Zion; The Lord hath redeemed his people, Israel, According to the election of grace, Which was brought to pass by the faith And covenant of their fathers" (84:99). *See also Jacob.*

ISRAELITES (SEE ISRAEL)

ITHAMAR

Ithamar (pronounced ith'-uh-mahr) was the youngest of Aaron's sons (see Exodus 6:23). All four sons—Nadab, Abihu, Eleazar, and Ithamar—were consecrated and anointed to serve in the priest's office (see Exodus 28:1). When Nadab and Abihu desecrated their office and perished by divine judgment (see Leviticus 10:1–2; Numbers 3:4), the priestly office was carried on by Eleazar and Ithamar (see Leviticus 10:6; Numbers 3:4), with Eleazar having seniority (Leviticus 10:12, 16; Numbers 3:32; 20:28; see also Numbers 4:17–28; 26:63; 27:19–21; 31:12; 31:29; Deuteronomy 10:6; Joshua 14:1).

JACOB

(Meaning: supplanter.) Jacob was the younger of the twin sons of Isaac and Rebekah. It was through Jacob and his seed that the covenant promises granted to Abraham and Isaac were continued: "And God said unto [Jacob], I am God Almighty: be fruitful and multiply; a nation and a company of nations shall be of thee, and kings shall come out of thy loins" (Genesis 35:11). The life of Jacob is unfolded in the latter part of the book of Genesis.

Of special interest is the question of the birthright and how it devolved upon Jacob. In ancient Israel, the birthright was the right and privilege of the oldest son. As the story unfolds, Esau comes home from hunting and is famished. Jacob, having just made some pottage, gives Esau a portion in exchange for the blessing of the birthright (see Genesis 25:32–34). Esau later laments his decision: "And when Esau heard the words of his father [who had given Jacob a birthright blessing—Genesis 27:28–29], he cried with a great and exceeding bitter cry, and said unto his father, Bless me, *even* me also, O my father" (Genesis

27:34). Isaac does indeed give Esau a blessing, but it is a blessing of service to Jacob (see Genesis 27:39–40). Having forfeited his birthright, Esau is full of hatred, and thus Rebekah sends Jacob away to her brother Laban for safety (see Genesis 27:41–43). Esau had confused his priorities, and valued his temporal comforts above his spiritual birthright. Jacob was valiant during his lifetime, according to eternal values, placing a priority on that which was of utmost importance.

In Genesis 49:26 we read that Jacob (Israel) conferred a splendid blessing upon the head of Joseph (who had been granted the birthright in place of the wayward Reuben—see 1 Chronicles 5:1). Through Joseph, the covenant blessings passed to his sons Ephraim and Manasseh—and on to the latter-day heirs of the divine gospel plan.

Modern scripture confirms the role of Jacob (Israel) in the design of the Lord to bless His children of all generations. Jacob (Israel) has a pervasive presence throughout the Book of Mormon as a representative of the founding patriarchal lineage of Abraham, Isaac, and

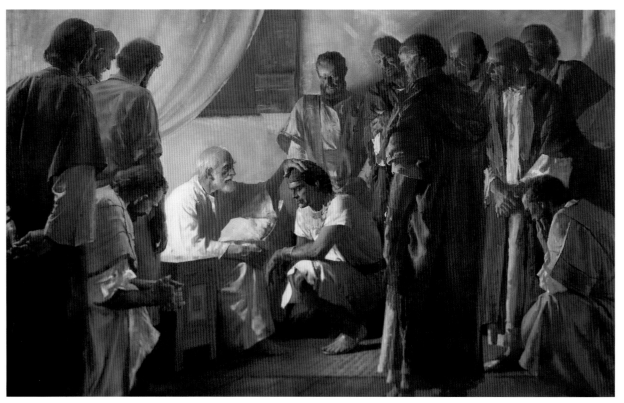

Jacob blessing Joseph

Jacob, and as the father of the twelve tribes of Israel. Lehi is identified as a descendant of Jacob through his son Joseph (see 1 Nephi 5:14)—and specifically through the line of Manasseh, son of Joseph (see Alma 10:3). In the wake of the seismic upheavals in ancient America that took place at the time of the death of the Savior, Mormon commented on the broader genealogical perspectives as evidence of the fulfillment of prophecy: "Behold, our father Jacob also testified concerning a remnant of the seed of Joseph. And behold, are not we a remnant of the seed of Joseph? And these things which testify of us, are they not written upon the plates of brass which our father Lehi brought out of Jerusalem?" (3 Nephi 10:17). When the resurrected Lord appeared to the ancient American Saints, He made reference to the covenant promises given to Jacob: "And it shall come to pass that I will establish my people, O House of Israel. And behold, this people will I establish in this land, unto the fulfilling of the covenant which I made with your father Jacob; and it shall be a New Jerusalem. And the powers of heaven shall be in the midst of this people; yea, even I will be in the midst of you" (2 Nephi 20:21–22).

The Doctrine and Covenants confirms that Jacob (Israel) was one of the patriarchs whose descendants carried forth the work of the Abrahamic covenant to spread the blessings of the gospel of salvation and the priesthood of God to the world (see Abraham 2:9–11). Jacob, whose exaltation is secured (see D&C 132:37), will be present at a future glorious sacrament meeting when all the faithful prophets of old will convene again (see D&C 27:10).

JAEL

(Meaning: mountain goat.) When the Israelites—under the leadership of Deborah, prophetess and judge—came against Jabin, king of the Canaanites, with his invading hosts under command of Sisera, the victory was with Deborah and her commander, Barak (see Judges 4:14, 23–24). The fleeing Sisera took refuge in the tent of Jael (pronounced jay'-uhl), wife of Heber the Kenite (a tribe related to the Midianites and friendly toward the Israelites). In the guise of serving and hiding Sisera, Jael stealthily brought an end to his life (see Judges 4:22). In their hymn of praise and celebration following the victory over the Canaanites, Deborah and Barak remembered the woman who silenced Sisera: "Blessed above women shall Jael the wife of Heber the Kenite be, blessed shall she be above women in the tent" (Judges 5:24).

JAHAZIEL

(Meaning: beheld by God or watched over by God.)

1. Jahaziel (pronounced jay'-huh-zy'-uhl or juh-hay'-zee-el) was a Benjamite chieftain named among the mighty men who joined with David in his ascendancy as king of Israel (see 1 Chronicles 12:4).

2. Jahaziel was a priest among those commissioned by King David to give service in connection with the removal of the ark to Jerusalem (see 1 Chronicles 16:6).

3. Jahaziel, third son of Hebron, was a Levite of the Kohathite order assigned to perform ministerial duties during the reign of King Solomon (see 1 Chronicles 23:19; 24:23).

4. Jahaziel was a Levite, the son of Zechariah of the line of Asaph, who rose up under the influence of the Spirit to give prophetic encouragement to Jehoshaphat in his quest to overcome the invading Ammonites, Moabites, and inhabitants of Mount Seir (see 2 Chronicles 20:15, 17).

On the morrow, the armies of the king, in their courageous advance, discovered that the enemy factions had battled amongst themselves and were totally destroyed (see 2 Chronicles 20:20–25).

5. Jahaziel was mentioned in reference to one of the family leaders ("son of Jahaziel"—Ezra 8:5) returning to Jerusalem from Babylonian captivity.

JANNES AND JAMBRES

Jannes (pronounced jan'-ees) and Jambres (pronounced jam-breez) were the sorcerers or magicians who confronted Moses in Egypt, as cited by Paul (see 2 Timothy 3:8). The names Jannes and Jambres do not occur in the Old Testament itself.

JAPHETH

Japheth (pronounced jay'-feth or jay'-futh) was the oldest son of Noah (see Genesis 5:32; see also Genesis 6:10; 7:13; 9:18, 23; Moses 8:12). Of this father-and-son circle the book of Moses states: "and [Noah] walked with God, as did also his three sons, Shem, Ham, and Japheth" (Moses 8:27). On one occasion Noah was sedated under the influence of wine when Ham came upon him in his nakedness and then informed his brothers, Shem and Japheth. These two discretely covered their father without viewing him. Noah later pronounced a curse on Ham for his indiscretion and blessed the other two sons. Of Japheth he said: "God shall enlarge Japheth, and he shall dwell in the tents of Shem; and Canaan [son of Ham] shall be his servant" (Genesis 9:27). The descendents of Japheth settled in a region extending from the eastern Mediterranean coasts to the Black Sea and the Caspian Sea. The sons of Japheth included "Gomer, and Magog, and Madai, and Javan, and Tubal, and Meshech, and Tiras" (1 Chronicles 1:5).

JAVAN

Javan (pronounced jay'-vuhn or jay'van) was one of the seven sons of Japheth, son of Noah (see Genesis 10:2; 1 Chronicles 1:5). Javan is considered the founder of the Greek race (see Isaiah 66:19; Ezekiel 27:13; Daniel 10:20; Zechariah 9:13).

JEBERECHIAH

(Meaning: whom Jehovah blesses.) Jeberechiah (pronounced juh-ber'-uh-ky'-uh) is mentioned only once in the Old Testament: "And I took unto me faithful witnesses to record, Uriah the priest, and Zechariah the son of Jeberechiah" (Isaiah 8:2; compare 2 Nephi 18:2).

JEBUSITES

The Jebusites (pronounced jeb'-yu-sites) were one of the indigenous peoples driven out by the influx of the Israelites into the promised land (see Deuteronomy 7:1–2; also Genesis 15:21; Exodus 3:8, 17; 13:5; 23:23; Numbers 13:29; Deuteronomy 20:17; Joshua 3:10; 12:8; 24:11; Judges 3:5; 19:11; 2 Samuel 5:6, 8; 1 Kings 9:20; 1 Chronicles 11:4, 6; 2 Chronicles 8:7; Ezra 9:1; Nehemiah 9:7–8).

JEHOAHAZ

1. Jehoahaz (pronounced juh-hoh'-uh-has, or jee-hoh'-uh-has), son of Jehu (see 2 Kings 10:35), was king of Israel for seventeen years, reigning in wickedness, following the pattern of Jeroboam, the first king of northern Israel. During his tenure, the judgments of God descended upon the nation in the form of invading Syrians, who wreaked havoc and great destruction (see 2 Kings 13:1–9, 25; compare 2 Chronicles 21:17). He was succeeded by his son Joash (also rendered *Jehoash*).

2. Jehoahaz, son of Josiah, was king of Judah for a period of three months before being deposed by Pharaoh-nechoh and replaced by Eliakim (renamed Jehoiakim—see 2 Kings 23:31–34; 2 Chronicles 36:1–4).

JEHOASH (SEE JOASH)

JEHOIACHIN

(Meaning: Jehovah shall establish.) Jehoiachin (pronounced juh-hoi'-uh-kin), son of Jehoiakim, was the eight-year-old king of Judah for a brief period of time in 598 BC. He was taken away to Babylon by Nebuchadnezzar and replaced by his brother Zedekiah (see 2 Chronicles 36:8–10; compare also 2 Kings 24:6–15; Ezekiel 1:2; some references make Zedekiah the uncle of Jehoiachin, as in Jeremiah 1:3; 37:1). Jehoiachin—sometimes referred to as Jeconiah (see 1 Chronicles 3:16–17; Esther 2:6; Jeremiah 24:1; 27:20; 28:4; 29:2) or Coniah (see Jeremiah 22:24, 28; 37:1)—was eventually released from captivity by the future king of Babylon, Evil-merodach, who treated him in a kindly fashion (see 2 Kings 25:27–29; see also Jeremiah 52:31–34).

JEHOIADA

(Meaning: Jehovah knows.)

1. Jehoiada (pronounced juh-hoi'-uh-duh or jee-hoi'-uh-duh) was the father of Benaiah, one of David's chief warriors (see 2 Samuel 8:18; 1 Chronicles 18:17).

2. Jehoiada was the leader of one of the contingents arrayed in support of David upon his ascension to the throne of Israel (1 Chronicles 12:27).

3. Jehoiada was the high priest who was instrumental in the overthrow of wicked Queen Athaliah, daughter of Ahab (king of Israel in the days of Elijah) and successor to her son Ahaziah, king of Judah. Jehoiada and his wife, Jehosheba, saved Joash (or Jehoash), surviving son of Ahaziah, elevating him six years later (at the tender age of seven) to the throne to replace the executed Athaliah (see 2 Kings 11:12, 13–21; 2 Chronicles 22:10–12; 23:15).

4. Jehoiada was a priest mentioned during the time of Jeremiah (see Jeremiah 29:26).

5. Jehoiada, son of Paseah, assisted in the repair of the old gate at Jerusalem (see Nehemiah 3:6).

JEHOIAKIM

Jehoiakim (pronounced juh-hoi'-uh-kim; originally called *Eliakim*) was elevated by the king of Egypt to the throne of Judah in place of his brother Jehoahaz (see 2 Kings 23:34). Jehoiakim ascended the throne at age twenty-five and reigned eleven years in wickedness (see 2 Chronicles 36:5). When Nebuchadnezzar invaded Judah, he carried away Jehoiakim prisoner (see Daniel 1:1–2), restoring him subsequently as a vassal king.

The word of the Lord through the prophet Jeremiah during those days proclaimed the impending downfall of Judah according to the judgments of God (see Jeremiah 36:1–3).

Jeremiah, a prisoner of the state at the time, caused these prophecies to be written down by the scribe Baruch and read to the people. When the king learned of this, he ordered the prophecies to be read before him. His angry reaction was to burn the written prophecy (see 36:23). Jeremiah responded quickly: "Then took Jeremiah another roll, and gave it to Baruch the scribe, the son of Neriah; who wrote therein from the mouth of Jeremiah all the words of the book which Jehoiakim king of Judah had burned in the fire: and there were added besides unto them many like words" (v. 32).

According to an earlier prophecy of Jeremiah, Jehoiakim would not be mourned after his death (see Jeremiah 22:18).

JEHONADAB

Jehonadab (pronounced juh-hahn'-uh-dab) was the son of Rechab and the principal founder of a tribe called the Rechabites (see 2 Kings 10:15, 23). Jeremiah pronounced God's blessings upon the Rechabites for their obedience (see Jeremiah 35).

JEHORAM (OR JORAM)

(Meaning: Jehovah exalted.)

1. Joram, son of Toi, king of Hamath, was dispatched to bestow congratulations upon David for his victory over Hadadezer, ally of the Ammonites (see 2 Samuel 8:10).

2. Joram was a Levite of the family of Gershom (see 1 Chronicles 26:25).

3. Jehoram (pronounced juh-hor'-uhm) was a priest sent by Jehoshaphat of Judah to instruct the people concerning the law of the Lord (see 2 Chronicles 17:8).

4. Jehoram (or Joram), son of Ahab and Jezebel, was the successor to his brother Ahaziah on the throne of Israel (see 2 Kings 1:17). Part of his reign was simultaneous with King Jehoram of Judah. Jehoram carried on the idolatrous culture of his parents, but with some reform (see 2 Kings 3:1–2). Through strategic alliances he was able to protect the land from Moabite subjection and Syrian invasion, though he was wounded in battle (the one during which the supportive prophet Elisha observed the protecting array of "chariots of fire"—2 Kings 6:17) and ultimately expired at the hand of Jehu (see 2 Kings 9:11–24) in fulfillment of the earlier prophecy of Elijah (see 1 Kings 21:29).

5. Jehoram (or Joram) succeeded Jehoshaphat as king of Judah (see 1 Kings 22:50). As king of Judah, Jehoram reigned in wickedness for eight years, having embraced the idolatrous practices of Ahab, king of Israel, whose daughter (Athaliah) he had married (see 2 Kings 8:16–24). Elijah prophesied that a plague would come upon the people and that Jehoram would perish—events that indeed transpired (see 2 Chronicles 21).

JEHOSHABEATH (OR JEHOSHEBA)

Jehoshabeath (pronounced jee-hoh-shab'-ee-ath), also rendered *Jehosheba* (pronounced jee-hosh'-ih-buh), was the daughter of King Joram (Jehoram) of Israel. She was also the half-sister of King Ahaziah of Judah, who ruled only one year before being succeeded by his ruthless mother, Athaliah. When Athaliah ordered the elimination of all the royal seed, Jehosheba courageously rescued the child Joash (or Jehoash), son of Ahaziah, and hid him away for six years until her husband, the high priest Jehoiada, could arrange for the lad to be enthroned in place of the subsequently executed Athaliah (see 2 Kings 11:2–3, 20–21; 2 Chronicles 22:2–12, 23:15).

JEHOSHAPHAT

(Meaning: Jehovah judged.)

1. Jehoshaphat (pronounced juh-hosh'-uh-fat') was an individual who served as recorder for David and later Solomon (see 2 Samuel 8:16; see also 2 Samuel 20:24; 1 Kings 4:3; 1 Chronicles 18:15).

2. Jehoshaphat was one of the priests who accompanied the transfer of the ark to Jerusalem (see 1 Chronicles 15:24).

3. Jehoshaphat was one of the princes in Solomon's court (see 1 Kings 4:17).

4. Jehoshaphat, son of Asa and Azubah (and great-great-great-grandson of Solomon—see 1 Chronicles 3:10), was a king of Judah who began his twenty-five-year reign at the time Ahab was king of Israel (see 1 Kings 22:41–42). He was renowned as a reformer and righteous monarch (see 1 Kings 22:43–44). A fitting epithet for Jehoshaphat is the remembrance that he "sought the Lord with all his heart" (2 Chronicles 22:9).

5. Jehoshaphat was the father of Jehu, king of Israel (see 2 Kings 9:2, 14).

JEHOVAH

(Meaning: the Unchangeable One.) Jehovah is a principal name for Jesus Christ, but is found only four times in the King James Version of the Old Testament (Exodus 6:2–3; Psalm 83:18; Isaiah 12:2; 26:4).

In addition, the Old Testament mentions the place name "Jehovah-jireh" (Genesis 22:14), so named by Abraham to memorialize the spot where he was about to sacrifice his son Isaac when the Lord intervened to provide a ram. *Jehovah-jireh* means "the Lord will see or provide."

Moreover, the name *Jehovah* appears a number of times in the Doctrine and Covenants (see 109:34, 42, 56, 68; 110:3; 128:9), the Pearl of Great Price (see Abraham 1:16; 2:8), and the Book of Mormon (see 2 Nephi 22:2). Especially notable is the concluding verse of the Book of Mormon, where Moroni proclaims: "And now I bid unto all, farewell. I soon go to rest in the paradise of God, until my spirit and body shall again reunite, and I am brought forth triumphant through the air, to meet you before the pleas-

ing bar of the great Jehovah, the Eternal Judge of both quick and dead. Amen" (Moroni 10:34). *See also the entry for Jesus Christ, which expounds further on the use and meaning of the name* Jehovah.

JEHU
(Meaning Jehovah is he.)

1. Jehu (pronounced jee'-hoo or jee'-hyoo) is mentioned among the posterity of Israel as the son of Obed and father of Azariah (see 1 Chronicles 2:38).

2. Jehu, son of Josibiah, is mentioned among the posterity of Israel (see 1 Chronicles 4:35).

3. Jehu is named as one of David's warriors (see 1 Chronicles 12:3).

4. Jehu, son of Hanani, was a prophet of Judah who pronounced the judgments of God upon Baasha, king of Israel, for his wickedness—resulting in Baasha's death at the hands of Zimri, one of his officers (see 1 Kings 16:1–2). Having been rebuked by Jehu for his alliance with wicked King Ahab, King Jehoshaphat of Judah took steps to cleanse the land of idolatry and induce the people to follow the pathway of righteousness (see 2 Chronicles 19).

5. Jehu, son of Jehoshaphat, was to become king of Israel in accordance with a prophecy of Elijah (see 1 Kings 19:16–17; 2 Kings 9:1–3). His twenty-eight-year tenure is marked by these actions: he dispatched Jehoram (Joram), king of Israel, with an arrow to the heart (see 2 Kings 9:24); ordered his warriors to fatally smite Ahaziah, king of Judah (see 2 Kings 9:27–28; 2 Chronicles 22:7–9); subjected Jezebel, the champion of idolatry, to an undignified death at Jezreel (see 2 Kings 9:30–37) in fulfillment of the prophecy of Elijah (see 1

Jehovah

Kings 21:23; 2 Kings 9:10); and then systematically cleansed the land of Baal worship (see 2 Kings 10:18–28), except for his tolerance of golden-calf worship at Dan and Bethel—for which the displeasure of the Lord was expressed through the destructive encroachments of the Syrians against the land (see 2 Kings 10:29–33).

JEPHTHAH

(Meaning: whom God liberates.) Jephthah (pronounced jef'-thuh), son of Gilead, was one of the judges in Israel (see Judges 11–12). In petitioning the Lord for victory against the Ammonite threat, Jephthah vowed to sacrifice "whatsoever cometh forth of the doors of my house to meet me, when I return in peace" (Judges 11:30–31). Regrettably, when it was his only daughter who appeared at the door of his house upon his return as victor, he had no choice but to honor his vow—something to which his daughter consented in meekness (see Judges 11:34–40).

JEREMIAH

(Meaning: raised up by Jehovah.) Jeremiah (pronounced jer'-uh-my'-uh) was a prophet of the Lord during the days of Lehi and Daniel. The books of Jeremiah and Lamentations (also written by Jeremiah) are two of the major prophetic books of the Old Testament, along with Isaiah, Ezekiel, and Daniel. Jeremiah prophesied during a forty-year period, from around 626 to 585 BC. His themes resound through the generations of time. He declares with power and authority the central governing principles of the gospel—that peace and happiness depend on obedience and honoring the covenants of the Lord, including

Jeremiah prophesies

developing a personal and spiritual relationship with Him; that the consequences of sin are destruction, scattering, and woe; that the Lord will chasten His people until they learn to be virtuous and righteous; and that He will eventually establish a new covenant with His faithful children and gather them in from the four quarters of the earth to be their King. Key sections of the Book of Jeremiah include: his prophecies during the reign of Josiah (626–608 BC—chapters 1–6), his prophecies during the reign of Jehoiakim (608–597 BC—chapters 7–20), his prophecies during the reign of Zedekiah (597–586 BC—chapters 21–38), the history of Jedekiah and other happenings after the fall of Jerusalem around 587 BC (chapters 39–45), his prophecies concerning foreign nations (chapters 46–51), and a historical conclusion (chapter 52).

The book of Lamentations post-dates the fall of Jerusalem (around 587 BC). Jeremiah laments the pitiful state of the great fallen city and bewails the fate of her lost citizens—but he does so in the spirit of a prophetic messenger commissioned to both cry repentance as well as confirm the mercies of a tender Lord. The people have brought upon themselves the judgments of God; still, despite the hardness of their hearts, He will remember them in His own due time following their chastening. For all the chaos depicted by Jeremiah as an eyewitness to the destruction in the streets of Jerusalem, he still maintains in his poetic discourse a solemn sense of governing order and design. The content of his composition reflects the reality of the turmoil and carnage before him; but the form reflects discipline and order.

Jeremiah's writings were included, in part, in the brass plates of Laban (see 1 Nephi 5:10–13; also 1 Nephi 7:14; Helaman 8:20). Nephi refers to Jeremiah in rebuking his rebellious brothers upon the return trip to guide Ishmael and his family to the encampment of Lehi: "For behold, the Spirit of the Lord ceaseth soon to strive with them [the people of Jerusalem]; for behold, they have rejected the prophets, and Jeremiah have they cast into prison" (1 Nephi 7:14). Many generations later, Nephi the son of Helaman, a few years before the birth of the Savior, invoked the name of Jeremiah, among many other prophets, to remind the people of the certainty of the coming of the Redeemer (see Helaman 8:19–20).

In terms of covenant history, Jeremiah's noble contemporary, Lehi, was obedient to the Lord in fleeing from Jerusalem with his family to preserve a branch of the House of Israel and to establish the foundation for the coming forth of a second testament of Jesus Christ—the Book of Mormon—that would rise from the dust as an integral part of the Restoration of the gospel in the latter days. Thus Jeremiah's ancient prophecy concerning a new covenant—even a new and everlasting covenant (see Jeremiah 31:31–34)—would be fulfilled in the return of the kingdom of God to earth prior to the Second Coming to extend the blessings of salvation and exaltation to all mankind, so that all who would choose to do so could know the Lord and follow in His footsteps.

JEREMIAS

Jeremias (jer'-uh-my'-as) is the New Testament version of Jeremiah (see Matthew 16:4). An alternate rendition is *Jeremy* (as in Matthew 27:9).

JEREMY

Jeremy (pronounced jer'-uh-mee) was a priesthood leader mentioned twice in the Doctrine and Covenants in connection with the lineage of the priesthood prior to the time of Moses: "And Elihu [received the priesthood] under the hand of Jeremy; And Jeremy under the hand of Gad" (84:9–10).

JEROBOAM

(Meaning: whose people are many.)

1. Jeroboam (pronounced jer'-uh-boh'-uhm) was the first in a long sequence of kings over the northern part of the House of Israel. Israel became divided into two parts around 975 BC, largely as a result of a revolt of the people against the heavy tax burden imposed by King Solomon. The northern part of the kingdom, headquartered at Shechem, comprised ten of the tribes, with Ephraim as the dominant

group. The southern part of the kingdom, headquartered at Jerusalem and governed by Solomon's successor, Reoboam, consisted chiefly of the tribes of Judah and Benjamin.

Jeroboam was promised by the prophet Ahijah that if he would walk in the ways of righteousness, his kingdom would be successful. However, he undertook initiatives that contravened the instructions of the prophet Ahijah. Jeroboam set up two golden calves (one in Bethel and one in Dan), telling the people to worship in those places rather than journeying to Jerusalem (where, he feared, they would be subjected to the influence of the rival king, Rehoboam). He also appointed priests from non-Levite ranks and established a feast day of his own contrivance (see 1 Kings 12:25–33; 2 Chronicles 13:9).

Subsequently, when Jeroboam was worshipping at the altar he had established at Bethel, a prophet of God from Judah came to the altar and rebuked him for his evil ways. At that moment Jeroboam reached forth his hand to command the arrest of the prophet, but the hand was rendered useless and the altar was rent. Only a petition to the prophet brought about a restoration of the hand (see 1 Kings 13:1–6), but Jeroboam did not restore righteousness to his reign.

When his young son Abijah was stricken with illness, Jeroboam sent his wife in disguise to inquire of the prophet Ahijah. Ahijah pronounced doom upon the house of Jeroboam for disregarding the Lord and worshipping idols. Ahijah prophesied that although the boy had good in him and would be mourned by all Israel, young Abijah would die as soon as his mother returned to the city (see 1 Kings 14:13). As prophesied, Abijah perished and Israel mourned (see 1 Kings 14:17–18). After a twenty-two-year reign, Jeroboam went to his grave as well (see 1 Kings 14:20; compare 2 Chronicles 13:20).

2. Jeroboam was king of Israel during the time of the prophets Amos (see Amos 1:1; 7:10–11), Hosea (see Hosea 1:1), and Jonah (see 2 Kings 14:25). He was the son and successor of Jehoash (or Joash), who was the son of Jehoahaz, who in turn was the son of Jehu (see 2 Kings 14:16). Jeroboam was highly successful in reclaiming Israelite territory taken over by enemy forces and building up the prosperity of the land (see 2 Kings 14:27–28). Morally, however, Jeroboam fell short: "And he did that which was evil in the sight of the Lord: he departed not from all the sins of Jeroboam the son of Nebat, who made Israel to sin" (2 Kings 14:24). Amos and Hosea denounced the wickedness rampant in the land (see Amos 1–2; 7:9–11; Hosea 1–2). Jeroboam reigned forty-one years (see 2 Kings 14:23) and was succeeded by his son Zachariah (see 2 Kings 14:29).

JERUBBAAL

(Meaning: He that contends with Baal.) Jerubbaal (pronounced jeh'-ruh-bay'-uhl) was the name that Gideon, the judge, received from his father, Joash, after Gideon had destroyed the altar of Baal according to a commandment from an angel of God (see Judges 6:32; 7:1; 9:1; 1 Samuel 12:11). *See Gideon.*

JERUBBESHETH

(Meaning: contender with the shame, i.e., with an idol, such as Baal.) Jerubbesheth is an additional name for Gideon, the judge/warrior (see 2 Samuel 11:21). *See Jerubbaal and Gideon.*

Jeshua (see Joshua)

Jesse

Jesse was the father of David and therefore in the direct line of descent leading to Christ (see Ruth 4:17, 22; 1 Chronicles 2:5–12; Matthew 1:5–6). After Saul had witnessed the miraculous conquest over Goliath by the fearless young man with the sling, he said: "Whose son art thou, thou young man? And David answered, I am the son of thy servant Jesse the Beth-lehemite" (1 Samuel 17:58). From that moment on, Jesse, as the father of David, was renowned throughout the land—just as his son was. Jesse is mentioned repeatedly in the scriptural accounts of the early history of David and also in the writings of Isaiah, who wrote, "And there shall come forth a rod out of the stem of Jesse, and a Branch shall grow out of his roots" (Isaiah 11:1; compare also Isaiah 11:10). This passage and similar ones in Isaiah are interpreted in Doctrine and Covenants section 113: "Who is the Stem of Jesse spoken of in the 1st, 2d, 3d, 4th, and 5th verses of the 11th chapter of Isaiah? Verily thus saith the Lord: It is Christ" (vv. 1–2).

Jesus Christ

Understanding the mission of the Lord gives us perspective on the unfolding panorama of God's dealings with His people in the Old Testament and the Pearl of Great Price. Jesus Christ is the central figure of these books, just as He is in the New Testament, Book of Mormon, and Doctrine and Covenants.

Not only was Jesus Christ the Lord of the Old Testament, but prophets throughout time foretold of His coming birth, life, and Atonement. Among the numerous offices and

Isaiah foretells the birth of Jesus Christ

titles of the Lord revealed through the scriptural record, the following six might be considered the predominant ones: (1) *Jehovah* ("Unchangeable One"), (2) *Messiah* or *Christ* ("Anointed One"), (3) *Creator*, (4) *Immanuel* ("God Among Us"), (5) *Jesus* ("God is help" or "Savior"), and (6) *King*. The names are often used interchangeably, and many of the qualities of each title overlap. But considering each title separately can shed light on the various offices and attributes of the Savior.

1. JEHOVAH. In the King James Version of the Old Testament, the word *Lord* (with each letter capitalized) signifies that the original text upon which the translation into English was based contained at that point the name *Jehovah*.

Out of respect for Deity, Jewish readers did not speak aloud the name *Jehovah* (or any of its variants), but substituted instead a Hebrew word such as *Adonai*, meaning "Lord."

The name *Jehovah* signifies the everlasting, endless, and eternal God, as well as a reflection of the supernal constancy of the word of God (see Isaiah 40:8). The nature of Jehovah as an eternal, unchanging, and everlasting Being derives from His relationship to, and grounding in, the Father, Elohim. Jehovah is in very deed the Son of God, even the Firstborn: "I will declare the decree: the LORD hath said unto me, Thou art my Son; this day have I begotten thee" (Psalm 2:7). Furthermore: "Also I will make him my firstborn, higher than the kings of the earth. My mercy will I keep for him for evermore, and my covenant shall stand fast with him. His seed also will I make to endure for ever, and his throne as the days of heaven" (Psalm 89:27–29). In the New Testament, Book of Mormon, and the Doctrine and Covenants,

this defining position as the "First as well as the Last," applied to Jesus Christ, is embodied in the appellation "Alpha and Omega" (see, for example, Revelation 1:8, 11; 21:6; 3 Nephi 9:18; D&C 19:1; 38:1; 4:7; 75:1; 81:7; 112:34; and 132:66).

Not only is Jehovah endless and eternal, He also serves everlastingly as a member of the Godhead under the direction of the Father and in conjunction with the Holy Ghost.

2. MESSIAH/CHRIST. *Messiah* is an Aramaic word meaning "the Anointed." Aramaic belongs to the Semitic language group (which also includes Hebrew and Arabic) and became the official language of the Assyrian and later the Babylonian and Persian empires. Aramaic was for centuries the dominant language in Jewish worship and daily life, with Jesus Himself speaking Aramaic.

The Greek equivalent of *Messiah* was "Christ." The word *Christ* does not appear in the King James Version of the Old Testament, but does appear in the book of Moses in the Pearl of Great Price (Moses 6:52, 57; 7:50; 8:24). The title *Messiah* appears only twice in the Old Testament (see Daniel 9:25 and 9:26) and only once in the Pearl of Great Price (see Moses 7:53). What is important about the terms *Messiah* and *Christ* is the underlying meaning of these titles as "the Anointed"— signifying that Jesus was divinely commissioned of the Father to carry out the work of redemption and Atonement on behalf of all mankind. He was foreordained to His supernal mission: "And the Lord said: Whom shall I send? And one answered like unto the Son of Man: Here am I, send me. And another answered and said: Here am I, send me. And the Lord said: I will send the first" (Abraham 3:27; compare Job 38:1–7; Isaiah 25:8–9).

Jesus—as the Messiah and the Christ—is the authorized and empowered agent of the Father with the express calling to carry out the divine mission of saving and exalting mankind in keeping with the eternal principles of truth and spiritual deliverance. Isaiah expresses this divine mission of the Anointed One in the following terms:

> The Spirit of the Lord GOD is upon me; because the LORD hath anointed me to preach good tidings unto the meek; he hath sent me to bind up the brokenhearted, to proclaim liberty to the captives, and the opening of the prison to them that are bound;
>
> To proclaim the acceptable year of the LORD, and the day of vengeance of our God; to comfort all that mourn;
>
> To appoint unto them that mourn in Zion, to give unto them beauty for ashes, the oil of joy for mourning, the garment of praise for the spirit of heaviness; that they might be called trees of righteousness, the planting of the LORD, that he might be glorified. (Isaiah 61:1–3)

To officiate in this singularly indispensable capacity as the Anointed One, Jesus must necessarily embody qualities such as being omnipotent, chosen, and mighty to effect change for good. The prophets of God throughout successive dispensations have promised and foretold the work and ministry of Jesus in this respect.

3. CREATOR. Jesus Christ served as the principal divine agent in laying the foundation of the world through the Creation itself: "I am the Lord that maketh all things; that stretcheth forth the heavens alone; that spreadeth abroad the earth by myself . . . " (Isaiah 44:24). The predominant quality of Jesus Christ as Creator is "One who completes," or One who—through faith, obedience, power, and divine light—generates and sustains life unto salvation. When God directed by His word that the Creation should proceed (see Genesis 1–2; Moses 2–3; Deuteronomy 4:32), it was through the Word of God (meaning Christ) that this divine process was initiated and completed (see Psalm 33:6). John the Apostle reaffirmed this verity: "In the beginning was the Word, and the Word was with God, and the Word was God. The same was in the beginning with God. All things were made by him; and without him was not any thing made that was made. In him was life; and the life was the light of men" (John 1:1–4; compare also Colossians 1:16; Revelation 5:13; 10:6; 2 Nephi 2:14; 29:7; Mosiah 4:2, 9; Mormon 9:11, 17; D&C 14:9).

What greater symbolic representation could there be of the office and function of the Creator than the image of being the "Light of the World"? In keeping with the essence of this divine capacity, the Psalmist wrote: "The LORD is my light and my salvation; whom shall I fear? the LORD is the strength of my life; of whom shall I be afraid?" (Psalm 27:1).

Many references from the Old Testament confirm and expand on the mission of the Lord as Creator. For example, the Lord asked Job, in his adversity: "Where wast thou when I laid the foundations of the earth? declare, if thou hast understanding. Who hath laid the measures thereof, if thou knowest? or who hath stretched the line upon it? Whereupon are the foundations thereof fastened? or who laid the corner stone thereof; When the morning stars sang together, and all the sons of God shouted for joy?" (Job 38:4–7; see also Job 10:8–12; 26:12–13).

Isaiah, Jeremiah, and Amos also proclaim through the voice of inspiration the Creator's power over the elements (see Isaiah 40:25–28; 45:11–14; 65:7; Jeremiah 51:15–16; Amos 4:13).

The Son of God governed and still governs the vital process of generating and preserving life itself—beginning with the Creation and continuing with the unfolding of the process of dynamic growth of all living things pertaining to this world and all other worlds: "And worlds without number have I created; and I also created them for mine own purpose; and by the Son I created them, which is mine Only Begotten" (Moses 1:33).

4. IMMANUEL. One of the greatest of all the miracles of the gospel is the condescension of the Father and the Son, that Jesus Christ should come among mortals to bring to pass for all mankind the effectual conditions for salvation and redemption. In this capacity, His office and title are known as *Immanuel* (also rendered *Emmanuel*)—that is, "God among Us." Isaiah prophecied that "a virgin shall conceive, and bear a son, and shall call his name Immanuel" (Isaiah 7:14).

Mary would come forth of the tribe of Judah via the Davidic lineage (see Psalm 132:11), just as Joseph, her husband (see Matthew 1). Gabriel would confirm this lineage to Mary when he announced, concerning her forthcoming son, "And the Lord shall give unto him the throne of his father, David" (Luke 1:32).

The chronicle of Immanuel's mortal experience is woven through prophetic utterance

The Savior Jesus Christ

into the fabric of the Old Testament. The Psalmist foresaw the work of the mortal Messiah: "The LORD is high above all nations, and his glory above the heavens. Who is like unto the LORD our God, who dwelleth on high, Who humbleth himself to behold the things that are in heaven, and in the earth!" (Psalm 113:4–6). Isaiah prophesied regarding the Savior's mortal birth and contrasted this with His great glory: "For unto us a child is born, unto us a son is given: and the government shall be upon his shoulder: and his name shall be called Wonderful, Counsellor, The mighty God, The everlasting Father, The Prince of Peace. Of the increase of his government and peace there shall be no end, upon the throne of David, and upon his kingdom, to order it, and to establish it with judgment and with justice from henceforth even for ever" (Isaiah 9:6–7; see also Genesis 49:10; Isaiah 10:27; 11:1–9).

Isaiah also envisioned the infinite humility of the Son in submitting Himself willingly to His detractors (see Isaiah 50:5–6). Continuing his inspired pronouncement, Isaiah articulates with consummate and unforgettable eloquence the pains of the Lord in doing the will of the Father upon the earth:

> He is despised and rejected of men; a man of sorrows, and acquainted with grief: and we hid as it were our faces from him; he was despised, and we esteemed him not.
>
> Surely he hath borne our griefs, and carried our sorrows: yet we did esteem him stricken, smitten of God, and afflicted.
>
> But he was wounded for our transgressions, he was bruised for our iniquities: the chastisement of our peace was upon him; and with his stripes we are healed.
>
> All we like sheep have gone astray; we have turned every one to his own way; and the LORD hath laid on him the iniquity of us all. (Isaiah 53:3–6)

Enoch saw in vision the Lord's mortal mission: "And behold, Enoch saw the day of the coming of the Son of Man, even in the flesh; and his soul rejoiced, saying: The Righteous is lifted up, and the Lamb is slain from the foundation of the world; and through faith I am in the bosom of the Father, and behold, Zion is with me" (Moses 7:47).

The all-encompassing view of the condescension of the Only Begotten is that of the Good Shepherd who tends His flocks personally as "the shepherd, the stone of Israel" (Genesis 49:24). This role is most memorably expressed in the twenty-third Psalm: "The LORD is my shepherd; I shall not want" (v. 1), but is also found in several other prophetic passages, including Psalm 95:7 (see also Zechariah 13:7). Perhaps the most detailed view of the Good Shepherd Immanuel is given in Ezekiel 34:11–19, including the statement, "I will feed them in a good pasture, and upon the high mountains of Israel shall their fold be: there shall they lie in a good fold, and in a fat pasture shall they feed upon the mountains of Israel" (Ezekiel 34:14).

As the Good Shepherd, Immanuel is clearly a very personal Savior, nurturing His flock with patience and love. The extraordinary record in the Pearl of Great Price concerning Moses' interaction with the Lord (see Moses

1) confirms the personal nature of God's interaction with His servants: "And I have a work for thee, Moses, my son; and thou art in the similitude of mine Only Begotten; and mine Only Begotten is and shall be the Savior, for he is full of grace and truth; but there is no God beside me, and all things are present with me, for I know them all" (Moses 1:6). The Psalmist reminds us to cultivate an openness to the Lord's invitation to achieve a personal relationship with Him: "O come, let us worship and bow down: let us kneel before the LORD our maker. For he is our God; and we are the people of his pasture, and the sheep of his hand" (Psalm 95:6–7).

In latter-day scripture, the Prophet Joseph Smith reemphasizes the counsel of the Lord that all should seek a personal relationship with Immanuel in order to enjoy the blessings of eternity: "And seek the face of the Lord always, that in patience ye may possess your souls, and ye shall have eternal life" (D&C 101:38).

5. JESUS. The name *Jesus* is the Greek form of the name *Joshua* or *Jeshua*, meaning "God is Help" (or "Jehovah is Help"), or in other words, Savior. The name implies the sacred office of Redeemer, Lamb of God, Bread of Life, the One who brings about the Atonement through the sacrificial crucifixion, the One who ushers in the process of the Resurrection, the One who is therefore, in all respects, the Life of the World. In this capacity as Savior, Jesus is the means for rescuing all mankind from the effects of the temporal death and enabling the faithful and obedient to escape the clutches of the second (or spiritual) death through compliance with the principles and ordinances of the gospel.

The Old Testament is a vibrant and compelling witness of the office of Savior and Redeemer as consummated in the crucifixion and Resurrection of Jesus: The Psalmist anticipated the express words of the sacrificial Lamb of God—"My God, my God, why hast thou forsaken me?" (Psalm 22:1)—and discerned in prophetic vision the process of the crucifixion: "the assembly of the wicked have inclosed me: they pierced my hands and my feet. I may tell all my bones: they look and stare upon me. They part my garments among them, and cast lots upon my vesture. But be not thou far from me, O LORD: O my strength, haste thee to help me" (Psalm 22:16–19). Isaiah foresaw in great detail the travail of the Lord on the cross (see Isaiah 53:5–12). Likewise, Zechariah was blessed to view spiritually the crucifixion and Atonement from the perspective of the Savior (see Zechariah 12:10; 13:6).

The glorious Atonement and Resurrection of the Savior was the crowning triumph of His ministry. The promise of the redeeming death of Christ as the Savior and Redeemer secured the faith and hope of His followers in all ages.

The concept of Jesus as the Lamb of God was made a regular part of the worship of ancient Israel through the ritual sacrifice of a lamb "without blemish" (Exodus 12:5)—one per household—during the Passover (see Exodus 12:13–14). Isaiah celebrated the symbolism of the Lamb of God with these words: "He is brought as a lamb to the slaughter, and as a sheep before her shearers is dumb, so he openeth not his mouth. . . . when thou shalt make his soul an offering for sin, he shall see his seed, he shall prolong his days, and the pleasure of the LORD shall prosper in his hand" (Isaiah 53:7, 10).

The qualities of Jesus as our Savior emerge sublime from the canon: loving, redeeming, spotless. He is so loving that He verily weeps when we fall short of our potential: "Wherefore, he suffereth for their sins; inasmuch as they will repent in the day that my Chosen shall return unto me, and until that day they shall be in torment; Wherefore, for this shall the heavens weep, yea, and all the workmanship of mine hands" (Moses 7:39–40). At the same time, He rejoices when we repent and follow in His footsteps (see D&C 18:11–13).

6. KING. The Firstborn of Elohim was anointed in the premortal realm as Messiah to lay the foundation of the world through the Creation and serve as the author of eternal salvation by coming to live among mortals (as "Immanuel"), in obedience to the will of the Father, for the purpose of completing His atoning mission as Jesus the Christ, thus becoming the Savior to all the world. In the final chapter of the history of this world, Jesus Christ will return in glory as King, Judge, Law-Giver, Mediator, Advocate, and Prince of Peace, to usher in the millennial reign and take His place as the covenant Father of all the righteous and redeemed. The Old Testament confirms this divine design through the voices of prophets such as David, Isaiah, Joel, and Zechariah.

The ushering in the of the millennial reign is a time of universal judgment, as the scriptural record confirms (see 1 Samuel 2:10; compare also Genesis 18:25; Deuteronomy 32:36; Judges 11:27): "And he shall judge the world in righteousness, he shall minister judgment to the people in uprightness" (Psalm 9:8).

As presented in the scriptural accounts of the final judgment, our King, the Great Jehovah, will be just, merciful, righteous, and full of grace. His judgments will be holy and glorious. Alma provides perhaps the most compelling summary of the qualities our Savior embodies as our Lord and King: "And thus he shall bring salvation to all those who shall believe on his name; this being the intent of this last sacrifice, to bring about the bowels of mercy, which overpowereth justice, and bringeth about means unto men that they may have faith unto repentance. And thus mercy can satisfy the demands of justice, and encircles them in the arms of safety, while he that exercises no faith unto repentance is exposed to the whole law of the demands of justice; therefore only unto him that has faith unto repentance is brought about the great and eternal plan of redemption" (Alma 34:15–16).

SUMMARY. The overarching reach of divine influence in the lives of God's children traces a pattern of magnanimous grace and love on the part of the Lord. We perceive in His divine career many titles and offices, but only one Lord; many qualities, but only one unified manifestation of divine love; many influences and interactions with mankind, but only one cause: "to bring to pass the immortality and eternal life of man" (Moses 1:39).

JETHRO

(Meaning: his excellence.) Jethro (also called *Reuel*), prince and priest of Midian, was the father-in-law of Moses. After Moses had fled from Egypt as a result of his having slain an Egyptian who was smiting an Israelite, he relocated to the land of Midian (see Exodus 2:11–16). While there, Moses observed at a well that shepherds were driving a group of young women away from the water. He interceded on behalf of the women—the seven daughters of Reuel (Jethro)—and watered their flock. Reuel was grateful to Moses and invited him to stay. Eventually Moses married Zipporah, one of Reuel's daughters (see Exodus 2:16–21). Moses also took over the responsibility to keep the flock of Jethro.

Jethro acted as a counselor to Moses regarding how to manage the heavy administrative burden of acting as judge over Israel. Jethro taught Moses effective principles of delegation and leadership development, rendering the task of governance more manageable (see Exodus 18:19–26).

The Doctrine and Covenants provides the added information that Moses received the Melchizedek priesthood from Jethro: "And the sons of Moses, according to the Holy Priesthood which he [Moses] received under the hand of his father-in-law, Jethro; And Jethro received it under the hand of Caleb" (84:6–7).

JEWS

The term *Jews*, in the most specific sense, refers to people of the lineage of Judah, son of Jacob. The earliest usage of the term in the Old Testament occurs in this passage: "At that time Rezin king of Syria recovered Elath to Syria, and drave the Jews from Elath" (2 Kings 16:6; around 740 BC). In a broader sense, the term can be applied to those, over the generations, who were citizens of Jerusalem, even though they were not of Jewish lineage. Thus, Lehi of the Book of Mormon was part of the Jewish community in his day (see 2 Nephi 30:4)—although he was by lineage from the tribe of Joseph through Manasseh, son of Joseph (see Alma 10:3), while Ishmael and his posterity derived from the tribe of Ephraim, son of Joseph (see *JD* 23:184–185).

The most frequent usage of the term *Jews* in the Doctrine and Covenants comes in passages distinguishing the flow of gospel truth—i.e., first to the Gentiles, and then to the Jews (see 20:9; 21:12; 107:33, 34; 133:8). However, in one passage concerning the Book of Mormon, the word *Jew* is used in the broader sense of the term: "Which is my word to the Gentile, that soon it may go to the Jew, of whom the Lamanites are a remnant, that they may believe the gospel, and look not for a Messiah to come who has already come" (19:27; compare 57:4). In this usage, the Lamanites are identified as a branch of the Jews. Such is indeed the case in regard to Lehi and his posterity being of Jewish citizenship (though of the lineage of Joseph). In a more direct sense, the Mulekites—as colonists to the New World who were later integrated into the Nephite generations under the leadership of Mosiah I—introduced the direct blood lineage of Judah into the Book of Mormon demographics, since Mulek was the surviving son of Zedekiah, king of Judah (see Helaman 8:21; Omni 1:12–16). Thus the Lamanites of the latter days could be thought of as Jewish in two senses: through the Jewish citizenship of Lehi and, in part, through the blood lineage of Mulek blended in with the Josephite lineage of Lehi and his descendants. *See Judah*.

JEZEBEL

(Meaning: chaste.) Jezebel, the notorious Phoenician princess, did not manage to live up to her name. Daughter of Ethbaal, king of the Zidonian, Jezebel married Ahab, king of Israel, and with him worshipped and served the idol Baal (see 1 Kings 16:30–33). Jezebel aggressively promoted idolatry in Israel and systematically attempted to exterminate the Lord's priests (see 1 Kings 18:4, 13). Elijah was sent by divine commission to obstruct and

The death of Jezebel

uproot this campaign of sacrilege (see 1 Kings 18:17–19).

In the celebrated contest between the forces of good and the forces of evil, Elijah calls down fire from heaven to confirm the power of God in a sacrificial ordinance and then destroys the impotent priests of Baal (see 1 Kings 18:2–40). Jezebel seeks to kill Elijah (see 1 Kings 19), but in the end is subjected to an ignoble death at Jezreel in fulfillment of the prophecy of Elijah and later of Elisha (see 2 Kings 9:7–10, 30–37). The name *Jezebel*, consequently, became a symbol for the kind of licentious idolatry to which gospel principles of purity stand in stark contrast (see Revelations 2:20).

JEZREEL

(Meaning: God will scatter.) Jezreel (pronounced jez'-ree-el or jez'-ree-uhl) was the name given to the oldest son of Hosea the prophet (see Hosea 1:4–5). Symbolically, the name *Jezreel* called to mind the scenes of carnage and destruction that occurred in the days of Jehu at the place of that name (see, for example, 2 Kings 10:11)—and thus reinforced the power of the prophecy being expressed for the future judgments of God.

JOAB

1. Joab—David's nephew, the oldest son of Zeruiah, David's sister (see 2 Samuel 2:18)—was "the general of the king's army" (1 Chronicles 27:34) and "the captain of the host" (2 Samuel 24:2). Joab was the acting general in all of David's major campaigns (see, for example, 2 Samuel 2:12–17; 10:6–19; 11:1; 1 Kings 11:15–16). During the days of conflict between Saul and David, Abner (Saul's commander) slew Asahel, the brother of Joab (see 2 Samuel 2:23). Joab then took action on his own to end the life of Abner (see 2 Samuel 3:27; compare 1 Kings 2:5, 32), causing the magnanimous David to mourn before the people (see 2 Samuel 5:3).

When Absalom, David's son, conspired against his father, Joab stood firm in support of David, who counseled against rash retribution: "Deal gently for my sake with the young man, even with Absalom. And all the people heard when the king gave all the captains charge concerning Absalom" (2 Samuel 18:5). But Joab took upon himself the initiative to slay Absalom (see v. 14), causing David deep anguish (see v. 33). David was then of a mind to elevate Amasa (captain of the army under Absalom—see 2 Samuel 17:25), but Joab slew Amasa (see 2 Samuel 20:9–10; see also 1 Kings 2:5, 32).

Joab later turned his support to Adonijah, David's upstart son, rather than to Solomon

Joash (3) ordered donated money be used to repair the temple

(see 1 Kings 1:5, 17–18). When Adonijah ascended the throne with the help of his allies, Joab and Abiathar the priest, the aging David gave the command that Solomon should be brought forth and anointed king amidst the sound of the trumpet while Adonijah and his insiders were celebrating what they considered a banquet of triumph (see 1:39–43). Under Solomon, the new king, Joab was executed for treachery and replaced by Benaiah (see vv. 34–35). Joab is a prime example of a man whose loyalty to his sovereign extends only to the boundaries of his own preferences.

2. Joab was one of the descendants of Kenaz mentioned in the Israelite genealogy (see 1 Chronicles 4:13–14).

3. Joab was an individual mentioned in Ezra 2:6; 8:9; and in Nehemiah 7:11.

JOASH (OR JEHOASH)

1. Joash was the father of Gideon, the warrior/judge (see Judges 6:11). When during the nighttime Gideon destroyed the altar of Baal and the associated grove (idol of nature worship), the citizens were outraged the next day but silenced by the courageous and moving defense of Joash (see Judges 6:31–32).

2. Joash was a son of King Ahab of Israel (see 1 Kings 22:26; 2 Chronicles 18:25; 25:23).

3. Joash, the son of Ahaziah, became king of Judah when brought as a lad from hiding and enthroned by the high priest Jehoiada (see 2 Kings 11–12, 14). Jehoiada then arranged for the execution of wicked Queen Athaliah, daughter of Ahab (king of Israel in the days of Elijah) and successor to her son Ahaziah, king of Judah (see 2 Kings 11:13–21; 2 Chronicles 22:10–12; 23:15). The land prospered under the leadership of Joash; however, upon the passing of Jehoiada, Joash allowed Judah to lapse once again into idolatry and was slain by his servants (see 2 Chronicles 24:20, 25).

4. Joash was king of Israel, son of Jehoahaz, and he reigned in wickedness (see 2 Kings 13:10–11). Elisha prophesied that Joash would defeat the Syrians three times—something that indeed occurred (see 2 Kings 13:14, 25). Joash also had occasion to battle against Amaziah, king of Judah, and prevailed (see 2 Kings 14:1–15; 2 Chronicles 25).

5. Joash was the name of two other individuals mentioned in genealogical listings (see 1 Chronicles 4:22; 7:8).

6. Joash was one of David's leading warriors (see 1 Chronicles 12:3).

Job and his family

7. Joash was an officer in the court of David and Solomon who oversaw the "cellars of oil" (1 Chronicles 27:28).

JOB

There are few treatises or narratives that plumb the potential of man, his interrelationships with others, and his integrity of heart with more depth or illumination than the book of Job. The book is one of the eleven books of the Old Testament belonging to the Hagiographa ("sacred writings") of the Jewish canon, along with Psalms, Proverbs, Song of Solomon, Ruth, Lamentations, Ecclesiastes, Daniel, Esther, Ezra-Nehemiah (counted as one book), and Chronicles (also counted as one book). The book of Job provides a poetic drama of unsurpassed intensity and meaning concerning the human condition, focusing on the misery and lowliness of man in comparison with the majesty and supremacy of God, the trials of life as a test of man's integrity and loyalty to his Creator (and not necessarily as evidence of unrighteousness), and the divine spark of testimony within man that God lives, guiding man toward a better state based on his obedience, patience, and willingness to endure to the end.

The book of Job comprises the following major sections: opening prologue and framework, teaching that God permits Satan to try to test Job, who encounters daunting adversity and decries his situation (chapters 1–3); Job's three friends (Eliphaz, Bildad, and Zophar) discuss with him the implications of his suffering, though not always with the most charitable spirit of understanding and encouragement (chapters 4–18); Job declares his faith in God's design and confirms his enduring testimony (chapter 19); Job continues his dialogue with his friends, with similar mixed outcomes and remaining questions (chapters 20–28); Job reviews his condition (chapters 29–31); Elihu intervenes with a sermon on man's weakness and God's majesty (chapters 31–37); God speaks with Job and teaches him truths from the divine perspective (chapters 38–41); Job repents and is blessed (chapter 42).

Echoing the spirit of Job, the Prophet Joseph Smith, while incarcerated in Liberty Jail (late Fall 1838 to early Spring 1839), cried unto the Lord, "O GOD, where art thou? And where is the pavilion that covereth thy hiding place? How long shall thy hand be stayed, and thine eye, yea thy pure eye, behold from the eternal heavens the wrongs of thy people and of thy servants, and thine ear be penetrated with their cries?" (D&C 121:1–2). The Lord responded with words of comfort and encouragement, also reminding Joseph, "Thou art not yet as Job; thy friends do not contend against thee, neither charge thee with transgression, as they did Job" (v. 10).

Having lost the fulness of his family and estate, having been afflicted with incapacitating ailments, having been accused unjustly of a wicked life, and having every ounce of hope and fortitude sapped from his system, Job nevertheless rose from the depths of adversity to exclaim: "For I know that my redeemer liveth, and that he shall stand at the latter day upon the earth: And though after my skin worms destroy this body, yet in my flesh shall I see God" (Job 19:25–26). Within his soul

unfolded the majesty of a son of God holding tightly to the assurance that his royal destiny would in no measure be compromised by the forces of tribulation around him: "But he [the Lord] knoweth the way that I take: when he hath tried me, I shall come forth as gold. My foot hath held his steps, his way have I kept, and not declined" (Job 23:10–11).

JOCHEBED

Jochebed (pronounced jock'-uh-bed) was the wife of Amram and the mother of Moses, Aaron, and Miriam (see Numbers 26:59; see also Exodus 6:20). It was Jochebed who hid the infant Moses in the bulrushes when Pharaoh ordered the execution of all the male children born to the Israelites (see Exodus 2:1–3). When Pharaoh's daughter rescued the babe, young Miriam arranged for Jochebed to nurse the child.

JOEL

Joel was a prophet of Judah. The time span of his writings is unknown—it could be as early as the ninth century or as late as the return from the Babylonian captivity following the decree of liberation of the Jewish people issued by Cyrus in 537 BC. Joel uses an occasion of dire famine and suffering to reflect on the perennial famine of truth among the unrighteous through the generations of time. Such a famine will be relieved through the eventual restoration of the Lord's kingdom on earth—a day when vision and prophesy will again be made manifest among the faithful and penitent and the Lord will reign supreme.

Joel was cited by Peter on the Day of Pentecost (see Acts 2:17) and by Moroni in

Jonah is cast ashore

his visitation to the Prophet Joseph Smith (see JS–H 1:41).

JONAH

Jonah lived during the reign of Jeroboam, king of Israel (see 2 Kings 14:25) from approximately 790 to 749 BC. During this same period, the prophets Hosea (see Hosea 1:1) and Amos (see Amos 7:10–11) were also active. The book of Jonah was written by an unknown later writer describing episodes from the prophet's life. The book of Jonah is one of the twelve shorter prophetic books of the Old Testament, and one of several books, like Job, that are poetic in structure. The writer of the book uses Jonah's experiences to confirm the Lord's universal love for His children of all nationalities and origins—even the population of the Assyrian capital city. Just as Jonah had to learn the magnanimous nature of the

Lord's charity and loving-kindness, so are we, as followers of Christ, enjoined to practice obedience, tolerance, and brotherly kindness in sharing the gospel with everyone.

The book of Jonah unfolds according to the following general pattern: Jonah's commission from the Lord and the consequences of his failure to obey (chapters 1–2); Jonah's mission to Nineveh (chapter 3); and Jonah's coming to terms with the mercy of the Lord (chapter 4). Highlights of Jonah's life include his call to preach repentance to the people of Nineveh, followed by his refusal and subsequent chastisement in being cast into the sea and being swallowed by a whale. He repents, is spared, and returns to Nineveh as the Lord has commanded him. During His earthly ministry, the Savior made specific mention of Jonah, using the episode with the whale as a symbol of the death and resurrection of the Messiah:

Jonathan and David

Then certain of the scribes and of the Pharisees answered, saying, Master, we would see a sign from thee.

But he answered and said unto them, An evil and adulterous generation seeketh after a sign; and there shall no sign be given to it, but the sign of the prophet Jonas [Jonah]:

For as Jonas was three days and three nights in the whale's belly; so shall the Son of man be three days and three nights in the heart of the earth.

The men of Nineveh shall rise in judgment with this generation, and shall condemn it: because they repented at the preaching of Jonas; and, behold, a greater than Jonas is here.

(Matthew 12:38–41; compare Luke 11:29–30)

JONATHAN

(Meaning: gift of Jehovah.)

1. Jonathan, the son of Gershom the Levite, served as a private priest in the household of Micah the Ephraimite, who had set up a molten image of his own (see Judges 18:30–31). When members of the tribe of Dan seized the image, they lured the priest away and took over the city of Laish, renaming it Dan. There they cultivated idol worship for generations, aided by Jonathan and his posterity (see Judges 17–18).

2. Jonathan, son of Saul, was known for his military prowess (see 1 Samuel 14:1–23). He and his father shared a reputation for speed and power: "They were [in the words of David] swifter than eagles, they were stronger than lions" (2 Samuel 1:23). Jonathan excelled especially in archery (see 2 Samuel 1:22). On one occasion where the forces of Jonathan had achieved a mighty triumph over the Philistines, Saul proclaimed a fast to ensure, as he said, "that I may be avenged on mine enemies" (1 Samuel 14:24). The penalty for failing to abide by the royal decree would be death; however, Jonathan, not knowing of the decree, partook of a little honey, much to the distress of those around him (see 1 Samuel 14:27–30). Learning of the action of his son, Saul confirmed the inevitability of the penalty. But the people defended Jonathan, saying unto the king, "Shall Jonathan die, who hath wrought this great salvation in Israel? . . . there shall not one hair of his head fall to the ground. . . . So the people rescued Jonathan, that he died not" (1 Samuel 14:45).

Jonathan is especially remembered for his enduring friendship with David, beginning with the miraculous slaying of Goliath, when "the soul of Jonathan was knit with the soul of David, and Jonathan loved him as his own soul" (1 Samuel 18:1), lasting until the end of Jonathan's life, when he fell by the sword along with his father, Saul, at the battle of Gilboa (see 1 Samuel 31:1–2). During his lifetime, Jonathan continually defended David before the murderous ambitions of Saul, the two young men having entered into a mutual covenant of security and devotion (see 1 Samuel 19:1–7; 20; 23:16–18). Upon the death of Jonathan, David prepared a moving eulogy (see 2 Samuel 1:17–27). David recovered the remains of Saul and Jonathan and buried them "in the country of Benjamin in Zelah, in the sepulchre of Kish his [Saul's] father" (2 Samuel 21:14; for the genealogy, compare 1 Samuel 9:1–3; 10:11, 21; 14:51).

3. Jonathan was a nephew of David who slew a mighty giant from Gath, home of Goliath (see 2 Samuel 21:21; 1 Chronicles 20:7).

4. Jonathan was the son of Abiathar (see 2 Samuel 15:27, 36; 17:17, 20), the priest whom Solomon suspended from the ministry for his support of the upstart son of David, Adonijah (1 Kings 1:7, 42; 2:26–27; compare 1 Samuel 2:31–35).

5. Jonathan was the name of various other individuals mentioned in the Old Testament (see 2 Samuel 23:32; 1 Chronicles 11:34; 27:25; Ezra 8:6; 10:15; Nehemiah 12:11, 14, 35; Jeremiah 37:15, 20; 40:8).

JORAM (SEE THE ENTRY FOR JEHORAM)

JOSEPH

(Meaning: increase.)

1. Joseph was the son of Jacob and Rachel (see Genesis 30:22–24) and holder of the birthright in Israel (see 1 Chronicles 5:1–2; the full panoramic story is given in Genesis 37–50). He married Asenath, who bore him two sons, Manasseh and Ephraim. His dealings with his errant brothers sent by Jacob to gather provisions in Egypt during the time of acute famine attest to Joseph's nature as one of compassion, mercy, and forgiveness—Christlike qualities in supreme measure (see Genesis 42–45). The fulfillment of the commission of the Abrahamic covenant to carry the gospel and the blessings of the priesthood to all nations of the earth (see Abraham 2:9–11) is accomplished largely through the lineage of Joseph.

On Joseph's rise to the stature of preeminence among his brethren, he encountered a

Joseph makes himself known to his brethren

107

great deal of opposition. Being favored of Jacob "because he was the son of his old age" (Genesis 37:3), Joseph became a target of malice on the part of his older brothers (see v. 4). Sharing freely his dreams—which predicted his future leadership over his brothers (see vv. 5–11)—Joseph managed to fuel his brothers' feelings of jealousy. Joseph's brothers considered killing him, but ultimately sold him into slavery instead, then led their father to believe Joseph had been killed by a wild animal (see vv. 18–35). The rent "coat of many colors" in this story becomes a lasting symbol of the ultimate preservation of the Lord's chosen lineage (see Alma 46:23–34).

Once in Egypt, Joseph became overseer of the house of Potiphar, captain of Pharaoh's guard. Refusing the advances of Potiphar's wife, Joseph was wrongly accused and imprisoned. Released after interpreting dreams for Pharaoh, Joseph eventually became a ruler over all Egypt. Joseph was reunited with his brothers and met his brother Benjamin once again (see Benjamin). His brothers begged his forgiveness and Joseph freely forgave them. Jacob and the rest of the family joined Joseph in Egypt (see Genesis 39–46).

In the contrast between the character of Joseph and the character of his brothers, we see played out in the starkest terms the preeminence of integrity over envy, honesty over jealousy, and (in the case of some of the brothers) virtue over moral laxity. Joseph built his life on a foundation of enduring principles and a commitment to follow the guidance of the Spirit. As such, his moral courage and leadership reflect the kind of strength, discipline, and stability that a great leader must always have. Let us consider two exemplary traits of Joseph: his purity and his spirit of forgiveness.

JOSEPH AS A PARAGON OF PURITY. Against the background of Joseph's removal to Egypt we can view one of his paramount qualities—that of virtue. Joseph's example of integrity and moral uprightness in Egypt is among the most celebrated instances of strength of character in all of holy writ.

Joseph's devoted effort and performance with his assigned duties brought favor with Potiphar; Joseph was a faithful servant, yet his allegiance was to the Lord (see Genesis 39:2–4). As the story unfolds, Joseph was accosted and tempted by Potiphar's wife. In response, Joseph said, "How then can I do this great wickedness, and sin against God?" (Genesis 39:9). Being of sterling character, Joseph took immediate action "and fled, and got him out" (Genesis 39:12).

JOSEPH AS A PARAGON OF FORGIVENESS. In addition to purity of character, Joseph reflects an extraordinary capacity to forgive. We recall the story of Joseph's brothers coming to Egypt for food during the acute famine and how Joseph interacts with them with magnanimity and forgiveness (see Genesis 42–45). It is evident that Joseph understands the necessity of his role in preserving Israel through dire circumstances:

> And Joseph said unto his brethren, Come near to me, I pray you. And they came near. And he said, I am Joseph your brother, whom ye sold into Egypt.
>
> Now therefore be not grieved, nor angry with yourselves, that ye sold me hither: for God did send me before you to preserve life. . . .

So now it was not you that sent me hither, but God: and he hath made me a father to Pharaoh, and lord of all his house, and a ruler throughout all the land of Egypt. (Genesis 45:4–5, 8)

Ultimately, all of Jacob's family members come to Egypt where Pharaoh, due to his great love and appreciation for Joseph, gives them and their posterity the land of Goshen (see Genesis 45–46).

The great principles of character exhibited by Joseph were his purity, his willingness to forgive, and his visionary understanding of the destiny of the House of Israel, including his own posterity. Joseph was ultimately buried by Moses and the Israelites in Canaan with his father and other ancestors (see Genesis 50:22–26; Exodus 13:19; Joshua 24:32).

Joseph was one of the great prophets of the House of Israel. That his branches did indeed "run over the wall" (Genesis 49:22) is confirmed by the record of Joseph contained in the Book of Mormon, dealing with the history of the Israelite immigrants to the New World. Joseph was the ancestor of Lehi through the lineage of Manasseh, Joseph's son (see Alma 10:3; 2 Nephi 3:4). Ishmael and his family, whom the Lord called to join with Lehi in the exodus to the promised land, descended from Ephraim, brother of Manasseh (see *JD* 23:184–185). With the coming forth of the Book of Mormon as an integral part of the Restoration of the gospel, the "stick of Joseph" foreseen by Ezekiel, the young contemporary of Lehi, was conjoined with the "stick of Judah" to confirm the eternal truths of the gospel of Jesus Christ to all the world (see Ezekiel 37:16–17; compare Isaiah 29).

The Book of Mormon provides an abundance of additional scriptural material concerning Joseph and his commission, including excerpts from his prophecies about a future seer of like name (Joseph Smith) who would bring forth the record of Joseph as a blessing for the world (see 2 Nephi 3:4–22; 4:2; compare JST, Genesis 50:24–38; also Alma 10:3; 46:23–27). The Doctrine and Covenants mentions Joseph as well. Key passages include a reference to the future event when Jesus Christ will participate in a glorious sacrament meeting with all of His holy prophets, including Joseph (see D&C 27:10), and in connection with a "rod" that should come forth "out of the stem of Jesse" (Isaiah 11:1; "stem of Jesse" refers to Jesus Christ—see D&C 113:1–2): "Behold, thus saith the Lord: It [the rod] is a servant in the hands of Christ, who is partly a descendant of Jesse as well as of Ephraim, or of the house of Joseph, on whom there is laid much power" (D&C 113:4; compare also verse 6 in connection with the "root" of Jesse). The terms *rod* and *root* very likely refer to the Prophet Joseph Smith.

2. Joseph was also the name of several other individuals mentioned in the Old Testament (see Numbers 13:7; 1 Chronicles 25:9; Ezra 10:42; Nehemiah 12:14).

JOSHUA

(Meaning: God is help.)

1. Joshua, son of Nun, was the one chosen to soldier with the leadership of the House of Israel following the days of Moses (see Numbers 27:18–23; Deuteronomy 1:38; 3:28). Of him it was said, "And Joshua the son of Nun was full of the spirit of wisdom; for Moses had laid his hands upon him: and the children

of Israel hearkened unto him, and did as the Lord commanded Moses" (Deuteronomy 34:9). The name *Joshua* has a number of variants in the Old Testament, including Jehoshua (see Numbers 13:16; 1 Chronicles 7:27), Hoshea (see Deuteronomy 32:44), and Jeshua (as in Ezra 2:2; 3:2, and many others). The name *Jesus* (from the Greek) is equivalent to the Hebrew name Joshua.

Traditionally, the authorship of the book of Joshua is assigned to Joshua himself, with the exception of the concluding section (see Joshua 24:29–33), which was added by another writer. The book of Joshua is the historical sequel to Deuteronomy, the last book of the Pentateuch (Genesis, Exodus, Leviticus, Numbers, and Deuteronomy—constituting the "Law" in terms of Jewish tradition). The book of Joshua stands as the first of the "Prophets" in this continuing tradition. The time span covered is from just after the passing (translation) of Moses until the death of Joshua (approximately 1427 BC).

The book of Joshua provides a chronicle of the fulfillment of the Lord's promise to lead Israel to the promised land and provide for them an inheritance, allocated by tribe. Thus ends the four-century-long exile in Egypt and the forty-year preparatory sojourn in the wilderness. The historical account is then overlaid with teachings and exhortations to the Israelites to honor their covenant vows and to choose to worship and follow the true and eternal God. Broadly speaking, the main sections comprise the history of the conquest of Canaan (chapters 1–12); the allotment of the land to the various tribes of Israel, with the appointment of the so-called cities of refuge and provision for the Levites (chapters 13–21); and the farewell address of Joshua, followed by the account of his death (chapters 22–24).

Joshua confronts Achan

Highlights from the book of Joshua include the drying of the waters of the River Jordan so that the ark of the covenant and the Israelites might pass over (chapters 3–4) and the bringing down of the walls of Jericho (see chapter 6).

Among Joshua's exhortations to Israel is the now-famous pronouncement, "Choose you this day whom ye will serve . . . but as for me and my house, we will serve the Lord" (Joshua 24:15).

2. Joshua was an individual of Beth-shemesh on whose property was located the stone marking the destination of the cart containing the ark of the Lord as it was returned by the Philistines (see 1 Samuel 6:10–18).

3. Joshua was a city governor (during the time of King Josiah) after whom a gate of the city was named (see 2 Kings 23:8).

4. Joshua, son of Josedech, was a high priest at the time of Zerubbabel, builder of the second temple (see Haggai 1:1, 14; 2:2, 4; rendered *Jeshua* throughout the books of Ezra and Nehemiah), likely the same as Joshua, the high priest mentioned in a vision granted to Haggai's contemporary, Zechariah, concerning the coming forth of the Messiah (referred to here as "the BRANCH"). This latter Joshua experienced a rite of purification, being clothed in clean garments and placed under a covenant of obedience while participating in an assemblage of associates—probably symbolic of the process of spiritual rejuvenation and recovery concerning the exiles returning from Babylonian captivity (see Zechariah 3:7–8).

JOSIAH

(Meaning Jehovah will heal or support.)

1. Josiah, son of and successor to Amon (see 2 Kings 21:24), was the great reform king of

Shaphan delivers the scrolls to King Josiah

Judah in the time frame 641–610 BC, concurrent with the early tenure of Jeremiah (see 2 Kings 22–24; 2 Chronicles 34–35): "Josiah was eight years old when he began to reign, and he reigned thirty and one years in Jerusalem. And his mother's name was Jedidah, the daughter of Adaiah of Boscath. And he did that which was right in the sight of the Lord" (2 Kings 22:1–2). Josiah commissioned Hilkiah, the high priest, to repair and purify the temple. While doing so, Hilkiah discovered, as he declared, "the book of the law in the house of the Lord" (2 Kings 22:8; compare 2 Chronicles 34:14–15). Upon reading the book, Josiah was struck with anxiety over the contrast between the wayward conduct of his people and the high standards engendered by the word of God. He therefore consulted the prophetess Huldah, who confirmed the word of the Lord concerning the judgments of God soon to fall upon the people for their iniquity. At the same time, the Lord recognized the humility and sorrow of the king and promised him he would die instead of witness the destruction that would come to his kingdom (see 2 Kings 22:19–20).

Stirred by this divine warning against the people, the king responded earnestly to the message of the book—also called "the book of the covenant" (2 Kings 23:2)—by having it read before all the people, then purging the nation of idolatry and directing everyone to turn to the Lord with a covenant to keep His commandments with full devotion (see vv. 1–25). In a subsequent military conflict with the Egyptians, Josiah was killed (v. 29; compare 2 Chronicles 35:20–25)—thus fulfilling the prophecy of Huldah that Josiah would depart this life prior to the time of the Lord's judgments upon the people (which was to come in the form of the impending Babylonian captivity).

2. Josiah was the son of Zephaniah (see Zechariah 6:10).

JOTHAM

(Meaning: God is upright or perfect.)

1. Jotham, the youngest son of the warrior/judge Gideon (or Jerubbaal), escaped the murderous rampage of Abimelech in the latter's ascent to the throne as king (see Judges 9). To assure his hegemony of power, Abimelech had gone to Shechem and slain all seventy of his brothers, save Jotham, who escaped and hid himself. From the top of mount Gerizim, Jotham courageously proclaimed a repudiation of Abimelech in the form of a parable about trees going "forth on a time to anoint a king over them" (Judges 9:8). Then Jotham revealed the key to the parable:

"Now therefore, if ye have done truly and sincerely, in that ye have made Abimelech king . . . then rejoice ye in Abimelech, and let him also rejoice in you: But if not, let fire come out from Abimelech, and devour the men of Shechem . . . and devour Abimelech" (Judges 9:16, 19–20). Three years from that time, Abimelech and many of the men of Shechem fell victim to internal conflicts among themselves and perished (see Judges 9:56–57).

2. Jotham is an individual mentioned among the descendants of the House of Israel (see 1 Chronicles 2:47).

3. Jotham, successor to Uzziah, was king of Judah in the time frame around 758–742 BC. His father, Uzziah (also referred to as Azariah), was the son and successor of Amaziah, king of Judah (see 2 Kings 14:21–22; 2 Chronicles 26:1–7). The fifty-two-year reign of Azariah (or Uzziah) commenced when he was but sixteen years old (see 2 Kings 15:1–2) and proceeded, for the most part, in righteousness (see 2 Kings 15:3–4). In his later years, because he suffered from leprosy, he arranged for his son Jotham to serve as administrator, a duty Jotham began when he was twenty-five years of age (see 2 Chronicles 26:21, 23; 27:1; also 2 Kings 15:5). Following the death of his father, Jotham became the reigning monarch, also serving for the most part in righteousness (2 Chronicles 27:2–4; compare also 2 Kings 15:34–35). Jotham prevailed over the Ammonites and reduced them to tributary status. The best epithet for summarizing his tenure is the following: "So Jotham became mighty, because he prepared his ways before the Lord his God" (2 Chronicles 27:6). Active during his tenure were the prophets Isaiah, Hosea, and Micah. Jotham was succeeded by Ahaz, his son (see 2 Kings 15:38; 2 Chronicles 27:9).

JUDA

Juda is the rendering of the name *Judah* in the New Testament (see Luke 3:33 for a reference to Juda, son of Jacob, in the genealogy of Jesus Christ; see Luke 3:27 for a reference to a later descendant also named Juda).

JUDAH

(Meaning: praise.) Judah, fourth son of Jacob and Leah (see Genesis 29:35; 37:26–27; 43:3, 8), was a principal figure in the perpetuity of the Abrahamic lineage as it extended down to Jesus Christ. Words from the final blessing of Jacob (Israel) upon the head of Judah bespeak the leadership role that this son was to fill: "Judah, thou art he whom thy brethren shall praise: thy hand shall be in the neck of thine enemies; thy father's children shall bow down before thee" (Genesis 49:8).

Judah was the one who stepped forward among the sons of Jacob to advance an alternative to slaying their brother Joseph, suggesting selling him instead (see Genesis 37:26–27). It was Judah who assumed the role of protector and guarantor of Benjamin when Jacob was persuaded to allow his youngest son to return to the Egyptian court where Joseph was in charge (see Genesis 43:8). When Joseph received the birthright by virtue of the moral laxity of Reuben, Judah nevertheless maintained a vital role: "For Judah prevailed above his brethren, and of him came the chief ruler; but the birthright was Joseph's" (1 Chronicles 5:2).

Judah had three sons by Shuah, a Canaanite woman: Er, Onan, and Shelah; Judah also had twin sons by Tamar (the widow of his son Er, conceived when she disguised herself as a harlot): Pharez and Zarah (see Genesis 38).

Moses pronounced the following blessing upon the posterity of Judah: "And this is the blessing of Judah: and he said, Hear, LORD, the voice of Judah, and bring him unto his people: let his hands be sufficient for him; and be thou an help to him from his enemies" (Deuteronomy 33:7). In keeping with this spirit, the tribe of Judah assumed a continual position of leadership in Canaan, just as Ephraim was to do over the generations.

From the word of the Lord to Joseph of Egypt included in the Book of Mormon we find confirmed the fact that the legacy of Judah is to serve as the wellspring of the Bible, just as the legacy of Joseph is contained in the Book of Mormon (see 2 Nephi 3:12–13; compare Ezekiel 37:15–19).

Judah is mentioned in the Doctrine and Covenants in the dedicatory prayer for the Kirtland Temple (see 109:63–64); in connection with the final gathering (see 133:12–13); and in relation to the eventual redemption of the house of Judah—"And they also of the tribe of Judah, after their pain, shall be sanctified in holiness before the Lord, to dwell in his presence day and night, forever and ever" (133:35). *See Jews.*

KENITES

(Meaning: smiths.) The Kenites were a tribe in Palestine friendly toward Moses and the Israelites during their journey through the wilderness, having accompanied them as far as Jericho (see Judges 1:16). The reference to the "Kenite" in this passage applies to Jethro, who is also called a Midianite (see Numbers 10:29) and a priest of Midian (see Exodus 2:16), implying that the Kenites were related to or a part of the Midianites. The friendly relations between the Kenites and the House of Israel continued (see Numbers 24:21–22; Judges 4:11, 17–21; 5:24; 1 Samuel 27:10; 30:29), Saul having spared this tribe from destruction during his campaign against the Amalekites (see 1 Samuel 15:6).

KETURAH

(Meaning: incense.) Keturah (pronounced kih-too'-ruh or kih-tyoor'-uh) became the wife of Abraham following the passing of Sarah: "Then again Abraham took a wife, and her name was Keturah" (Genesis 25:1; compare 1 Chronicles 1:32–33). The posterity of Abraham and Keturah included various tribes, among them the Midianites (after their son Midian—see Genesis 25:4; 1 Chronicles 1:33).

KOHATH

(Meaning: assembly.) Kohath was the second of the three sons of Levi, son of Jacob (see Genesis 46:11). Kohath had four sons, the first of whom was Amram (see Exodus 6:18), who married his father's sister Jochebed, and was the father of Moses and Aaron (see Exodus 6:20). The Kohathite line of Levitical priests performed important duties associated with the Tabernacle (see Numbers 3:27; 4:18, 34, 37; 10:21; 1 Chronicles 15:5; see also 1 Chronicles 6:61, 70).

KORAH

1. Korah was a son of Esau, son of Isaac (see Genesis 36:5, 14, 18; 1 Chronicles 1:35).

2. Korah, son of Eliphaz, was a grandson of Esau (see Genesis 36:16).

3. Korah was a son of Hebron, as indicated in

The death of Korah

a listing of the Israelite descendants (see 1 Chronicles 2:43).

4. Korah was the son of Izhar, who in turn was the son of Kohath, son of Levi (see Exodus 6:21, 24; 1 Chronicles 6:22). Because Korah and two other dissenting leaders combined forces with 250 of the princes of Israel to defy Moses and Aaron in seeking more priestly power (see Numbers 16:3), they were censured by Moses and subsequently swallowed up in the earth (see Numbers 16:7, 28, 31–23; 26:9–11; 27:3; see also Jude 1:11, where the name is spelled *Core*). The later descendants of Korah (Korahites or Korathites) were part of a guild of performing musicians (see the headings to Psalms 42, 44–49, 84–85, 87–88), while others of this particular Levite lineage were appointed to serve as porters, gatekeepers, bakers, and the like (1 Chronicles 9:17–19, 31).

KORASH

An ancient god worshipped by the idolatrous people in Ur of the Chaldees at the time of Abraham (see Abraham 1:13).

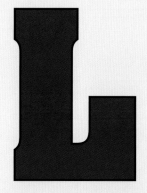

LABAN

(Meaning: white.) Laban was the son of Bethuel, who was the youngest son of Nahor, brother of Abraham (see Genesis 22:22–23). Both Bethuel and Laban concurred with the proposal of Abraham's servant that Rebekah (Laban's sister) should become the wife of Isaac (see 24:50–51; compare 25:20). Years later, Isaac sent his son Jacob to Laban to seek a wife (28:1–5), resulting (after some subterfuge on the part of Laban) in Jacob's marrying not only Leah (Laban's older daughter), but also her sister Rachel, whom Jacob had initially chosen (see 29:18–20, 25–26; see also 31:36–38, 41; 43–55).

LAMECH

1. Lamech is the fifth in descent from Cain, son of Adam, as follows: Cain, Enoch, Enoch, Irad, Mehujael, and Lamech (see Genesis 4:17–18). The sons of Lamech were Jabal, Jubal, and Tubal-cain (see Genesis 4:20–22; compare Moses 5:43–48). The account in the Pearl of Great Price extends our knowledge about Lamech:

For Lamech having entered into a covenant with Satan, after the manner of Cain, wherein he became Master Mahan, master of that great secret which was administered unto Cain by Satan. . . .

Wherefore Lamech, being angry, slew [Irad], not like unto Cain, his brother Abel, for the sake of getting gain, but he slew him for the oath's sake.

For, from the days of Cain, there was a secret combination, and their works were in the dark, and they knew every man his brother.

Wherefore the Lord cursed Lamech, and his house, and all them that had covenanted with Satan; . . . and their works were abominations, and began to spread among all the sons of men. . . .

Wherefore Lamech was despised, and cast out, and

116

came not among the sons of men, lest he should die. . . . (Moses 5:49–52, 54)

2. Lamech was the seventh in descent from Seth, son of Adam, as follows: Seth, Enos, Cainan, Mahalaleel, Jared, Enoch, Methuselah, Lamech (see Genesis 5:6–25). Lamech was the father of Noah (see Genesis 5:25–31; 1 Chronicles 1:3; compare Luke 3:36; Moses 8:5–11). Lamech is mentioned once in the Doctrine and Covenants in connection with the lineage of the priesthood: "Lamech was thirty-two years old when he was ordained under the hand of Seth" (107:51).

LEAH

(Meaning: weary.) Leah was the oldest daughter of Laban, son of Bethuel, the latter being the youngest son of Nahor, brother of Abraham (see Genesis 22:22–23). When Rebekah and Isaac sent their son Jacob to Laban (Rebekah's brother), Jacob was well received and labored seven years for the hand of Laban's daughter Rachel (see Genesis 28:1–5; 29:13–20). At this time, Rachel's older sister Leah was also an eligible bride, being however "tender eyed" compared to Rachel, who was "beautiful and well favoured" (Genesis 29:17). After Jacob had served his seven years for the hand of Rachel, Laban adjusted the unfolding of events on the marriage day by sending a veiled Leah that evening to be Jacob's wife. The next morning the truth was discovered by Jacob: "And it came to pass, that in the morning, behold, it *was* Leah: and he said to Laban, What *is* this thou hast done unto me? did not I serve with thee for Rachel? wherefore then hast thou beguiled me? And Laban said, It must not be

so done in our country, to give the younger before the firstborn" (Genesis 29:25–26). Jacob, having agreed to serve Laban yet another seven years, was soon thereafter favored with the bride of his choice—Rachel. In all, Jacob served Laban for a total of twenty years before returning to Canaan (see Genesis 31:38, 41).

Leah bore unto Jacob six sons: Reuben, Simeon, Levi, Judah (see Genesis 29:32–35), and later Issachar and Zebulun (see Genesis 30:17–20; compare Genesis 35:23). Leah also bore unto Jacob a daughter by the name of Dinah (see Genesis 30:21). All of these children were born before Rachel was able to conceive and give birth to her first child Joseph (see Genesis 30:22–24). Upon her passing, Leah was buried in the cave of Machpelah, the resting place of Abraham, Sarah, Isaac, and Rebekah (see Genesis 49:31).

LEVI

(Meaning: joined or adhered to.) Levi was the third son of Jacob by Leah (see Genesis 29:34; 35:23). The motivation for naming him thus was explained as follows: "And she conceived again, and bare a son; and said, Now this time will my husband be joined unto me, because I have born him three sons: therefore was his name called Levi" (Genesis 29:34). Leah was ever hopeful that her husband's affection would turn to her rather than her sister Rachel, who had been unable to bear children.

Later in their careers, Levi and Simeon were responsible for the callous campaign of vengeance against the Hivite community when Shechem, the son of Hamor the Hivite, fell in love with Dinah (Levi's sister) and defiled her. Executing the ultimate response to this misdeed, Simeon and Levi fell upon the

Hivite community, killed all of the males, "and took Dinah out of Shechem's house, and went out" (Genesis 34:26). They then despoiled the city and took all the survivors captive. When Jacob learned of their actions, he was greatly distressed and gathered his people together and moved away to Beth-el at the command of God (see Genesis 34:30; 35:1–5). Levi's and Simeon's cruelty is called to mind once again in the final blessing that Jacob gave to them (see Genesis 49:5–7).

The blessing pronounced by Moses on the tribe of Levi (of which he and Aaron were members) included the promise of priestly assignments: "They shall teach Jacob thy judgments, and Israel thy law: they shall put incense before thee, and whole burnt sacrifice upon thine altar. Bless, LORD, his substance, and accept the work of his hands" (Deuteronomy 33:10–11). These words reflect the perpetual assignment given to the sons of Levi to provide service in support of the work of the priesthood on behalf of the House of Israel under the direction of Aaron and his sons (see Numbers 3, 4, 8). It was the Levites who rose up in support of Moses at the time the people had called on Aaron to make them a golden calf (see Exodus 32:26). In particular, the descendants of Levi as a tribe were given the work of assisting the priests in the sanctuary of the Lord (see Numbers 3:5–10; 18:1–7). The Levites performed a variety of functions, including providing musical offerings (see 1 Chronicles 6:16–31; 15:16; Nehemiah 11:22); preparing the sacrificial animals (see 2 Chronicles 29:34; 35:9–11; Ezra 6:20); and assisting with temple duties, having as it were "the oversight of the outward business of the house of God" (Nehemiah 11:16). The Levites did not receive a regional inheritance in the promised land, but were assigned cities and given resources in support of their service (see Numbers 18:21–24; 35:6; Deuteronomy 12:17–19; 14:27, 29).

Levi is mentioned in the Doctrine and Covenants in the expression "sons of Levi" used by John the Baptist in connection with the restoration of the Aaronic Priesthood in the latter days (see D&C 13:1; compare also D&C 124:39; 128:24).

LIBNAH

Ancient god worshipped by the idolatrous people at the time of Abraham in Ur of the Chaldees (see Abraham 1:13).

LO-AMMI

(Meaning: not my people.) Lo-ammi (pronounced loh-am'-y) was the name given by the prophet Hosea to his second son to reflect, symbolically, the rejection of Israel at that time by the Lord because of its wickedness (see Hosea 1:9).

LO-RUHAMAH

(Meaning: uncompassioned.) Lo-ruhamah (pronounced loh'-roo-hay'-muh) was the name given by the prophet Hosea to his daughter to signify the Lord's withholding mercy from Israel (the northern kingdom) on account of its wickedness (see Hosea 1:6–7). However, in the last days, the mercy of the Lord will again be shown Israel (see Hosea 2:23).

LOT

(Meaning: a covering.) Lot, son of Haran and nephew of Abraham, joined with the family entourage leaving Ur of the Chaldees for their

Lot flees Sodom

journey to the land of Canaan (see Genesis 11: 27, 31; 12:4–5; 13:1, 5; Abraham 2:4–5, 14–15). The estate of Abraham and the estate of Lot were so abundant that a separation of the two family groups was necessitated in order to find terrain of sufficient size for both. When Abraham granted Lot a choice of where he would reside, Lot favored the verdant plains, so "Abram dwelled in the land of Canaan, and Lot dwelled in the cities of the plain, and pitched his tent toward Sodom" (Genesis 13:12).

Later, Chedorlaomer, king of Elam, in league with three princes of Babylon, defeated the kings of Sodom, Gomorrah, and several other cities in that area of the land who had revolted from their agreement to be subservient to Chedorlaomer (see Genesis 14:1–10). In the battle among these kings, the victors "took all the goods of Sodom and Gomorrah, and all their victuals, and went their way. And they took Lot, Abram's broth-er's son, who dwelt in Sodom, and his goods, and departed" (Genesis 14:11–12). Learning of this abduction, Abraham went out with 318 of his own men and routed the forces of Chedorlaomer, rescuing Lot and his family (see 14:16).

But Lot and his family were not altogether liberated from danger, for they dwelt by choice in a wicked city. Thus messengers were sent to warn Lot to remove his family from the midst of evil, lest they should be present when the impending destruction from heaven should take place (see Genesis 19). When Lot seemed to resist, the messengers took forceful action, bringing Lot and his family out of the city (see v. 16). One of the messengers urged them to escape to the mountain and not look back, but Lot persuaded the messenger that he could go to the small city of Zoar instead (see vv. 17–22). As the sun rose, the family entered Zoar, and "the LORD rained upon Sodom and upon Gomorrah brimstone and fire from the LORD out of heaven" (v. 24; see also v. 23). Unfortunately, Lot's wife did look back at Sodom and Gomorrah, "and she became a pillar of salt" (v. 26). Lot left Zoar and dwelt on the mountain, where he fathered two sons, Moab and Ammon, who became the ancestors of the Moabites and Ammonites (see Genesis 19; Deuteronomy 2:9, 19).

We can look back on the experience of Lot and avoid following his example when he "pitched his tent toward Sodom" (Genesis 13:12). We can also avoid the experience of Lot's wife by being obedient to the counsels of the messengers of God. We are counseled well to focus our view on eternal things rather than on the enticements of the world.

LOT'S WIFE (SEE LOT)

119

LUCIFER

(Meaning: the shining one, light bringer, son of the morning.) Lucifer is Satan, the "father of all lies" (2 Nephi 2:18; Ether 8:25; Moses 4:4). The name *Lucifer* is used only once in the Bible, concerning his rebellion in the premortal existence:

> How art thou fallen from heaven, O Lucifer, son of the morning! how art thou cut down to the ground, which didst weaken the nations!

For thou hast said in thine heart, I will ascend into heaven, I will exalt my throne above the stars of God: I will sit also upon the mount of the congregation, in the sides of the north:

I will ascend above the heights of the clouds; I will be like the most High.

Yet thou shalt be brought down to hell, to the sides of the pit. (Isaiah 14:12–15; compare Luke 10:18)

See Satan.

Lucifer is rebuked after tempting Jesus

MAGOG

(Meaning: covering.) Magog was one of the sons of Japheth, son of Noah (see Genesis 10:2; 1 Chronicles 1:5). The term *Magog* is also used in reference to a nation (see Ezekiel 38:2; 39:6), specifically in the context of the battle of Gog and Magog that will represent the triumph of the forces of heaven over the forces of evil in the final days—initiated at the time of the Second Coming and finalized in the closing battle against Satan and his forces at the end of the millennial period (see Ezekiel 38:16; 39:6–7; compare Revelation 20:8).

MAHALALEEL

1. Mahalaleel (pronounced muh-hay'-luh-lee'-uhl) was the son of Cainan and great-great-grandson of Adam and Eve (see Genesis 5:4–17; 1 Chronicles 1:2; Moses 6:10–20). He is also mentioned twice in the Doctrine and Covenants (see D&C 107:46, 53). The name is rendered *Maleleel* in Luke 3:37.

2. Mahalaleel was one of those who dwelt in Jerusalem following the return from Babylonian exile (see Nehemiah 11:4).

MAHMACKRAH

Mahmackrah was an ancient god worshipped by the idolatrous people in Ur of the Chaldees at the time of Abraham (see Abraham 1:13).

MALACHI

(Meaning: my messenger.) Malachi was the last of the Old Testament prophets. The book of Malachi was written around 430 B.C. Its central purpose was to call the people and their priests to repentance for gross shortcomings and remind them to prepare for the Second Coming and the judgments of the Lord.

Malachi taught the people of his day—and ours—that we should honor God (see Malachi 1:5), bring a "pure offering" before Him in righteousness (1:11; 3:3), give glory to Him (2:2), walk with God "in peace and equity" (2:6), remain faithfully within the covenant bounds in marriage (see 2:11), care for the poor and needy (see 3:5), return to God (see 3:7), pay tithes and offerings (see 3:8–10; compare D&C 64:23–25; 59:20–21), fear God and always keep Him in one's thoughts (see 3:16), avoid pride (see 4:1), and (under the influence of the sealing power of the priesthood) cultivate a godly and eternal disposition of oneness among families (see 4:5–6).

Malachi is remembered especially for his reference to tithes and offerings: "Bring ye all the tithes into the storehouse, that there may be meat in mine house, and prove me now herewith, saith the LORD of hosts, if I will not open you the windows of heaven, and pour you out a blessing, that there shall not be room enough to receive it" (3:10).

He also prophesied with great power regarding Elijah and the last days: "Behold, I will send you Elijah the prophet before the coming of the great and dreadful day of the LORD: And he shall turn the heart of the fathers to the children, and the heart of the children to their fathers, lest I come and smite the earth with a curse" (Malachi 4:5–6).

Six years after the publication of the Book of Mormon in this dispensation, the Savior appeared to Joseph Smith and Oliver Cowdery in the Kirtland Temple on April 3, 1836, accompanied by other heavenly beings, including Elijah, in fulfillment of the prophecy of Malachi (see D&C 110:13–16; compare D&C 128:17).

Malachi was the grand prophet of transition: transition from the Old Testament to the New Testament, and from these sacred volumes to the Book of Mormon and the Doctrine and Covenants. Malachi is often cited in subsequent prophetic discourse and scripture. The Lord made reference to the passage in Malachi 3:1 ("Behold, I will send my messenger") in speaking of John the Baptist:

"For this is he, of whom it is written, Behold, I send my messenger before thy face, which shall prepare thy way before thee" (Matthew 11:10; see also Mark 1:2). So important were the words of Malachi, including truths about the law of tithing and the sealing commission of Elijah, that the resurrected Savior quoted them to the ancient American Saints during His visit (see 3 Nephi 24 and 25, which include Malachi 3 and 4) and commanded that these words be written down. The Savior then declared: "These scriptures, which ye had not with you, the Father commanded that I should give unto you; for it was wisdom in him that they should be given unto future generations" (3 Nephi 26:2).

Malachi is included among the elect whom President Joseph F. Smith beheld during his vision of the work of salvation going on in the spirit world: "And Malachi, the prophet who testified of the coming of Elijah—of whom also Moroni spake to the Prophet Joseph Smith, declaring that he should come before the ushering in of the great and dreadful day of the Lord—[was] also there" (D&C 138:46).

MAMRE

Mamre (pronounced mam'-ree) was an Amorite ally of Abram (Abraham) in Canaan. When Chedorlaomer, king of Elam, in league with three princes of Babylon, defeated the kings of Sodom, Gomorrah, and several other cities in that area of the land, the victors seized much spoil and also carried away Lot, Abram's brother's son (see Genesis 14:1–12). It was Mamre who apprised Abram of the circumstances, allowing him to organize a campaign to rout the forces of Chedorlaomer and liberate Lot (see Genesis 14:13, 16). (Compare

Mamre as a place name: see Genesis 23:17–19; 25:9; 50:13.)

MANASSEH

(Meaning: forgetting.)

1. Manasseh (pronounced muh-na'-suh or muh-nas'-uh) was the firstborn son of Joseph of Egypt and Asenath (see Genesis 41:50). In his ailing years, Jacob (Israel) was visited by Joseph, with his sons Manasseh and Ephraim, who received blessings from the patriarch:

> And when Joseph saw that his father laid his right hand upon the head of Ephraim, it displeased him: and he held up his father's hand, to remove it from Ephraim's head unto Manasseh's head.
>
> And Joseph said unto his father, Not so, my father: for this is the firstborn; put thy right hand upon his head.
>
> And his father refused, and said, I know it, my son, I know it: he also shall become a people, and he also shall be great: but truly his younger brother shall be greater than he, and his seed shall become a multitude of nations.
>
> And he blessed them that day, saying, In thee shall Israel bless, saying, God make thee as Ephraim and as Manasseh: and he set Ephraim before Manasseh. (Genesis 48:17–20)

Thus Ephraim, the younger son, was placed in the primary position regarding the blessing of his posterity. Ephraim and Manasseh are both mentioned in the blessing of Moses upon the descendants of Joseph many years later (see Deuteronomy 33:17), as well as in Joshua's explanation of inheritances in the promised land (see Joshua 17:17–18).

Gideon, the warrior/judge, was of the tribe of Manasseh (see Judges 6:15). Lehi of the Book of Mormon was also a descendant of Manasseh (see Alma 10:3).

2. Manasseh was the son of King Hezekiah and successor to the throne of Judah (see 2 Kings 20:21; 2 Chronicles 32:33). From the start, Manasseh's reign was marked by evil practice (see 2 Kings 21:1–4; compare 2 Kings 23:12, 26; 24:3; 2 Chronicles 33:1–10; Jeremiah 15:4). In judgment against Judah, the Lord sent upon them the Assyrian hosts. Manasseh was taken captive to Babylon and subjected to odious treatment, causing him to reform his ways (see 2 Chronicles 33:12–13). As a result, Manasseh took steps to cleanse the land of idolatry and repair the altar of the Lord for genuine sacrifices (see vv. 14–21). Upon his passing, he was succeeded by his son Amon, who reigned but a brief time in wickedness before his own son, Josiah, the great reformer, came to power (see vv. 21–25; 34:1–2).

3. Manasseh was the name of two individuals mentioned as having taken non-Israelite wives at the time of the return from the Babylonian captivity (see Ezra 10:30, 33).

MEDAD (SEE ELDAD AND MEDAD)

MEDES

The Medes were an ancient people from the country of Media, which Cyrus integrated into the Persian kingdom around 550 BC.

Thereafter we often find references to the *Medes and Persians* (see Daniel 5:28; 6:8, 12, 15). It was in the province of the Medes that Darius found and renewed the decree of Cyrus (537 BC) authorizing the return of the Jewish people to Jerusalem following the Babylonian conquest (see Ezra 6:1–12; compare Isaiah 13:17, 2 Nephi 23:16–17).

MELCHIZEDEK

(Meaning: king of righteousness.) Melchizedek, king of Salem (Jerusalem), was the great high priest and prophet who lived at the time of Abraham, around 2,000 years before Christ.

The story of Melchizedek is the story of peace, for it represents the transformation of a wayward society through the redemptive power of spiritual principles of faith, repentance, and

Melchizedek ordaining Abraham

committed righteousness. When Melchizedek assumed the office of prophet/leader, Salem (later called Jerusalem) was under a veil of spiritual darkness and rebellion, "yea, they had all gone astray" (Alma 13:17). But Melchizedek was well prepared for his mission: "Now Melchizedek was a man of faith, who wrought righteousness; and when a child he feared God, and stopped the mouths of lions, and quenched the violence of fire. And thus, having been approved of God, he was ordained an high priest after the order of the covenant which God made with Enoch" (JST Genesis 14:26). What Melchizedek accomplished was nothing short of a miracle, for his influence on the people had the astounding effect of bringing them all back into the fold (see Alma 13:18–19).

Melchizedek was placed in charge of the abundance of the Lord's kingdom as "the keeper of the storehouse of God; Him whom God had appointed to receive tithes for the poor" (JST Genesis 14:37–38; compare Genesis 14:18–20). Of the meeting where Abraham paid tithes to Melchizedek, the Apostle Paul said, "Now consider how great this man was, unto whom even the patriarch Abraham gave the tenth of the spoils" (Hebrews 7:4). The Prophet Joseph Smith confirmed: "The King of Shiloam (Salem) had power and authority over that of Abraham, holding the key and the power of endless life" (*TPJS*, 322).

The Apostle Paul describes the meeting of Abram and Melchizedek and also expounds on Melchizedek's priesthood (see Hebrews 7:1–4), but this account could easily be misinterpreted. Thus, the Joseph Smith Translation records for Hebrews 7:3 the following: "For this Melchizedek was ordained a priest after the order of the Son of God, which order was without father, without mother, without descent, having neither beginning of days, nor end of life. And all those who are ordained unto this priesthood are made like unto the Son of God, abiding a priest continually" (compare Hebrews 7:3).

Knowing that "Melchizedek was ordained a priest after the order of the Son of God" (JST Hebrews 7:3), it may seem confusing that the New Testament describes Jesus Christ as "called of God an high priest after the order of Melchisedec" (Hebrews 5:10; see also Hebrews 6:20; Psalm 110:4). Melchizedek was honored to have the priesthood called after his own name (D&C 107:2–4).

What made Melchizedek so great? Why was he so honored to have the Lord's priesthood named after him? The answer is that he "exercised mighty faith" (Alma 13:18), magnified his holy office in the priesthood, preached repentance, and was unmatched in his righteousness. Melchizedek's success in bringing his people to repentance is reflected in the outcomes of his labors. His people became a holy people like unto the people of Enoch, for that is what Melchizedek sought: "And his people wrought righteousness, and obtained heaven, . . . And this Melchizedek, having thus established righteousness, was called the king of heaven by his people, or, in other words, the King of peace" (JST Genesis 14:34, 36).

MEPHIBOSHETH

1. Mephibosheth (pronounced muh-fib'-oh-sheth') was one of two sons of Saul whom David turned over to the Gibeonites in "atonement" (2 Samuel 21:3) for Saul's having slain the Gibeonites in violation of Israel's oath of peace (see vv. 3, 8–9). The Gibeonites then hanged the two, along with five others from Saul's family circle, in settlement of their grievance.

2. Mephibosheth, son of Jonathan, lost his father and grandfather (Saul) when he was but five years old. During the political turmoil of the day, "his nurse took him up, and fled: and it came to pass, as she made haste to flee, that he fell, and became lame" (2 Samuel 4:4). David, in later seeking to locate those remaining of the house of Saul and show them benevolence, located Mephibosheth with the help of Ziba, one of Saul's servants, and treated both Mephibosheth and the somewhat contentious Ziba with kindness and understanding (see 2 Samuel 9:7, 12–13; 16:1–4; 2 Samuel 19:29)—largely as a result of David's covenant of loyalty and friendship with Jonathan (see 2 Samuel 21:7).

MERODACH

(Meaning: death or slaughter.) Merodach (pronounced mer'-oh-dak) was the name of a Babylonian god whose destruction was prophesied by Jeremiah (see Jeremiah 50:2).

MERODACH-BALADAN

Merodach-baladan (pronounced mer'-oh-dak-bal'-uh-dan) was a king of Babylon who sent a delegation to King Hezekiah of Judah to express best wishes upon his recovery from an illness. Having shown his visitors his entire inventory of wealth, Hezekiah then heard from Isaiah a prophecy concerning the eventual captivity of the people at the hands of the Babylonians (see Isaiah 39:6–8; compare 2 Kings 20:12, where the name is rendered *Berodach-baladan*)—something that was fulfilled around 587 BC.

MESHA

(Meaning: freedom or deliverance.)

1. Mesha was the king of Moab defeated by the alliance of Jehoram of Israel and Jehoshaphat of Judah, as predicted by the word of the Lord through Elisha the prophet (see 2 Kings 3).

2. Mesha was an individual mentioned in the listing of Israelite descendants (see 1 Chronicles 2:42).

3. Mesha was an individual listed in the lineage of Benjamin (see 1 Chronicles 8:9).

MESHACH

Meshach (pronounced mee'-shak) was a Jewish youth captured along with Daniel and several others (including Azariah—later called Abed-nego—and Hananiah—later called Shadrach) by the forces of the Babylonian king Nebuchadnezzar and taken to Babylon to the palace of the king on the eve of the conquest of Jerusalem around 587 BC (see Daniel 1:6–7). His real name was Mishael, but he was given the name Meshach by the prince of the eunuchs (see v. 7). *See Shadrach for more details (see also vv. 13–30).*

MESSIAH

(Meaning: the Anointed One.) Messiah is the Aramaic name that is equivalent to Christ (from the Greek). The name *Messiah* occurs only twice in the King James Version of the Old Testament (see Daniel 9:25, 26), but is used frequently in the Book of Mormon (see, for example, 1 Nephi 1:19; 10:4, 5, 7; 15:13; 2 Nephi 1:10; 2:6, 8, 26; 26:3; Jarom 1:11; and Helaman 8:13). *See Jesus Christ.*

METHUSELAH

(Meaning: man of the dart or javelin.) Methuselah, son of Enoch, was the longest surviving of the ancient patriarchs (see Genesis 5:21–27; 1 Chronicles 1:3; Moses 6:25; 8:2–7; and Luke 3:37—where the name is rendered *Mathusala*). He died at the age of 969 (see Genesis 5:27). Methuselah "was ordained under the hand of Adam" (D&C 107:50) and was present in the assembly of elect individuals gathered together by Adam to receive his benedictory blessing (see D&C 107:53).

MICAH

(Meaning: who is like Jehovah?)

1. Micah (pronounced my'-kuh) was an Ephraimite after the days of Samson who, having set up a molten image within his own household, hired Jonathan, the son of Gershom the Levite, to serve as a private priest (see Judges 17–18; see also Jonathan 1).

2. Micah was the son of Mephibosheth, the son of Jonathan (Saul's son). *See Mephibosheth.*

3. Micah was a descendant of Joel the Reubenite (see 1 Chronicles 5:5).

4. Micah the Moresthite was a prophet of Judah who prophesied during the reign of King Hezekiah (see Micah 1:1). Hezekiah ascended the throne around 728 BC and reigned for twenty-nine years. Thus Micah was a contemporary of Isaiah, whose ministry extended from around 740 BC to 701 BC. Micah echoes the recurrent theme of all the prophets: that the Lord will bring judgment upon evildoers while showing mercy and forgiveness to those who repent and follow His statutes and remember His covenants. Goodness and truth—as evidenced in the coming forth of the Messiah to be

Micah

born at Bethlehem—will eventually triumph over degeneracy and rebellion. The Lord's kingdom of glory and salvation will rise in the latter days as a compelling beacon to all peoples.

The Book of Micah comprises three major divisions: prophecies of judgment and destruction because of idolatry and sinfulness (chapters 1–3), prophecies concerning the Restoration and the Messianic mission (chapters 4–5), and prophetic statements concerning the goodness of the Lord and His expectations of the covenant people (chapters 6–7).

MICHAEL

(Meaning: who is like God?)

1. Michael was the father of Sethur, one of the twelve spies sent by Moses to scout out the land of Canaan (see Numbers 13:13).

2. Michael was an individual of the lineage of Gad (son of Jacob and Zilpah—see Genesis 30:10–12; 35:26) who is mentioned as being among those who settled in the land of Bashan (see 1 Chronicles 5:13).

3. Michael was another individual of the lineage of Gad who was an ancestor of the tribal leader Abihail (see 1 Chronicles 5:14).

4. Michael was a member of the Levite tribe during the time of David (see 1 Chronicles 6:40).

5. Michael is listed as an individual from the tribe of Issachar during the time of David (see 1 Chronicles 7:3).

6. Michael is listed as an individual from the tribe of Benjamin during the time of David (see 1 Chronicles 8:16).

7. Michael was one of David's "mighty men of valour, and were captains in the host" (1 Chronicles 12:21; see also v. 20).

8. Michael (of the tribe of Issachar) was the father or perhaps ancestor of Omni, one of the officers in David's court (see 1 Chronicles 27:18).

9. Michael was one of the sons of King Jehoshaphat of Judah executed by Jehoram, firstborn son and successor to the throne (see 2 Chronicles 21:1–4).

10. Michael, listed as the son or perhaps ancestor of Zebadiah, was among those returning to Jerusalem from the Babylonian captivity (see Ezra 8:8).

11. Michael, the prince and archangel, is another name for Adam, the first man. The name *Michael* is generally used to refer to him in a premortal or post-mortal capacity. John the Revelator confirmed regarding the role played by Michael in the premortal existence: "And there was war in heaven: Michael and his angels fought against the dragon; and the

dragon fought and his angels, And prevailed not; neither was their place found any more in heaven" (Revelation 12:7–8). In the last days, he will defend and deliver Israel: "And at that time shall Michael stand up, the great prince which standeth for the children of thy people: and there shall be a time of trouble, such as never was since there was a nation even to that same time: and at that time thy people shall be delivered, every one that shall be found written in the book" (Daniel 12:1; compare also Daniel 10:13, 21). *See Adam.*

MICHAL

Michal (pronounced like "Michael") was the younger of Saul's two daughters, the first-born being Merab (see 1 Samuel 14:4–9). Michal loved David and was given to him by the king to be his wife (see 18:20, 27–28). Committed to the elimination of David, Saul took steps to fulfill his evil purpose, but was thwarted on one occasion by his daughter's cleverness:

> Saul also sent messengers unto David's house, to watch him, and to slay him in the morning: and Michal David's wife told him, saying, If thou save not thy life to night, to morrow thou shalt be slain.
>
> So Michal let David down through a window: and he went, and fled, and escaped.
>
> And Michal took an image, and laid it in the bed, and put a pillow of goats' hair for his bolster, and covered it with a cloth.
>
> And when Saul sent messengers to take David, she

said, He is sick. (1 Samuel 19:11–14)

When the messengers ultimately took possession of the bed-ridden "David," they learned that they had seized a mannequin, much to the disappointment of Saul (see 1 Samuel 19:15–17).

Subsequently, Saul gave Michal to another man (see 1 Samuel 25:44); however, David later reclaimed her from her second husband (2 Samuel 3:13–16). Unfortunately, on the occasion of the return of the Ark of the Covenant to Jerusalem, Michal was offended by David's celebratory display (see 2 Samuel 6:14–16; see also 1 Chronicles 15:29). Upon David's return, she reproached him, but he justified his behavior rather than apologizing. Readers are left to guess at the implication of the verse that follows this argument: "Therefore Michal . . . had no offspring unto the day of her death" (v. 23; compare 2 Samuel 21:8, where Michal should likely have been rendered *Merab*).

MIDIAN

(Meaning: judgment.) Midian was one of the six sons of Abraham and Keturah (see Genesis 25:1–2; compare 1 Chronicles 1:32). *See Midianites.*

MIDIANITES

The Midianites were a dominant nomadic people associated with the lineage of Midian (son of Abraham and Keturah) living principally in the northern region of the Arabian Peninsula and emerging from time to time in the chronicles of Israelite history: Joseph being sold to a caravan of Midianites by his jealous brethren (see Genesis 37:28); Moses fleeing from Egypt and living among the Midianites where he married Zipporah, daughter of Reuel (or Jethro), the prince of Midian (see Exodus 2:11–21; 3:1; 4:19); the Midianites providing guidance to Moses and the Israelites during their wanderings in the wilderness (see Numbers 10:31); divine judgment against the Midianite kings during the days of Balak and Balaam (see, for example, Numbers 22:4–7, 12, 22; 25; 31:1–2; compare Joshua 13:21–22); and the defeat of the Midianite oppressors by Gideon, the warrior/judge (see Judges 6–8; Psalm 83:9; Isaiah 9:4; 10:26).

MILCOM

(Meaning: their king.) Milcom was a heathen god whose worship king Solomon facilitated among his people (see 1 Kings 11:5). Because of this wickedness, the Lord sent word through the prophet Ahijah that Jeroboam would displace Solomon and his followers—something that happened in due time (see 1 Kings 11:33; 12:20; 14:6–16). Generations later, Josiah the great reform king eradicated the worship of false gods such as Milcom (see 2 Kings 23:13)—also identified with such terms as *Molech* (see Leviticus 18:21; 20:2–5), *Moloch* (see Amos 5:26), and *Malcham* (see Zephaniah 1:5).

MIRIAM

(Meaning: exalted.)

1. Miriam the prophetess, daughter of Amram and his wife Jochebed, was the sister of Moses and Aaron (see Numbers 26:59; 1 Chronicles 6:3). It was Miriam who, observing the daughter of Pharaoh as she discovered her younger brother hidden in the bulrushes, arranged for

Miriam watches over Moses

"a nurse of the Hebrew women" (her own mother Jochebed) to come into service to care for Moses (Exodus 2:7). It was later Miriam, by now a leader among her people, who raised an anthem of praise to the Lord following the deliverance of Israel through the Red Sea: "And Miriam the prophetess, the sister of Aaron, took a timbrel in her hand; and all the women went out after her with timbrels and with dances. And Miriam answered them, Sing ye to the Lord, for he hath triumphed gloriously; the horse and his rider hath he thrown into the sea" (15:20–21). On one occasion during the wandering in the wilderness, Miriam and Aaron murmured against Moses for having taken to wife an Ethiopian woman: "And they said, Hath the Lord indeed spoken only by Moses? hath he not spoken also by us? And the Lord heard it" (Numbers 12:2). As a result, the Lord confirmed to them both the preeminence of Moses the prophet. For her

129

lapse, Miriam was rendered leprous, causing an anguished Aaron to appeal to Moses to intercede with the Lord on her behalf—which he did, resulting in her return after seven days of recovery (see Numbers 12:10–16; compare Deuteronomy 24:9). Miriam passed away at Kadesh and was buried there (see Numbers 20:1).

Though her life was marked by an occasion of murmuring, Miriam nevertheless remained stalwart and noble in the history of the covenant people—and thus remembered of the Lord alongside her brothers as being a blessing to His people: "And I sent before thee Moses, Aaron, and Miriam" (Micah 6:4).

2. Miriam was an individual listed among the descendants of Judah (see 1 Chronicles 4:17).

MISHAEL (SEE MESHACH)

MIZRAIM

Mizraim (pronounced miz-ray'-im or miz'-ray-im) was one of the sons of Ham, son of Noah (see Genesis 10:6; 1 Chronicles 1:8). The descendants of Mizraim (the Hebrew word for "Egypt") included the Hamitic peoples of Egypt and Canaan, the latter being the source of the Philistines (see Genesis 10:13–14; 1 Chronicles 1:11–12).

MOAB/MOABITES

Moab was the son of Lot by his oldest daughter, the child being conceived by an incestuous union unbeknownst to the sedated and sleeping Lot (see Genesis 19:37). The Moabites were a people who frequently warred with the Israelites.

The most often-cited episode concerning conflict with the Moabites is the campaign of Balak, king of the Moabites, to bring down a curse upon the Israelites, perceived as a distinct threat to the Moabites and their confederate associates, the Midianites. When the hosts of Israel were encamped on the plains of Moab east of the Jordan River near Jericho, Balak took action to retain the services of Balaam—who apparently had the reputation of divine influence—for the purpose of cursing Israel (see Numbers 22:6). Balaam agreed to approach the Lord on their behalf—but the message from the Lord was consistently in favor of blessing, rather than cursing, Israel (see Numbers 22:12, 22, 27–35; 23:19–24; *see Balaam*).

As the Israelites had intimate contact with the Moabites, they began to assimilate their pagan practices and immoral ways. Thus the Lord commanded Moses to strike out against the indigenous peoples and eliminate the evil influence of the Moabites and Midianites (see Numbers 31:8; also Joshua 24:9–10; Nehemiah 13:2; 2 Peter 2:15; Jude 1:11; Revelation 2:14).

Over time, the Moabites and Israelites repeatedly confronted one another, but eventually, the Moabites came under the yoke of Assyria and Chaldea according to the judgments of the Lord (see Zephaniah 2:8–11; compare 2 Kings 24:2; Ezekiel 25).

MOLECH

Molech was a fire god worshipped by the Ammonites, who made their children pass through or be consumed by a ceremonial fire (see 2 Kings 23:10; Deuteronomy 18:10; 2 Chronicles 28:3). From time to time the Israelites lapsed into this form of idolatry, always with devastating consequences (see 1 Kings 11:5, 7; 2 Kings 16:3; 17:17; Jeremiah 7:31).

MORDECAI

(Meaning, variously, little man, warrior, follower of Marduk, the Babylonian war god, or servant of God.) Mordecai (pronounced mor'-duh-ky, mor'-dee-ky, or mor-dee-kay'-uh), a Jewish official of Benjamite extraction at the court of King Ahasuerus of Persia (most likely Xerxes), was the foster father of his young orphan cousin, Esther, who became the queen of the realm in place of the deposed Vashti (see Esther 1–2). Mordecai, a man of high principles, was despised by Haman, the king's chief officer, who concocted an insidious plan to exterminate him, together with all the Jews (see chapter 3). In response, Mordecai called for a period of national mourning and fasting by the Jewish people—inspiring Esther to come courageously before the king and have the decree reversed (see chapters 4–5). Haman was executed and the Jewish people were spared. Mordecai was raised in honor to a position next only to Ahasuerus (see 10:3) and became, along with Esther, the cause for national celebration (see Esther 8:15–16). These events provided the historical context for the establishment of the annual Feast of Purim among the Jewish people (see chapter 9). Thus Mordecai, whose name, according to some etymological sources implies "little man," was a giant of deliverance for his people.

MOSES

(Meaning of the name is disputed, with alternatives such as drawn or pulled out [of the water], son, has provided, and others.) Moses

Moses presents the brass serpent to the Israelites

was the prophet of God who prefigured Christ's redeeming mission by liberating the Israelites from Egyptian bondage, sustaining them in their journeys, serving as the agent for the revelation of the Ten Commandments, establishing the presence of the Tabernacle among the people, and providing leadership to guide them to the gateway of the promised land. Though he was "very meek, above all the men which were upon the face of the earth" (Numbers 12:3), his service is marked throughout by divine station and transcending power.

1. THE MISSION OF LIBERATION. The story of Moses is legendary. He was rescued from the bulrushes by a princess, nursed clandestinely by his Hebrew mother, grew up as a child in the court of the pharaoh, cultivated a passion for protecting his people—as evidenced by his action in killing the Egyptian who was smiting

a Hebrew—and then had to flee Egypt fearing for his life. He went north in the desert of the Arabian Peninsula to the land of Midian, where he helped the daughters of Reuel (Jethro) and was given Zipporah to be his wife. She then bore him a son named Gershom (see Exodus 2).

Meanwhile, the Israelites in Egypt were praying for deliverance from their crushing burdens of slavery. The Lord heard their prayers and visited Moses on Mount Horeb, appearing in the midst of a burning bush (see chapter 3). The Lord told Moses that he would be sent as the deliverer of Israel (see vv. 10–12, 16–17).

Moses—along with his brother Aaron—did as the Lord commanded and sought freedom for their people from the pharaoh, but Pharoah refused, instead increasing the daily quota of required bricks, including the gathering of their own straw. Moses and his people were disheartened, but the Lord said to Moses, "Wherefore say unto the children of Israel, I am the Lord, and I will bring you out from under the burdens of the Egyptians, and I will rid you out of their bondage, and I will redeem you with a stretched out arm, and with great judgments" (Exodus 6:6–7).

When the Israelites would not hearken to Moses, the Lord unfolded a design to show the Egyptians as well as the Israelites that He was God over all the earth and had power to do all things. As time proceeded, signs and plagues were sent upon the Egyptians, showing the might and power of the God of Israel (see chapters 7–10). With each curse the pharaoh promised to let the people go if Moses would stop the plague, only to relinquish his word when relief came.

Finally the Lord told Moses that the firstborn child in every Egyptian home was to die.

To protect their own households, the Israelites were to slay a lamb without blemish and administer the blood to the lintel and side posts of their entry doors (see 12:3–14, 22–24). In the Egyptians' homes the firstborn child was taken by the destroying angel of the Lord. That was the crucial intervening act that caught the pharaoh's attention in earnest, "for there was not a house where there was not one dead" (v. 30)—and among the dead was the pharaoh's own son (see v. 29). Finally the pharaoh told Moses and Aaron to take the children of Israel and leave (see vv. 30–38)—thus the Lord led the Israelites to freedom.

Still desirous to retain the slavery of the Israelites, the pharaoh followed after them with his hosts. Moses, endowed with the power of the Lord, parted the Red Sea, allowing the Israelites to walk across on dry ground. The Egyptians followed, only to be swallowed by the resurging waters (see Exodus 14:5–30). Finally, the Israelites were free. In gratitude, Moses led the Israelites in a chorus of praise to the God of deliverance (see chapter 15).

Just as the Lord liberated the captive Israelites from Egyptian bondage, He has also put in place the saving truths, ordinances, and powers that can bless our lives with redeeming grace through the Atonement of Jesus Christ. "Let my people go" was the watchword for the Exodus (5:1). Similarly, the gospel of Jesus Christ provides the means and power to "let people go" from the bondage of sin and pass through the waters of baptism toward a new life following in the footsteps of the Lord.

2. SUSTENANCE FOR THE JOURNEY. The experiences of the liberated Israelites in the wilderness became a time of preparation. Trials and

tests of their faith in God marked their journey. There was no water to be found for three days. When they found water, it was bitter to the taste, and the people began to murmur. Moses "cried unto the Lord; and the Lord shewed him a tree, which when he had cast into the waters, the waters were made sweet . . ." (Exodus 15:25). But the Lord also took this opportunity to teach his people, "and said, If thou wilt diligently hearken to the voice of the Lord thy God, and wilt do that which is right in his sight, and wilt give ear to his commandments, and keep all his statutes, I will put none of these diseases upon thee, which I have brought upon the Egyptians: for I am the Lord that healeth thee" (v. 26). This defined the covenant with the Lord—obedience results in great heavenly blessings.

The Israelites continued to travel in the wilderness, struggling for food and at times becoming angry with Moses and Aaron. Moses told them, "and what are we? Your murmurings are not against us, but against the Lord" (Exodus 16:8). Again the Lord blessed them with food—manna from heaven (and later quail as well—see chapter 16). Manna is explained in the Bible Dictionary as follows: "The children of Israel called it manna (or man-hu in Hebrew)—which meant 'What is it?'—because they did not know what it was (Exodus 16:15). It was also called 'angels' food' and 'bread from heaven' (Ps. 78:24–25; John 6:31). It was a symbol for Christ, who would be the Bread of Life (John 6:31–35)."

When again the people became angry with Moses for lack of water, he "cried unto the Lord, saying, what shall I do unto this people? They be almost ready to stone me" (Exodus 17:4). The Lord instructed His prophet to "smite the rock" at Horeb to bring forth water (see 17:5–6). Again Moses had gone to the Lord with the needs of his people, and again the Lord responded to his pleadings and met their needs.

3. REVELATION OF THE LORD'S COMMANDMENTS. The Ten Commandments were given through Moses to guide Israel into the proper pathways for honoring that covenant (see Exodus 20). The tablets on which were inscribed the Ten Commandments were not, however, the first tablets prepared for Moses (see Exodus 31:18, 32–34. In *Answers to Gospel Questions*, President Joseph Fielding Smith explains how the two sets of stone tables Moses brought down from Mount Sinai relate to the law of Moses and the priesthood:

> When Israel came out of Egypt it was the intention of the Lord to make of Israel a royal priesthood. That is to say, that he was to give them the Melchizedek Priesthood and the principles of exaltation. When Moses went up into the mount and was gone forty days, Israel sinned a very serious sin and turned back to the worship of the Egyptians and had Aaron make for them a golden calf. When Moses came down from the mountain, in his anger, he threw down the tables and broke them. Then at the command of the Lord he went back into the mountain, and the Lord gave him other tables on which he wrote with his finger [see Exodus 20; Deuteronomy 5].
>
> The Lord did not write the same things on the second

Moses and the commandments on stone tablets

tables that were on the first, but confined Israel to the Aaronic Priesthood and denied the Melchizedek Priesthood to the tribes of Israel except in special cases with certain prophets like Isaiah, Jeremiah and others. These prophets had the Melchizedek Priesthood by special appointment. The Lord gave to Israel the carnal law and said that they should not enter into his rest while they were in the wilderness.

The Ten Commandments were in existence long before Moses' time, and the Lord only renewed them in the days of Moses, just as he has done in our day. (D. & C. 84:19–27.)

(Joseph Fielding Smith, *AGQ* 3:154–155)

In living the Ten Commandments we fulfill the two great commandments spoken of by our Savior when He was queried, "Master, which is the great commandment in the law? Jesus said unto him, Thou shalt love the Lord thy God with all thy heart, and with all thy soul, and with all thy mind. This is the first and great commandment. And the second is like unto it, Thou shalt love thy neighbour as thyself. On these two commandments hang all the law and the prophets" (Matthew 22:36–40).

4. ESTABLISHMENT OF THE TABERNACLE. Since the beginning of time the Lord has desired to come to His people in His House that He might bless them. The Lord commanded Moses, "And let them make me a sanctuary; that I may dwell among them" (Exodus 25:8).

The children of Israel obeyed the Lord and sacrificed their precious things for the building of the Tabernacle (see 36:21–29). Moses truly was joyful over the building of the Tabernacle, blessing it and those who helped in its construction. Then the power, glory, and blessings of the Lord were manifested and continued with the Israelites as they traveled (see 40:34–38; compare the similar divine counsel and promises given through the modern-day prophet, Joseph Smith, as recorded in D&C 124:38–44).

5. HOMEWARD GUIDANCE. Moses was the paragon of the spiritual guide, the exemplar of how to succor others in their mortal journey toward the promised land. The Lord's people must be tried. It is in trials and tribulations that we are humbled and turn to the Lord so that He can nurture and succor us in all of our afflictions (see Alma 7:11–12). The wilderness

sojourn for the Israelites after the Exodus from Egypt was indeed a difficult experience. They struggled. They murmured. The Lord sent them manna. They grew tired of manna and wanted meat. The Lord sent them quail. They were still anxious and desirous for better conditions. Finally they came to the land of Canaan. Moses sent a spy delegation consisting of a leader from each of the twelve tribes. Except for the words of Caleb and Joshua, the report came back: Canaan was indeed a land of milk and honey, but the inhabitants were too strong for the Israelites to defeat. Once more the seeds of doubt were sown and the people, lacking in faith, again became angry with Moses. In Numbers 14:26–27, 30–31, we read about the Lord's reaction to their anger and the consequence they reaped therefrom.

The Lord had made the Israelites "wander in the wilderness forty years, until all the generation, that had done evil in the sight of the LORD, was consumed" (Numbers 32:13). But the youth—those who had been children at the start of the journey—He would spare and guide into the promised land (see 14:29). Traditions have power—for good or bad—and the Israelites suffered because of their wicked traditions. Hence a new generation born of righteousness was required to qualify for entrance into the promised land.

Upon the completion of his years in the wilderness, Moses did not die in the literal sense (as implied in Deuteronomy 34:5–7) but was translated, enabling him to complete his mission of conveying essential priesthood keys on the Mount of Transfiguration in the meridian of time (see Matthew 17:3; compare Alma 45:19) and then as a resurrected being during the Restoration in the latter days (see D&C 110:11; 133:54–55).

Modern scripture sheds additional light on the mission and person of Moses. It was Moses who appeared to Joseph Smith and Oliver Cowdery in the Kirtland Temple on April 3, 1836, to restore the keys of "the gathering of Israel from the four parts of the earth, and the leading of the ten tribes from the land of the north" (D&C 110:11). Moses is mentioned many times throughout the Doctrine and Covenants. Some of the key passages depict Moses as an exemplar of one who receives and acts on the spirit of revelation (see D&C 8:3); as the prototype for the ministry of Joseph Smith—that is, the only one appointed to receive commandments and revelations for God's people in a given dispensation (see D&C 28:2); as a key figure in the lineage of the priesthood (see D&C 84:6); as one given the mission to sanctify his people "that they might behold the face of God" (D&C 84:23); as the forebear of those "sons of Moses" who shall serve with devotion in the temples of God and fulfill the commission of the Abrahamic covenant (D&C 84:31–34); as the prototype of the president of the high priesthood, who is to "preside over the whole church, and to be like unto Moses" (D&C 107:91); as the one who built the Tabernacle of the Lord as an ancient model of the temple (see D&C 124:38); as one of the "great and mighty ones" assembled in the "vast congregation of the righteous" perceived in vision by Joseph F. Smith (D&C 138:38)—plus many passages concerning the law of Moses.

Moses' remarkable qualities and accomplishments are also celebrated throughout the pages of the Book of Mormon, including references to the dividing of the Red Sea (see 1 Nephi 4:2); his authoring the five initial books of the Bible (see 1 Nephi 5:11); his smiting the rock to obtain water for the Israelites (see 1

Nephi 17:29); the deliverance of Israel from Egypt (see 2 Nephi 3:10); his radiant countenance while on the mount (see Mosiah 13:5); his prophecies of the coming of the Messiah (see Mosiah 13:33); his references to the Son of God (see Alma 33:19); his lifting of the brazen serpent as a type of the Savior (see Helaman 8:14); and many others. Of major significance as a theme in the Book of Mormon is the fulfillment of the law of Moses through the ministry and Atonement of the Savior. The Bible Dictionary describes the law of Moses as "the whole collection of written laws given through Moses to the House of Israel, as a replacement of the high law that they had failed to obey." The resurrected Lord declared to the Saints in Bountiful that the law of Moses was now fulfilled (see 3 Nephi 15:4–8).

From the very beginning of the Book of Mormon, the transcendence of the Atonement as the key to salvation and exaltation is emphasized; the law of Moses is respected as a preparatory protocol pointing to the Savior and His redeeming mission (see 2 Nephi 2:5–8).

It is from chapter one of Moses in the Pearl of Great Price that we have the priceless verity about the purpose of God: "For behold, this is my work and my glory—to bring to pass the immortality and eternal life of man" (v. 39).

MULEK

Mulek (not mentioned specifically in the Bible) was the only surviving son of King Zedekiah, last king of Judah at the time of the Babylonian conquest of Jerusalem around 587 BC (see 2 Chronicles 36:11). Jeremiah reported that the sons of Zedekiah were slain by the king of Babylon (see Jeremiah 52:10–11; 2 Kings 25:7), but the Book of Mormon account makes it clear that Mulek survived and was led by the Lord to ancient America, where he founded a nation later integrated with the Nephites (see Helaman 6:10; 8:21; Omni 1:12–16).

N

NAAMAN

(Meaning: pleasantness.)

1. Naaman (pronounced nay'-uh-muhn), son of Bela, was an individual of the family of Benjamin who journeyed to Egypt with the entourage of Jacob (see Genesis 46:21; Numbers 26:40; 1 Chronicles 8:4, 7).

2. Naaman was a nobleman in the royal court of Syria who had leprosy (see 2 Kings 5:1). Naaman's wife had a maid who had been captured from among the Israelites by the Syrians. This young girl was concerned about Naaman's disease and said to her mistress, "Would God my lord were with the prophet that is in Samaria! for he would recover him of his leprosy" (v. 3). When the prophet Elisha heard that the Syrian king (Ben-hadad II) had sent a letter of request to the king of Israel (Joram) on behalf of Naaman, Elisha, knowing of the hesitancy of the king of Israel concerning the matter, declared: "Let him come now to me, and he shall know that there is a prophet in Israel" (v. 8). So Naaman and his company came before the house of Elisha, seeking a blessing. "And Elisha sent a messenger unto him, saying, Go and wash in Jordan seven times, and thy flesh shall come again to thee, and thou shalt be clean" (v. 10), but Naaman was upset that Elisha hadn't come himself, nor had the prescribed cure seemed spectacular enough to him (see vv. 11–12).

Naaman is cured of leprosy

Fortunately one of his servants persuaded him to follow Elisha's counsel and he was healed (see vv. 13–14).

Returning whole to the house of Elisha, Naaman declared: "Behold, now I know that there is no God in all the earth, but in Israel: now therefore, I pray thee, take a blessing of thy servant" (v. 15). Elisha refused compensation for his services, but Gehazi, servant of Elisha, followed after Naaman and accepted for himself gifts of silver and raiment; upon learning this, Elisha pronounced a severe judgment upon Gehazi, who then himself became a leper (see v. 27).

The story of Naaman and his recovery was recalled by Jesus on one occasion while speaking in a synagogue at Nazareth: "And many lepers were in Israel in the time of Eliseus [Elisha] the prophet; and none of them was cleansed, saving Naaman the Syrian" (Luke 4:27). The implication was that Naaman, a Syrian, had more faith and a higher degree of obedience than was to be found among the Israelites.

NABAL

(Meaning: foolish or villainous.) Nabal, husband of Abigail, was an affluent estate holder in Carmel who refused to assist David and his army fleeing the murderous campaigns of King Saul (see 1 Samuel 25:10–11). When David was about to launch a vengeful attack against Nabal and his family, Abigail, on her own initiative, came before David with courage and pled for forgiveness and compassion, thus softening his heart and deflecting his action (see vv. 27–33). Following the death of Nabal, David sent for Abigail and took her as his wife (see 1 Samuel 25:37–38, 42).

NABOTH

(Meaning: fruits.) Naboth (pronounced nay'-bahth) was a Jezreelite who owned a vineyard near the palace of Ahab, king of Israel. Desiring to possess this land, Ahab offered to buy the land or exchange it for a better piece of land (see 1 Kings 21:2), but Naboth refused on the basis that an inheritance from his fathers could not be sold. At that point, Jezebel, Ahab's wife, caused the people to stone Naboth to death based on fraudulent incriminations (see vv. 10–13). Soon thereafter, the prophet Elijah, confronting Ahab in the vineyard of Naboth, pronounced the ultimate judgment of God upon the idolatrous house of Ahab (see vv. 19, 27–29)—something carried out in due time by the hand of Jehu, the rising new king of Israel (see 2 Kings 9:11–26, 30–37; 10:11).

NADAB

(Meaning: liberal.)

1. Nadab (pronounced nay'-dab) was the eldest son of Aaron and Elisheba (see Exodus 6:23; compare Numbers 3:2; 26:60; 1 Chronicles 6:3; 24:1). Nadab was among the group of leaders privileged to view the Lord on Sinai (see Exodus 24:1–2, 9–11).

Nadab and his three brothers were consecrated to the office of priest (see Exodus 28:1). However, despite the glorious blessings accorded them from the Lord, Nadab and Abihu profaned their office and brought the judgment of the Lord upon their heads (see Leviticus 10:1–2; compare Numbers 3:4; 26:61; 1 Chronicles 24:2).

2. Nadab was an individual mentioned in the lineage of Judah (see 1 Chronicles 2:28, 30).

3. Nadab was an individual listed among the leaders of the tribe of Benjamin (see 1 Chronicles 8:30; compare 1 Chronicles 9:36).

4. Nadab was the son and successor of Jeroboam, king of Israel (see 1 Kings 14:20). In all, Nadab reigned two years: "And he did evil in the sight of the Lord, and walked in the way of his father, and in his sin wherewith he made Israel to sin" (1 Kings 15:26). While Nadab was sustaining a siege against the Philistine stronghold at Gibbethon, Baasha took his life and assumed the throne (see 1 Kings 15:27–28).

NAHOR

1. Nahor (pronounced nay'-hor) was the father of Terah, who was the father of Abram, later named Abraham (see Genesis 11:24 and 1 Chronicles 1:26; see also Luke 3:34, where the name is rendered *Nachor*).

2. Nahor was the son of Terah (see Genesis 11:26; 22:20, 23; 24:15, 24; 29:5; 31:53; Abraham 2:2). Nahor married Milcah (the daughter of his brother Haran, future father of Lot—see Genesis 11:29), who bore him a son named Bethuel, future father of Rebekah, the wife of Isaac (see Genesis 24) and aunt of Leah and Rachel (future wives of Jacob—see Genesis 31).

NAHUM

(Meaning: consoler.) Nahum (pronounced nay'-hum) was a prophet of the Lord. Scholarly opinion varies concerning the date of composition of the book of Nahum; some judge that it was written during the latter part of the eighth century BC (during the reign of Hezekiah), and others conclude that it was written in the mid to late seventh century BC. The book reveals the Lord's design in bringing mercy to the righteous and judgment to the wicked and then details the fate of Nineveh as an archetype of the degenerate kingdom of pride and idolatry (see passages such as Nahum 1:7, 15; compare similar imagery in Isaiah 52:7 and Mosiah 15:13–18).

NAOMI

(Meaning: pleasant.) Naomi (pronounced nay-oh'-mee or nah'-oh-mee) was the wife of Elimelech, the mother of two sons (Mahlon and Chilion), and the mother-in-law of Ruth. After Naomi's family moved from Bethlehem-Judah to Moab to seek relief during a severe famine, her husband passed away. Her two sons each married a Moabite woman and then, tragically, also passed away. When Naomi decided to return alone to Bethlehem, one of

Naomi and her daughter-in-law Ruth

her two daughters-in-law, Ruth, was desirous of remaining with her (see Ruth 1). Naomi gladly consented, and when they returned to Bethlehem, Ruth went forth to glean in the fields of their kinsman, Boaz. Naomi then played an active role in encouraging a union between Boaz and Ruth (see chapters 2–3). Boaz and Ruth were married and soon favored with a son, thus providing a direct link to the future descendant of David, Jesus Christ (see Ruth 4:17).

NAPHTALI

(Meaning: wrestlings.) Naphtali (pronounced naf'-tuh-ly) was the fifth son of Jacob (Israel) by Bilhah, Rachel's handmaid (see Genesis 30:8; 35:25; 46:24; Exodus 1:4). For a segment from the blessing later pronounced upon Naphtali and his posterity by Jacob, see Genesis 49:21 (compare Moses' blessing upon this tribe given in Deuteronomy 33:23, also Joshua 19:32–39). One celebrated member of the tribe was Barak, who responded to the commission of Deborah, judge of Israel, to wage the triumphant battle against the encroaching Canaanites under command of Sisera (see Judges 4–5).

NATHAN

(Meaning: he has given.)

1. Nathan was a son of David and Bathsheba (see 2 Samuel 5:14; 1 Chronicles 3:5; 14:4; Zechariah 12:12; Luke 3:31).

2. Nathan was a prophet of the Lord during the time of David. Through Nathan, the Lord declared to David that the commission to build a temple unto God would devolve upon his son (see 2 Samuel 7:12–13; compare 1 Chronicles 17:11–12). Through Nathan as

well, the Lord reproved David for his serious lapse of moral rectitude in regard to Bathsheba and Uriah. The inspired words of Nathan in this case—including a parable (a rarity in the Old Testament)—constitute one of the most powerful calls to repentance in all of holy writ (see 2 Samuel 12:1–10). The parable describes a rich man with many flocks and a poor man with only one lamb, a pet much beloved; the rich man wishes to prepare a meal and kills the pet rather than taking from his own flock. When David hears the story he is outraged, saying, "The man that hath done this thing shall surely die: And he shall restore the lamb fourfold" (vv. 5–6). But Nathan responded:

Thou art the man. . . . I anointed thee king over Israel, and I delivered thee out of the hand of Saul;

And I gave thee thy master's house, and thy master's wives into thy bosom . . .

Wherefore hast thou despised the commandment of the LORD, to do evil in his sight? thou hast killed Uriah the Hittite with the sword, and hast taken his wife to be thy wife, and hast slain him with the sword of the children of Ammon. (2 Samuel 12:7–9)

Nathan continued to be of service to David after this episode, including assisting him to organize the protocols of public worship (see 2 Chronicles 29:25). Later, Nathan was instrumental in facilitating the enthronement of Solomon, the legitimate successor to the throne of Israel (see 1 Kings 1; see also *Bathsheba*).

Nathan apparently also wrote a book concerning the reign of David (see 1 Chronicles 29:29) as well as the reign of Solomon (see 2 Chronicles 9:29), though we do not have these writings today. Nathan is mentioned once in the Doctrine and Covenants concerning David and the doctrine of plural marriage (see D&C 132:39).

3. Nathan was an individual listed in connection with David's guard (see 2 Samuel 23:36; 1 Chronicles 11:38).

4. Nathan was an individual listed as the father of two of the officers (Azariah and Zabud) associated with Solomon's court (1 Kings 4:5; compare 1 Chronicles 2:36).

5. Nathan was an individual mentioned among those who returned to Jerusalem from the Babylonian captivity (see Ezra 8:16), possibly the same as the Nathan listed among those of this group who married non-Israelite wives (see Ezra 10:39).

NAZARITE

(Meaning: one separated unto the Lord, a consecrated man.) A male or female under the vow of a Nazarite would abstain from strong drink, avoid cutting his or her hair from the head, and avoid any contact with persons deceased (see Numbers 6). The Nazarite vow could be for life, as in the case of Samson (see Judges 13:5, 7; 16:17) or Samuel (see 1 Samuel 1:11)—or for only a shorter, defined period of time (see also Amos 2:11–12; compare Luke 1:15 concerning John the Baptist). The record does not indicate that Nazarite vows are associated with physical strength, as in the case of Samson; however, vows of spiritual

Daniel interprets Nebuchadnezzar's dream

commitment surely lead to enhanced spiritual strength and vitality.

NEBO

Nebo was a Babylonian god of wisdom decried in the words of Isaiah as powerless by contrast with the true God (see Isaiah 46:1–2, 5, 8–9).

NEBUCHADNEZZAR

(Meaning: Nebo, protect the crown (or landmark).) Nebuchadnezzar, king of Babylon in the period 604–561 BC, besieged Jerusalem and took away many captive to his country, including Zedekiah, king of Judah, and most of his subjects (see 2 Kings 24–25; Daniel 1–5; 1 Chronicles 6:15; 2 Chronicles 36:6–7, 10–13, Jeremiah 27–28; 29:1, 3; 34:1; 39:5). And Nebuchadnezzar burned down all the great houses of the city, including the palace and the Lord's house, the temple (see 2 Kings 25:9–11).

In the second year of Nebuchadnezzar's reign, he dreamed of a stone hewn from the mountain without hands that destroyed a mighty image in human form. The king's wisemen were powerless to discover the secret of the dream, but Daniel was able to unfold its mystery through the blessings of the Spirit. When the answer came to Daniel "in a night vision" (Daniel 2:19), he immediately blessed the name of God and gave humble thanks and praise for the divine gift (see Daniel 2:23). Daniel was able to save all condemned wisemen in the kingdom by advising Nebuchadnezzar correctly concerning the dream. The stone "cut out of the mountain without hands" (v. 45) is the kingdom of God, which is to supersede all earthly kingdoms and fill the world with a heavenly dominion of truth and light under the supreme rulership of the Redeemer and Lord of Lords.

But the king refused nevertheless to relinquish his idolatry, and dreamed a second dream depicting the king as a great and mighty tree that was hewn down at the behest of "an holy one coming down from heaven" (Daniel 4:23). Daniel interpreted this dream as foretelling the king's loss of power and position, and counseled the king to refrain from sin and show "mercy to the poor" (v. 27). But "at the end of twelve months" (v. 29), as Nebuchadnezzar was extolling his own greatness, a voice came from heaven reaffirming Daniel's interpretation (see vv. 30–32), and "the same hour was the thing fulfilled" (v. 33). Stripped of his opulence, the deposed king later blessed and praised God (see vv. 34–37).

NECHO

Necho was an Egyptian king at the time of Josiah, king of Judah. Having proclaimed war against Assyria, Necho sought passage through the kingdom of Judah but was confronted by Josiah and his warriors in the valley of Megiddo. (See 2 Kings 23:29–30; 2 Chronicles 35:20–25; see also 2 Chronicles 36:1–4 and Jeremiah 46:2, where he is designated *Pharaoh-necho*.)

NEHEMIAH

(Meaning: comfort of the Lord.)

1. Nehemiah, apparently of the tribe of Judah, was an officer in the court of Artaxerxes of Persia—his "cupbearer," in fact (Nehemiah 1:11). Responding to the dire reports from his Jewish colleagues visiting him, Nehemiah obtained from the king a commission to rebuild the walls and structures of Jerusalem—

a task he performed in subsequent years with honor as the governor of Judah (see Nehemiah 5:14, 18; 12:26). The chronicle of his tenure is contained in the book of Nehemiah, a sequel to the book of Ezra historically (the two are regarded as one in the Jewish canon). The book of Ezra covers the return of a second wave of Jewish people from the Babylonian captivity for resettlement in Jerusalem. The book of Nehemiah then covers the associated project of rebuilding the walls of Jerusalem. The time span of the book of Nehemiah is either contemporaneous with the later ministry of Ezra or shortly thereafter, beginning perhaps around 444 BC. The book closes the historical account of the Old Testament, as the prophet Malachi—author of the last book—was a contemporary with Nehemiah.

The book of Nehemiah comprises three main sections: a record of the rebuilding of the wall of Jerusalem, including an account of the register Nehemiah discovered of those who had returned from Babylon (chapters 1–7); a record of the manner of religious practice being conducted among the Jewish people of this period, including the remarkable and precedent-setting public reading of the law of God by the priest Ezra (chapters 8–10); and reforms and civic practices among the people, including the dedication of the wall of Jerusalem (chapters 11–13).

2. Nehemiah was an individual listed among those who accompanied Zerubbabel with the first influx of people returning from the Babylonian captivity (see Ezra 2:2; Nehemiah 7:7).

3. Nehemiah, son of Azbuk, was an individual who assisted with the work of repairing the walls of Jerusalem under the leadership of

Nehemiah views the ruined walls of Jerusalem

the governor—also named Nehemiah (see Nehemiah 3:16).

NERGAL-SHAREZER

(Meaning: Nergal protect the king.) Nergal-sharezer (pronounced nuhr'-gal-shar-ee'-zuhr) was one of the princes accompanying Nebuchadnezzar in the siege of Jerusalem around 587 BC (see Jeremiah 39:3, 13).

NIMROD

Nimrod was the son of Cush, (who was the son of Ham). Nimrod was "a mighty hunter before the LORD" (Genesis 10:9; see also 1 Chronicles 1:10).

In one passage, Assyria is referred to as "the land of Nimrod" (Micah 5:6). During the period of the Tower of Babel, as presented in the Book of Mormon, the Lord initially directed the brother of Jared and his group to take their provisions and travel to a valley northward, where they would receive further instructions: "and the name of the valley was Nimrod, being called after the mighty hunter" (Ether 2:1).

NISROCH

Nisroch (pronounced nis'-rock or nis'-roke) was a god worshipped by the Assyrians. It was in the temple of Nisroch in Nineveh that Sennacherib, king of Assyria, was slain by his sons following the defeat of his forces through an act of God during the reign of Hezekiah, king of Judah (see 2 Kings 19:37; Isaiah 37:38).

NOAH

(Meaning: rest.) Noah, son of Lamech, was a leading patriarch of the Old Testament (see Genesis 5:28–29; compare Luke 3:36, where he is designated as *Noe*). He had three sons: Japheth, Ham, and Shem. In later accounts he is also known for his role as the angel Gabriel (see Gabriel).

From latter-day scripture, we learn that Noah, when ten years old, was ordained to the priesthood by Methuselah (see D&C 107:52). Noah was a just and righteous man (see Moses 8:27; Genesis 6:9). Like all the Lord's prophets, Noah was commanded to call the people to repentance so that they might avoid being destroyed. Full of pride, the people would not listen, even when Noah prophesied of floods to come upon them if they didn't repent; instead, they desired to kill him. Noah prayed to the Lord in sorrow, and the Lord told Noah He would "destroy all flesh from off the earth" (Moses 8:30).

The Lord established a covenant with Noah, commanding him to build an ark,

Noah gathers animals in the ark

gather provision and animals, and preserve his family (see Genesis 6:14–22; compare Hebrews 11:7; 1 Peter 3:20; 2 Peter 2:5). Covering the entire earth, the waters flooded and surged for forty days (see Genesis 7:12, 17). Everything was destroyed—only Noah and those on the ark were preserved. The waters prevailed for another 150 days (see Genesis 8:3), eventually subsiding to allow the ark and its passengers to come to rest on "the mountains of Ararat" (Genesis 8:4). The Lord had preserved the life of mankind and earthly creatures. A new era of life was about to begin.

The Prophet Joseph Smith describes Noah as next to Adam in priesthood authority (see *TPJS*, 157). Noah is mentioned in the text of the Doctrine and Covenants in connection with the descent of the priesthood (see 84:14, 15; 107:52); the assembly of elect prophets who will meet the Savior at His Second Coming (see 133:54); and the vision granted to President Joseph F. Smith concerning the cause of salvation in the spirit world (see 138:9, 28, 41).

Noah is also mentioned in the Book of Mormon. In one passage, Amulek warns the people of his native city, Ammonihah, to repent and avoid the judgments of God: "Yea, and I say unto you that if it were not for the prayers of the righteous, who are now in the land, that ye would even now be visited with utter destruction; yet it would not be by flood, as were the people in the days of Noah, but it would be by famine, and by pestilence, and the sword" (Alma 10:22). In the book of Ether, the barges of the Jaredites are compared in tightness with the ark built by Noah (see Ether 6:7).

OBADIAH

(Meaning: servant of the Lord.)

1. Obadiah (pronounced oh'-buh-dy'-uh) was a person of high responsibility in the court of Ahab, king of Israel. He was a God-fearing man who respected the Lord's messengers (see 1 Kings 18:3–4). While fulfilling the king's request to search out grass for the royal horses and mules during the severe drought of the day, Obadiah encountered the prophet Elijah, who requested that he inform Ahab that he (Elijah) was located in that place. Obadiah was fearful that Elijah would not be available for a meeting with the king, and that his own life would thus be at risk; Elijah reassured him that the meeting would take place, and Obadiah complied and informed Ahab as requested by the prophet (see 1 Kings 18:13–15).

2. Obadiah was an individual listed among the descendants of Solomon (see 1 Chronicles 3:21).

3. Obadiah was an individual listed as belonging to the tribe of Issachar (see 1 Chronicles 7:3).

4. Obadiah was an individual listed among the descendants of Saul (see 1 Chronicles 8:38).

5. Obadiah was listed as one of the Levite service-providers in Jerusalem (see 1 Chronicles 9:16).

6. Obadiah was another individual listed among the descendants of Saul (see 1 Chronicles 9:44).

7. Obadiah was included in a listing of the mighty men of David (see 1 Chronicles 12:9).

8. Obadiah was listed among the leaders of the tribe of Zebulun in the days of David (see 1 Chronicles 27:19).

9. Obadiah was one of the princes in the court of Jehoshaphat of Judah (see 2 Chronicles 17:7).

10. Obadiah was one of the overseers associated with the repair of the house of the Lord during the reign of Josiah, king of Judah (see 2 Chronicles 34:12).

11. Obadiah was an individual listed among those returning to Jerusalem from the Babylonian captivity (see Ezra 8:9).

12. Obadiah was an individual listed among those who covenanted to marry in Israel, honor the Sabbath, pay tithes, and keep the commandments (see Nehemiah 10:5).

13. Obadiah was among the Levites appointed to provide services associated with the temple (see Nehemiah 12:25).

14. Obadiah was a prophet of the Lord who prophesied the downfall of Edom—a worldly kingdom of degeneracy and godless values. Nothing is known of Obadiah's personal life. The time of writing is not known with certainty; however, the book was written in the context of the capture of Jerusalem, probably referring to the capture by the Chaldeans around 587 BC. The book of Obadiah comprises a single chapter concerning the shame of Edom for participating in the program to attack Jerusalem and destroy the Lord's covenant people (see vv. 1–16)—followed by the fall of Edom and the triumph of the Lord's work and glory for the salvation and exaltation of the faithful, including a declaration of the ultimate victory of truth and right associated with the Second Coming (see vv. 17–21).

Obadiah prophesied that Mount Zion is to prevail in the triumph of the Lord's plan for the redemption of the righteous (see v. 21). In a discourse on May 16, 1841, the Prophet Joseph Smith made reference to "saviours . . . on mount Zion" (v. 21) as follows: "The election of the promised seed still continues, and in the last day, they shall have the Priesthood restored unto them, and they shall be the 'saviors on Mount Zion,' the ministers of our God; if it were not for the remnant which was left, then might men now be as Sodom and Gomorrah" (*TPJS*, 189; see also *TPJS*, 191, 223).

OBED

(Meaning: servant.)

1. Obed was the son of Ruth and Boaz: "And the women her neighbours [that is, the neighbors of Naomi, Ruth's mother-in-law] gave it a name, saying, There is a son born to Naomi; and they called his name Obed: he is the father of Jesse, the father of David" (Ruth 4:17, 21–22; see also 1 Chronicles 2:12; Matthew 1:5; Luke 3:2).

2. Obed was an individual listed among the descendants of Israel (see 1 Chronicles 2:37–38).

3. Obed was one of the mighty men of David (see 1 Chronicles 11:47).

4. Obed was one of the porters (or gatekeepers) assigned to provide service in connection with the temple during the days of David (see 1 Chronicles 26:7).

5. Obed was the father of Azariah (see 2 Chronicles 23:1), who was one of the captains of hundreds assisting the priest Jehoiada in elevating Joash (or Jehoash) as king of Judah and slaying the notorious Athaliah—the daughter of Ahab (king of Israel in the days of Elijah) and Jezebel (Ahab's Phoenician wife)—who had taken over throne upon the death of her son Ahaziah (see 2 Chronicles 23:2–21).

OBED-EDOM

(Meaning: servant of Edom.)

1. Obed-edom (pronounced oh'-bed-ee'-duhm) was a Levite who hosted the ark of the covenant for three months during its transition to Jerusalem (see 2 Samuel 6:10–12; compare 1 Chronicles 13:13–14; 15:25). Obed-edom served as a door keeper of the ark in Jerusalem (see 1 Chronicles 15:24–25).

2. Obed-edom was an individual (perhaps the same as the aforementioned) who performed duties in connection with the ark (see 1 Chronicles 16:5, 38). His sons assisted with the work (see 1 Chronicles 26:4, 8, 15; 2 Chronicles 25:24).

OG

(Meaning: giant, or long-necked.) Og (pronounced ahg or ohg) was king of Bashan—"the land of giants" (Deuteronomy 3:13)—at the time Moses and the Israelites were advancing into Canaanite territory. After the defeat of the Amorites, Moses and his army were assaulted by Og and his forces, a race of large-statured people. In the strength of the Lord, the Israelites triumphed (see Numbers 21:33–35; Deuteronomy 1:4; 3:1–6, 11; 4:47; 29:7; 31:4; Joshua 2:10; 9:10; 12:4; Psalm 135:10–12; 136:18–21).

OMRI

1. Omri (pronounced om'ry) was "captain of the host" under Elah, king of Israel (1 Kings 16:16). When Elah was murdered by Zimri, one of the high-ranking officers, Omri was elevated by the people to the throne of Israel and established his authority by emerging victorious in a four-year civil war (see vv. 21–24). His leadership was marked by unprincipled and evil conduct that was prolonged and augmented by his son and successor, Ahab (see vv. 25–29).

2. Omri was an individual mentioned as a descendant of Benjamin (see 1 Chronicles 7:8).

3. Omri was an individual mentioned among the descendants of Judah (see 1 Chronicles 9:4).

4. Omri is mentioned as a leader in the tribe of Issachar in the days of David (see 1 Chronicles 27:18).

ON

On (pronounced ohn) was a Reubenite among the 250 leaders in the camp of Israel who were swallowed up in the earth as a result of their rebellion against Moses (see Numbers 16:1, 2–35).

ONAN

Onan (pronounced oh'-nan or oh'nuhn) was one of the three sons of Judah by a Canaanite woman, the daughter of Shuah (see Genesis 38:4, 8–9; 46:12; Numbers 26:19; 1 Chronicles 2:3). Onan and his brother Er perished by the hand of the Lord because of wickedness (see Genesis 38:7–9).

PATRIARCH(S)

The word *patriarch* is a title that applies to all the early prophets/fathers in the Old Testament account (see Bible Dictionary). The term is not used in the King James Version of the Old Testament; however, in ref-

Melchizedek teaching his family as its patriarch

erence to Old Testament figures it is used in the New Testament: concerning "the patriarch David" (Acts 2:29); regarding "the patriarch Abraham" (Hebrews 7:4); and in Stephen's recounting of the history of Israel and the sons of Jacob (called "patriarchs"—Acts 7:8, 9). In the Pearl of Great Price, Abraham refers to his fathers as "patriarchs" (Abraham 1:31).

PEKAH

(Meaning: open-eyed.) Pekah (pronounced pee'-kah or pee'-kuh) was the son of Remaliah, a captain in the army of Pekahiah, king of Israel. Aided by a band of Gileadites, Pekah slew the king and took his place on the throne (see 2 Kings 15:25), ruling in wickedness until he was slain by Hoshea (see vv. 29–30).

PELEG

(Meaning: division.) Peleg was the son of Eber, of the lineage of Shem (see Genesis 11:16–19). In the days of Peleg, the earth was "divided" (Genesis 10:25; compare 1 Chronicles 1:19). Modern revelation indicates that this division spoken of will be reversed at the Second Coming: "He [the Lord] shall command the great deep, and it shall be driven back into the north countries, and the islands shall become one land; And the land of Jerusalem and the land of Zion shall be turned back into their own place, and the earth shall be like as it was in the days before it was divided" (D&C 133:23–24).

PERIZZITES

The Perizzites were one of the indigenous peoples driven out or overcome by the influx of the Israelites into the promised land (see Deuteronomy 7:1–2; 1 Kings 9:20; Joshua 3:10; 17:15; Nehemiah 9:7–8).

PHARAOH

(Meaning: great house.) Pharaoh was the title of the kings of Egypt, many of whom are

Joseph interprets the Pharaoh's servants' dreams

identified in the Old Testament by that title alone. Several were described by their relationships with other Old Testament figures: father-in-law of Mered of the tribe of Judah (see 1 Chronicles 4:18); brother-in-law of Hadad the Edomite (see 1 Kings 11:18–20); and father-in-law of Solomon (see 1 Kings 9:16). A few are described by more detailed names, such as Pharaoh-nechoh (or Necho) who slew Josiah, king of Judah (see 2 Kings 23:29–30; 2 Chronicles 35:20–24); Pharaoh-hophra at the time of Zedekiah, king of Judah (see Jeremiah 37:5–11; 44:30; Ezekiel 17:11–18); "So king of Egypt" at the time of Hoshea, king of Israel (2 Kings 17:4); and "Shishak king of Egypt" at the time of Jeroboam (1 Kings 11:40). See also Abraham 1 concerning the pharaoh at the time of Abraham (also the notations for figures 4 and 9 in Facsimile 1; figures 2 and 4 in Facsimile 3). Pharaoh, ruler of Egypt at the time of the Exodus, is mentioned two times in the Book of Mormon in connection with the destruction of the Egyptian armies during the episode of the parting of the Red Sea (see 1 Nephi 4:2; 17:27).

PHILISTINES

The Philistines (pronounced fih'-luh-steens or fih-lis'-teens) were an ancient tribe, or group of tribes, that contended from time to time with the Israelites, particularly during the time of King Saul and, to a declining degree, King David.

They are first mentioned in the Old Testament in connection with Abraham, who made a covenant of peace with Abimelech, king of the Philistines in Gerar, a region located in the Western Negev not far from Gaza (to the northwest) and Beersheba (to the southeast). (See Genesis 21:32–34.) It was rarely such an amicable spirit that characterized the relationship between the Philistines and the people of the Lord. The intense and lethal conflict between the Philistines and Samson is well known (see Judges 14–16), as is David's defeat of the Philistine giant, Goliath (see 1 Samuel 17:49–51). Saul and his three sons (Jonathan, Abinadab, and Malchi-shua) were slain in battle against the Philistines (see 1 Samuel 31), but after being anointed king of Israel, David subjected the Philistines to a definitive defeat (see 2 Samuel 5). Under Hezekiah, king of Judah, the Philistines were again brought under subjection (see 2 Kings 18:8), though their animosity against the Israelites continued to fester (see Ezekiel 25:15–17).

Originally, the Philistines resided in "Caphtor" (Amos 9:7), thought to be the island of Crete or perhaps part of the Egyptian delta. Eventually they established a powerful confederacy of five key cities (Ashdod, Gaza, Askelon, Gath, and Ekron) in the territory between Judea and Egypt (see 1 Samuel 6:17; compare Exodus 13:17; Joshua 13:3). The name *Palestine*, a word designating the Holy Land itself, derives from the name of the Philistines.

PHINEHAS

1. Phinehas (pronounced fin'-ee-us or fin'-ee-huhs) was the son of Eleazar, son of Aaron (see Exodus 6:25; 1 Chronicles 6:4, 50). When many of the Israelites were giving themselves over to the perverted ways of the Midianites, intermingling with non-Israelite women and practicing idolatrous forms of worship, the Lord commanded Moses to eliminate such traitors to the covenant and thus put a stop to

the plague of retribution that had broken out with devastating consequences among the people (see Numbers 25:9). In obedience, Phinehas rose up and did away with one such rebellious couple in the midst of the people. In response, the Lord blessed Phinehas and his posterity for his zeal (see Numbers 25:11–13). Soon thereafter Moses sent an army of twelve thousand, accompanied by Phinehas, to inflict destruction on the Midianites for having corrupted the lifestyle of the Israelites (see Numbers 31:6; Psalm 106:30).

Later, as Joshua discharged the tribe of Reuben, the tribe of Gad, and half the tribe of Manasseh to take possession of their region of inheritance in Gilead beyond the Jordan River, these people, in their journeying, erected a prominent altar by the Jordan River. The remainder of the Israelites, dismayed and angered, having interpreted this act as a return to the idolatry of the Midianites, sent Phinehas and ten princes to warn the builders of the altar of the dire consequences of their actions. Phinehas was relieved to discover that the monument was not idolatrous in purpose (see Joshua 22:28).

On another occasion, when all Israel was rising up against the tribe of Benjamin in the city of Gibeah because of a serious moral crime perpetrated by a group of unnamed and protected Benjamites, Phinehas served as commander under commission from God to root out the evil, which he successfully accomplished (see Judges 20:28–48).

Phinehas also provided leadership in connection with services rendered for the Tabernacle (see 1 Chronicles 9:20). The descendants of Phinehas are listed among those returning from the Babylonian captivity (see Ezra 7:5; 8:2, 33).

2. Phinehas was the second son of Eli. *See Eli.*

POTIPHAR

(Meaning: he whom Ra [the sun-god] gave.) Potiphar (pronounced pot'-uh-fahr or pot'-uh-fuhr) was captain of the bodyguard of the pharaoh and benefactor of Joseph when he was sold into slavery (see Genesis 37:36). Potiphar, a wealthy man, saw that everything Joseph did was blessed by the Lord and flourished, thus he made Joseph overseer of his house. Potiphar's wife made multiple attempts to persuade him to lie with her. Joseph resisted honorably, and when the woman then falsely accused Joseph of licentious behavior, Potiphar became angry and put Joseph in the king's prison (see Genesis 39).

POTIPHAR'S WIFE (SEE POTIPHAR AND JOSEPH)

POTIPHERAH

(Meaning: devoted to the sun.) Potipherah (pronounced pah-tih'-fuh-ruh or pah-tih-fur'-ruh) was a priest of On (Heliopolis) and father of Asenath, Joseph's wife in a marriage arranged by the pharaoh (see Genesis 41:45, 50; compare Genesis 46:20, where the name is spelled *Poti-pherah*).

PRIEST(S)

The office of priest was bestowed over the generations upon the worthy sons of Aaron (see Numbers 18:1–2, 7; see also Numbers 16:5, 40; Hebrews 5:4) in connection with their rendering such services as blessing the people, offering sacrifices, teaching the principles of the

Priests and scribes

law, and communicating the will of the Lord (see Leviticus 10:10–11; Numbers 6:22–27; Deuteronomy 33:10, Malachi 2:7). The priests were supported from portions of the offerings given by the people (see Leviticus 7:8, 34; Numbers 15:20–21; 18:9; Deuteronomy 8:3–5; Nehemiah 10:35–37) and given certain cities in the Holy Land (see Numbers 18:20; Joshua 21:13–19). See the Bible Dictionary entry *Priests* for greater detail.

PROPHET(S)

The Old Testament provides comprehensive and compelling evidence of the divine commission and indispensable service of the prophets of the Lord in all ages—from Adam through Malachi and beyond. Amos confirmed: "Surely the Lord GOD will do nothing, but he revealeth his secret unto his servants the prophets" (Amos 3:7). The gift of the prophet is to confirm for mankind, through the power of the Holy Ghost, that God lives; to communicate God's divine will for the blessing of all His children; and to uphold, sustain, and further the designs of heaven for the eternal salvation and exaltation of the sons and daughters of God, all dimensions of the plan being empowered through the sacred Atonement of Jesus Christ.

PROPHETESS

The term "prophetess" is used in the Old Testament to refer to Miriam, sister of Moses (see Exodus 15:20); Deborah, the judge (see Judges 4:4); Huldah, at the time of King Josiah of Judah (see 2 Kings 22:14; 2 Chronicles 34:22); the wife of Isaiah (see Isaiah 8:3); and Noadiah, a false prophetess at the time of Nehemiah (see Nehemiah 6:14). In addition, in the New Testament the term is applied to Anna, at the time of Christ's birth (see Luke 2:36), and Jezebel, the false prophetess mentioned by John the Revelator (see Revelation 2:20). The term conveys a sense of honor for the leadership women provide in Israel, that a woman has the spiritual gift of discernment, or that she may prophesy.

An Old Testament prophet

In its universal application, the term might well apply to all women who have been blessed with a testimony of the divinity of Jesus Christ—just as the term *prophet* might be applied to all men blessed with such a testimony. John confirmed that "the testimony of Jesus is the spirit of prophecy" (Revelation 19:10), and Paul declared that "no man [or, by extension, woman] can say that Jesus is the Lord, but by the Holy Ghost" (1 Corinthians 12:3). Thus any individual, man or woman, who bears witness by the Spirit that the Atonement of Jesus Christ and the principles and ordinances of the gospel lead to salvation and exaltation is speaking prophetically. The scriptures expressly include prophecy as one of the gifts of the Spirit (see 1 Corinthians 12:10; Moroni 10:13; D&C 46:22).

President Joseph Fielding Smith said, "Our sisters are entitled just as much to the inspiration for their needs of the Holy Spirit as are the men. They are entitled to the gift of prophecy concerning matters that would be essential for them to know as it is for the men" (Joseph Fielding Smith, *Take Heed to Yourselves* [Salt Lake City: Deseret Book, 1966], 259). It should be understood that *prophetess* is not meant to be used as a parallel for the special priesthood title of *prophet* (as in the expression "prophets, seers, and revelators").

PUL

Pul was the king of Assyria who received a large tribute from Menahem, king of Israel (see 2 Kings 15:19). Pul was probably the same as Tiglath-pileser, founder of the second Assyrian empire (see 16:7–9; spelled *Tilgath-pilneser* in 1 Chronicles 5:26).

Queen of Sheba

The queen of Sheba visited King Solomon at his court and acclaimed his renown (see 1 Kings 10:6–9; compare 2 Chronicles 9:5–8). The queen came from Sheba, a country in southern Arabia. The Savior referred to the queen of Sheba as the "queen of the south" (Matthew 12:42).

Solomon receiving the queen of Sheba

RACHEL

(Meaning: ewe.) Rachel was the younger of the two daughters of Laban, son of Bethuel, who was the youngest son of Nahor, brother of Abraham (see Genesis 22:22–23). When Isaac and Rebekah sent their son Jacob to Laban (who was Rebekah's brother), Jacob joyously met Rachel for the first time as she brought her father's sheep to the well (see Genesis 29:1–14).

Jacob loved Rachel, and agreed to serve Laban for seven years in exchange for her hand in marriage—"and they seemed unto him but a few days, for the love he had to her" (Genesis 29:20). At the same time, Rachel's older sister Leah was also an eligible bride. Though he had promised the hand of Rachel to Jacob, Laban adjusted the unfolding of events on the marriage day by sending the veiled Leah that evening to be Jacob's wife. The next morning, when the truth was discovered by Jacob (see Genesis 29:25–26), he agreed to serve Laban yet another seven years, and was soon thereafter favored with the bride of his choice—Rachel. In all Jacob served Laban for a total of twenty years before returning to Canaan (see Genesis 31:38, 41).

While Leah bore Jacob many children, Rachel seemed unable to conceive, so Rachel gave unto Jacob her maid Bilhah, who bore two sons, Dan and Naphtali (see Genesis 30:1–8). Evenutally Rachel was also blessed with a son, Joseph (see Genesis 30:22–24).

On the family's journey back to Canaan, Rachel was pregnant once again, and she went into labor, but it was obviously difficult, as Rachel died in childbirth (see Genesis 35:16–20; compare Genesis 46:19; 48:7).

Jeremiah uses Rachel as an emblem of the lamentation of Israel in the face of calamities: "Thus saith the LORD; A voice was heard in Ramah, lamentation, and bitter weeping; Rahel [Rachel] weeping for her children refused to be comforted for her children, because they were not" (Jeremiah 31:15–17; compare Matthew 2:18, where the same invocation of mourning is used in reference to the slaying of infants in Bethlehem at the hands of Herod). The hope that Jeremiah unfolds for his listeners in reference to Rachel is none other than the Restoration of the gospel of Jesus

Christ in the latter days (see Jeremiah 31:31–34). It was especially through Joseph, son of Rachel and Jacob, that the power and blessings of the Abrahamic covenant would be made available to all quarters of the earth in the latter days.

RAHAB

(Meaning: broad or large.) Rahab (pronounced ray'-hab) was a woman in Jericho who sequestered the two spies sent by Joshua to survey the city in preparation for the Israelite advance into Canaan (see Joshua 2:1).

When the king of Jericho got word of the spies' whereabouts, he sent to Rahab, demanding she bring the men out (see vv. 2–3). Courageously, Rahab, having concealed the men under stalks of flax on her roof, claimed that the fugitives had escaped in the night. Why would she have rescued the Israelite enemy spies in this fashion? According to her own witness to them, she and her household were persuaded that the Israelite cause was of divine making (see vv. 9–11). She then requested of the men that they spare her family during the impending invasion, something they agreed to do in exchange for her silence concerning their mission. To secure the members of her family gathered within the walls of her house, which was located on the wall of the city, she was to tie a scarlet thread in her window (see vv. 12–22). As promised, her family was withdrawn to safety on the day that Jericho was destroyed by the armies of Joshua (see Joshua 6:17–25).

Paul later recounted this event in his lecture on the principle of faith: "By faith the walls of Jericho fell down, after they were compassed about seven days. By faith the harlot Rahab perished not with them that believed not, when she had received the spies with peace" (Hebrews 11:30–31). In another passage, James uses the incident concerning Rahab's decisive initiative to illustrate the principle that "faith without works is dead" (James 2:26).

In other passages of scripture, the word *Rahab* is used in a different sense—to identify, symbolically, a force of worldly pride, such as Egypt (see Psalm 87:4; 89:10; Isaiah 51:9). Presumably the two usages are not related.

RAPHAEL

Raphael was a heavenly messenger among the ranks of elect figures such as Michael and Gabriel. Though not mentioned in the Old Testament, Raphael is included in the Doctrine and Covenants in one verse concerning the manifestations of various divine messengers during the foundation period of the Restoration (see D&C 128:21). We are not told in the scriptures anything further concerning the identity and character of Raphael.

REBEKAH

(Meaning: that which binds or secures.) Rebekah was the wife of Abraham's son Isaac. She was the sister of Laban and the daughter of Bethuel, son of Nahor, Abraham's brother (see Genesis 22:23)—thus she was Isaac's cousin.

The story of how Rebekah came to be Isaac's wife is told in Genesis 24. Abraham had arranged for his servant to seek a wife for Isaac within the extended family circle. Having arrived at the Mesopotamian city of Haran in the Padan-aram region, the abode of Abraham's kin, the servant of Abraham prayed for guidance in identifying Isaac's bride (see vv. 13–14.)

The servant's prayer was answered before he had even finished as the very pretty Rebekah approached, a pitcher balanced on her shoulder (see Genesis 24:16). There was an amicable period of introductions, followed by the arrival of Laban, Rebekah's brother, who extended the hand of hospitality to the visitor. In an atmosphere of friendship and goodwill among all members of the family circle, the arrangement for the marriage was soon agreed upon.

Though the family expressed a preference for Rebekah to delay her departure by a few days, they deferred to the anxiety of the servant of Abraham to return to his master forthwith, something to which Rebekah readily consented. The family then "blessed Rebekah, and said unto her, Thou art our sister, be thou the mother of thousands of millions, and let thy seed possess the gate of those which hate them" (Genesis 24:60). Isaac and Rebekah were soon married, and Isaac loved his wife.

After a lengthy period of not being able to bear children, Rebekah became the mother of Esau and Jacob, her husband having supplicated the Lord on her behalf (see Genesis 25:20–28). During her pregnancy, Rebekah prayed to the Lord concerning her condition, receiving this answer: "And the LORD said unto her, Two nations are in thy womb, and two manner of people shall be separated from thy bowels; and the one people shall be stronger than the other people; and the elder shall serve the younger" (v. 23). Her disposition, therefore, was in favor of the second of the twins, Jacob, though her husband favored Esau (see vv. 27–28).

Following the encounter in which Esau sold his birthright to Jacob for pottage (see Genesis 25:29–34), Isaac removed his family to Gerar, a Philistine stronghold, to find relief from the famine in the land. While there, Isaac

Rebekah at the well with the servant of Abraham

identified Rebekah as his sister, rather than his wife, being concerned that her beauty would induce the men of the community to kill him so they could take her for themselves. But his secret was soon discovered (see 26:8). Confronted with this reality, Isaac confessed his reasons for the secrecy. Subsequently, good relations were again restored in the land, lasting until Isaac's unfolding prosperity and power caused unease among the Philistines. They induced him to move away, though they afterwards entered into a covenant of friendship with him (see vv. 28–29).

Rebekah figures prominently in the final chapter of Isaac's life, when he decided to bestow a benedictory blessing on the head of Esau, his firstborn son. Having learned that Isaac had sent Esau into the countryside to obtain and prepare venison for him, and no doubt remembering the Lord's promise to her that "the elder shall serve the younger" (Genesis 25:23), Rebekah arranged for Jacob to play the role of Esau by disguising himself strategically. Isaac, now poor of vision, granted the blessing, much to the distress of Esau when he discovered the deception. Jacob gave Esau a blessing of his own, but he was still angry at his brother, so Rebekah and Isaac dispatched Jacob to remain with her brother Laban in Haran for a period of time until the venomous anger of Esau subsided (see chapter 27). The transition also served the purpose of encouraging Jacob to choose a wife from within the extended family circle rather than from among the indigenous non-covenant tribes (see 27:46; 28:1–5). Eventually Jacob married Leah and Rachel, daughters of Laban, Rebekah's brother (see chapters 28, 29) and made reconciliation with Esau (see chapter 33).

Upon her death, Rebekah was buried "in the cave that is in the field of Machpelah, which is before Mamre, in the land of Canaan" (Genesis 49:30)—the resting place for Abraham, Sarah, Isaac, and Leah (see 49:31).

Rechabites

The Rechabites (pronounced ree'-kuh-bytes) were a tribe related to or belonging to the Kenites (see 1 Chronicles 2:55). The name derives from an individual named Rechab, who was the father of Jehonadab, the founder of the Rechabites (see 2 Kings 10:15, 23). Jeremiah pronounced God's blessings upon the Rechabites for their obedience (see Jeremiah 35).

Rehoboam

(Meaning: enlarger of the people.) Rehoboam (pronounced ree'-uh-boh'-uhm) was the son of

Solomon and the Ammonitess Naamah, and successor to the throne (see 1 Kings 11:43; 14:21, 31; 1 Chronicles 3:10; 2 Chronicles 9:31; Matthew 1:7). During the days of Rehoboam, around 975 BC, Israel became divided into two parts (see 1 Kings 12; 2 Chronicles 10:19), largely as a result of a revolt of the people against the heavy tax burden imposed by King Solomon.

When Rehoboam attained the throne, he continued his father's practice of exacting heavy taxes from the people. He said, "My father made your yoke heavy, and I will add to your yoke: my father *also* chastised you with whips, but I will chastise you with scorpions" (1 Kings 12:14; compare 2 Chronicles 10:11). The ten tribes took decisive action against Rehoboam's regime: "So Israel rebelled against the house of David unto this day. And it came to pass, when all Israel heard that Jeroboam was come again, that they sent and called him unto the congregation, and made him king over all Israel: there was none that followed the house of David, but the tribe of Judah only" (1 Kings 12:19–20).

Rehoboam, having been warned by Shemaiah, a man of God, not to go up to battle against the northern kingdom (see vv. 21–24; compare 2 Chronicles 11:2–4), left things as they were for a season. Meanwhile, Jeroboam rebuilt Shechem but then also undertook initiatives that contravened the instructions of the prophet Ahijah, who had warned him to walk in the ways of the Lord (see 11:33, 37–38). Jeroboam set up two golden calves (one in Bethel and one in Dan) and instructed the people to worship in those places rather than journeying to Jerusalem where, he feared, they would be subjected to the influence of Rehoboam. He also appointed priests from non-Levite ranks and established a feast day of his own contrivance (see 12:25–33; 2 Chronicles 13:9). Thus both kings—one over Judah and one over Israel—failed to walk in the footsteps of their righteous predecessors, causing the Lord to withdraw His blessings. Not long thereafter, Rehoboam's power was greatly weakened as a result of an invasion by the Egyptians under Shishak, king of Egypt—something Shemaiah had warned him about (see 1 Kings 14: 25–31; 2 Chronicles 12:9–12). The northern and southern kingdoms, both having ripened in iniquity, made war one with another for many years (see 1 Kings 15:6).

REMALIAH

(Meaning: adorned by the Lord.) Remaliah (pronounced rem'-uh-ly'-uh) was the father of Pekah, one of the kings of Israel (see 2 Kings 15:25–37; 16:1–5; 2 Chronicles 28:6). In this connection, Remaliah is also mentioned several times in the Book of Mormon in quotations from Isaiah 7 and 8 (see 2 Nephi 17:1, 4, 5, 9; 18:6).

REPHAIM(S)

(Meaning: giants.) The Rephaim (pronounced ref'-ay-im) were a pre-Israelite people who were especially large of stature. At the time of Abraham, Chedorlaomer, king of Edom, defeated this tribe and several others (see Genesis 14:5). According to the covenant promises given of the Lord to Abraham and his seed, the Rephaim and other indigenous peoples were to be supplanted or subjected by the Israelites (see Genesis 15:18–21; see also other references concerning tribal giants in Deuteronomy 2:11, 20; 3:11, 13; Joshua 12:4; 13:12; 17:15; for references to the "valley of Rephaim"—usually in connection with the activities of the Philistines—see 2 Samuel 5:22; 23:13; 1 Chronicles 11:15; 14:9; Isaiah 17:5).

REUBEN

(Meaning: behold a son.) Reuben, son of Leah, was Jacob's first-born son (see Genesis 29:32). Though Reuben was the firstborn son and thus heir to the primary blessings of the lineage, his immoral act with Bilhah, his father's concubine, cost him his birthright (see 35:22).

Reuben was part of the vile conspiracy with his brethren to do away with their brother Joseph (see Genesis 37:18–20), but he influenced his brothers instead to abandon Joseph in a pit. Reuben intended to retrieve him later and return him to Jacob, but meanwhile his brethren sold Joseph to the Ishmaelite band (vv. 21–22, 29). Reuben again showed a certain valor when he guaranteed to protect the life of Benjamin should Jacob permit this youngest son to return with the brothers to the court of Joseph (see 42:37).

By the time Jacob and his family moved to Egypt, Reuben had a total of four sons (see Genesis 46:9), but since Reuben had been displaced out of his birthright position, Jacob

Reuben and his brothers sell Joseph

transferred that blessing to Joseph (see 1 Chronicles 5:1–2) and accepted Joseph's two sons, Ephraim and Manasseh, as participants in the right of inheritance (see Genesis 48:5). Jacob's final blessing on the head of Reuben and his posterity included the following words: "Reuben, thou art my firstborn, my might, and the beginning of my strength, the excellency of dignity, and the excellency of power: Unstable as water, thou shalt not excel; because thou wentest up to thy father's bed; then defiledst thou it: he went up to my couch" (Genesis 49:3–4). Later, Moses bestowed the following blessing upon the tribe of Reuben: "Let Reuben live, and not die; and let not his men be few" (Deuteronomy 33:6).

The tribe of Reuben inherited a fertile area east of the Jordan River (see Numbers 32). When Joshua discharged the tribe of Reuben, the tribe of Gad, and half the tribe of Manasseh to take possession of their region of inheritance beyond the Jordan River, these people, in their journeying, erected a prominent altar by the Jordan River. The remainder of the Israelites, dismayed and angered—having interpreted this act as a return to the idolatry of the Midianites—sent Phinehas and ten princes to warn the builders of the altar of the dire consequences of their actions. But the builders from Reuben, Gad, and half of Manasseh assured the delegation that the monument was not idolatrous in purpose, but simply a witness of the commitment to honor the covenants of the Lord over the generations (see Joshua 22). On a later occasion, Deborah rebuked the Reubenites for failing to stand forth with courage at a time of great peril for the nation under siege by the Canaanites (see Judges 5:15–16). Eventually the Reubenites, Gadites, and half the tribe of Manasseh were carried away captive by the Assyrians (see 1 Chronicles 5:26).

REUEL

(Meaning: friend of God.) Reuel (pronounced roo'-el) was the son of Esau and the father-in-law of Moses. Reuel was also called Jethro. *For details, see Jethro.*

REZIN

Rezin (pronounced ree'-zin) was a king of Syria who entered into an alliance with Pekah, king of Israel, and besieged Jerusalem during the reign of Ahaz, king of Judah (see 2 Kings 15:37; 16:5; 2 Chronicles 28:6; Isaiah 7:1). King Ahaz induced the Assyrians to advance on Damascus, causing Rezin to return to his own domain where he was slain (see 2 Kings 16:9). Isaiah refers to these events in a celebrated passage prophesying the future birth of Immanuel (see Isaiah 7:7–9, 14–16; compare also the same reference quoted by Nephi in 2 Nephi 17:7–9, 14–16; see other references to Rezin in the Book of Mormon in quotations from Isaiah 7, 8, and 9; 2 Nephi 17:1; 18:6; 19:11).

RIMMON

1. Rimmon, of the tribe of Benjamin, was the father of Baanah and Rechab, the two captains of Ish-bosheth, king of Israel. Baanah and Rechab, having murdered the king and delivered his head to David, king of Judah, were then executed by David (see 2 Samuel 4:2–10).

2. Rimmon was a Syrian idol (see 2 Kings 5:18), likely associated with the sun god Hadadrimmon (see Zechariah 12:11).

ROOT OF JESSE

The root of Jesse is an individual referred to by the prophet Isaiah in relation to latter-day events: "And in that day there shall be a root of Jesse, which shall stand for an ensign of the people; to it shall the Gentiles seek: and his rest shall be glorious" (Isaiah 11:10; compare Romans 15:12; 2 Nephi 21:10; compare the commentary in D&C 113:6). The root of Jesse is most probably the Prophet Joseph Smith (see Hoyt W. Brewster, Jr., *Doctrine and Covenants Encyclopedia* [Salt Lake City: Bookcraft, 1996], 479).

RUTH

Ruth was a Moabite woman who became the daughter-in-law of Naomi and a progenitor in the lineage leading to Jesus Christ (see Matthew 1:5). Ruth was "a model of ideal womanhood" (Thomas S. Monson, "Models to Follow," *Ensign*, Nov. 2002, 60).

Compiled and authored by an unnamed writer, the book of Ruth, along with the book of Judges, presents all of the Hebrew history available concerning events during the period of time commencing with the death of Joshua and extending to the birth of Samuel. The time span of the book of Ruth was likely the middle part of the twelfth century BC, since Ruth was the great-grandmother of David (who was born around 1096 BC). The book of Ruth is a story of unsurpassed beauty and tenderness illustrating loyalty and devotion within the family—especially in the context of the integration of a non-Israelite into the fold of Israel. Some of the most memorable words in the Old Testament were spoken by Ruth in her declaration of loyalty to her mother-in-law (Ruth 1:16).

The four chapters of the book cover the transition of the Elimelech family to Moab, the marriages and deaths within the family, and the return of Naomi and Ruth to Bethlehem (chapter 1); the courtship of Boaz and Ruth (chapters 2–3); and the marriage of Boaz and Ruth (chapter 4).

It is important to remember that Ruth was of the Moabite lineage, one of the indigenous cultures remaining in the Holy Land after the return of Israel from Egypt. The original Moab was the son of Lot's oldest daughter (see Genesis 19:37), and thus the Moabites were distant kin to the Israelites but represented a different way of life and religion. Ruth wholeheartedly embraced the Israelite way of life, though it was different from her own. She was welcomed into her new environment and became instrumental in continuing the promised lineage via David to the Savior Himself. It is a reminder that converts to the Church and kingdom of God are welcome from all kindreds, nations, tongues, and peoples.

Ruth in the fields of Boaz

SABAOTH

(Meaning: hosts.) Sabaoth (pronounced sab'-ay-oth) refers to the armies arrayed to sustain the cause of the Lord—whether on earth or in heaven. *Lord of Sabaoth* as a title for Jehovah does not occur in the Old Testament, but is found elsewhere in the scriptures (Romans 9:29; James 5:4; D&C 87:7; 88:2; 95:7; 98:2), with the more common equivalent title *Lord of hosts* occurring many times throughout holy writ, especially in the Old Testament (as in the famous words of David spoken to Goliath and recorded in 1 Samuel 17:45: "I come to thee in the name of the LORD of hosts"). The expression *Lord God of hosts* is also encountered frequently in the scriptures.

SABEANS

The Sabeans (pronounced suh-bee'-uns) were an Arab tribe mentioned specifically in four passages of scripture (see Job 1:15; Isaiah 45:14; Ezekiel 23:42; and Joel 3:8).

SAMARITANS

The Samaritans were a people who populated Samaria following the Assyrian captivity of the northern kingdom of Israel around 721 BC. Samaria, located in the mountainous region of Palestine, had originally been established as a stronghold capital by Omri, king of Israel (see 1 Kings 16:23–24). The Samaritans were in general descendants of the colonists placed in that territory by the Assyrian conquerors (see 2 Kings 17:23–24). Though initially idolatrous and thus incurring the judgments of heaven, these colonists were taught to fear the Lord by a priest sent from among the captive circle of Israelites by the Assyrian king (see 2 Kings 17:25–41). Generations later, upon the return of Judah from the Babylonian captivity of the sixth century BC, the Samaritans desired to assist in the rebuilding of the temple at Jerusalem—a privilege denied them by the Jewish leaders (see Ezra 4:1–3).

Angered, the Samaritans turned against Judah with much animosity and later erected a temple of their own on Mount Gerizim (pronounced gair'-uh-zim). Gerizim thus became for the Samaritans what Jerusalem was for the Jewish people. Later, it was to this site upon Gerizim that the Samaritan woman referred when she was being counseled by the Savior at the well: "The woman saith unto him, Sir, I perceive that thou art a prophet. Our fathers worshipped in this mountain; and ye say, that in Jerusalem is the place where men ought to worship" (John 4:19–20). Despite the intolerance of the Jewish people for the Samaritans living among them (see, for example, Matthew 10:5; Luke 9:51–56; Luke 10:33; 17:16; John 4:9, 39; 8:48), the Samaritans were able, in their time, to receive the gospel message from the disciples of Jesus (see Acts 1:8; 8:4–15).

SAMSON

(Meaning: of the sun.) Samson, famous for his astounding strength, was the twelfth in a sequence of judges serving in Israel (see Judges 13–16). At a time when the Israelites had been in bondage to the Philistines for four decades, an angel of the Lord came to the wife of Manoah, a member of the tribe of Dan, and pronounced a wondrous blessing upon her head (for she had been barren): "For, lo, thou shalt conceive, and bear a son; and no razor shall come on his head: for the child shall be a Nazarite unto God from the womb: and he shall begin to deliver Israel out of the hand of the Philistines" (Judges 13:5). The rise of Samson was marked by several notable milestones: his slaying of a lion with his bare hands during the time he was courting a Philistine woman (see Judges 14); his slaying of a thousand Philistines with the jawbone of an ass in connection with bitter disappointments concerning his marriage (see chapter 15); and his fatal interaction with Delilah, a woman from the valley of Sorek whom he loved (see 16:4).

Samson and the Philistines

The Philistines bribed Delilah to discover the secret of Samson's astounding strength. Three times in sequence she induced him to share the information with her—but each time he provided her a ficticious explanation. She persisted until Samson relented (see Judges 16–17). *See also Delilah.*

Then Delilah caused his hair to be shaved while he slept, leaving him powerless: "And he wist not that the Lord was departed from him" (Judges 16:20). The Philistines then put out Samson's eyes and imprisoned him at Gaza. Later—after Samson's hair had grown long once again (see 16:22)—the Philistines assembled a vast throng of people to celebrate their victory and to make sport of Samson. It was then that he called one last time upon the Lord and pulled down the pillars of the house, destroying himself and all three thousand of the celebrants who were therein (see 16: 28–30).

SAMUEL

(Meaning: name of God or God has heard.) Samuel, a great prophet in ancient Israel at the time of Saul and David, was the son of Elkanah and Hannah. Hannah had desired greatly to become a mother and promised the Lord that if she could bear a son, she would dedicate his life to the Lord's service: "I will give him unto the Lord all the days of his life, and there shall no razor come upon his head" (1 Samuel 1:11; compare Judges 13:5 concerning the vow of a Nazarite). Her prayers were answered in the birth of Samuel (see also *Hannah*). True to to her vow, Hannah brought young Samuel to the temple after he was weaned and put him in the care of Eli the priest.

One night, Samuel heard a voice during the night calling his name (see 1 Samuel 3:4). Assuming it was Eli calling him, Samuel ran to the elderly priest's bedside, but Eli told him it wasn't he who called and had him return to his own bed. After this scene repeated itself twice more, Eli told him it was the Lord calling and that he should return to his bed and if the voice called again, he should say, "Speak Lord; for thy servant heareth" (v. 9). Samuel followed Eli's instructions and the Lord revealed to Samuel the sad news of Eli's sons and their unrighteousness, and the dire consequence to Eli's family (see vv. 11–14). Subsequently, Eli's sons were killed in battle (see 4:11) and Eli, as a feeble ninety-eight-year old, passed away in a tragic accident (see v. 18). Samuel continued in righteousness and became the prophet of the Lord (see 1 Samuel 3:19–20).

The books of 1 and 2 Samuel cover the time period from the birth of Samuel (shortly before 1125 BC) to a period just prior to the death of David (around 1015 BC)—a span of

Samuel hears the voice of the Lord

some 130 years. Samuel himself, however, passed away prior to the end of 1 Samuel. The book of 1 Samuel sets forth the commencement of the history of Israel under King Saul and his successor, King David. Against the backdrop of intrigue and pride reflected in the vacillating character of Saul, we perceive the principled ministry of the prophet Samuel as a mirror of divine purpose and truth. We also see the magnanimous character of the young David as he emerges from obscurity to a position of prominence as a great leader in Israel.

The Psalmist remembered Samuel in this inspiring exhortation: "Exalt ye the LORD our God, and worship at his footstool; for he is holy. Moses and Aaron among his priests, and Samuel among them that call upon his name; they called upon the LORD, and he answered them" (Psalm 99:5–6).

SANBALLAT

Sanballat (pronounced san-bal'-at), known as the "Horonite" (Nehemiah 2:10), was a leader among the people of Samaria who opposed Nehemiah in the mission of rebuilding the walls of Jerusalem following the return of the Jewish people from Babylonian captivity (see Nehemiah 2:19; 4:1, 7; 6:1–14). Sanballat had a son-in-law who was a priest, but Nehemiah, after reprimanding the priests who had married non-Israelite women, said he "chased" this priest from him (see Nehemiah 13:28).

SARAH/SARAI

(Meaning: princess.) Sarah, wife of Abraham, was originally known as Sarai (pronounced sair'-y or sair'-ay-y). Sarai's childlessness was a burden to her for many years, though Abram (later named Abraham) was blessed by the

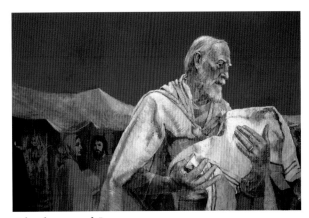
Abraham and Isaac

Lord: "And I will make of thee a great nation" (Genesis 12:2). A famine in Canaan caused Abram and Sarai to move for a time to the land of Egypt, where Abram instructed his wife, who was "a fair woman to look upon" (Genesis 12:11), to present herself as his sister, lest the Egyptians should kill him in order to take her as their own (see Genesis 12:10–20; compare Genesis 20 for a similar episode concerning Abimelech, king of Gerar). Upon returning to Canaan, Abram yearned for his promised posterity, and the Lord sent words of comfort: "And he brought him forth abroad, and said, Look now toward heaven, and tell the stars, if thou be able to number them: and he said unto him, So shall thy seed be" (Genesis 15:5).

After ten years in Canaan with no children, Sarai, in accordance with the cultural practice of her time, gave unto Abram her Egyptian handmaid, Hagar, as a wife. The Doctrine and Covenants confirms:

> God commanded Abraham, and Sarah gave Hagar to Abraham to wife. And why did she do it? Because this was the law; and from Hagar sprang many people. This, therefore,

was fulfilling, among other things, the promises.

Was Abraham, therefore, under condemnation? Verily I say unto you, Nay; for I, the Lord, commanded it. (D&C 132:33–34; see also D&C 132:65)

Subsequently, Hagar gave birth to Ishmael (see Genesis 16). Several years later, the Lord confirmed to Abram the covenant promise of great increase and changed his name to Abraham, "father of many nations" (Genesis 17:5). Sarai, too, received a new name—Sarah—and was blessed that she would bear a son and "be a mother of nations; kings of people shall be of her" (17:16).

This promise of Sarah's pending motherhood was confirmed somewhat later by three holy men visiting Abraham and Sarah at their encampment. When the aged Sarah overheard the statement that she would conceive and bear a son, she also laughed to herself, but the Lord responded to Abraham, "Is any thing too hard for the LORD? At the time appointed I will return unto thee, according to the time of life, and Sarah shall have a son" (Genesis 18:14).

Sarah did indeed bear a son, who was given the name *Isaac* (meaning "he laughed"—see Genesis 21:1–3). Some years later Sarah was vexed by Ishmael's mocking and insisted he and his mother be sent away. Abraham was grieved to lose this son, but the Lord assured him he should hearken to Sarah in the matter (see 21:12–13).

Sarah passed away at age 127, and "Abraham came to mourn for Sarah, and to weep for her" (Genesis 23:2). She was buried "in the cave of the field of Machpelah before Mamre: the same *is* Hebron in the land of Canaan" (Gensis 23:19).

Paul celebrated the faith of Sarah: "Through faith also Sara herself received strength to conceive seed, and was delivered of a child when she was past age, because she judged him faithful who had promised" (Hebrews 11:11). And Peter elevated Sarah as a beacon of obedience in the cause of the Lord (see 1 Peter 3:6).

SARGON

Sargon was an Assyrian king during the days of Isaiah (see Isaiah 20:1).

SATAN

(Meaning: adversary.) Satan, who is Lucifer, is the principal devil and primordial enemy to God. Understanding some of the many names for Satan can help us understand his nature and circumstances. In one passage of the Doctine and Covenants (76:25–29), Satan is mentioned with seven different designations: fallen angel, Perdition, Lucifer, son of the morning, Satan, old serpent, and devil.

Satan was a fallen angel in that he is a child of God who, in rebelling against God, was ejected from God's heavenly home. The word *Perdition* in English usage comes from the Latin verb *perdere*, meaning to lose. Assuredly Satan is the archetype of the loser, for as an angel in authority in the premortal realm who rebelled against the Almighty God, he lost forever the divinely appointed opportunity to receive an inheritance of glory and exaltation (see Isaiah 14:12–15; compare Luke 10:18). The name *Lucifer* means literally "the shining one" or "the lightbringer" (see Bible Dictionary, 726). This name, which derives from the Latin word for "light" (compare the related word *lucid*), is the equivalent of the appellation "son of the morning," and suggests that Satan has not always been the dark force he is now. The name *Satan* in its Greek, Latin, and Hebrew sources, means "adversary"—the perfect characterization of Satan's defining role in opposing the Father's plan of redemption and rejecting the choice of Jehovah as Redeemer from the foundations of the world. The word *devil* in its Latin and Greek etymological derivation means "slanderer"—a further characterization of the fallen angel's strategy in opposing the eternal source of truth.

The case of Satan is the most fundamental example of irony in the scriptures, for how could a being of light transform himself into the archetypal representative of darkness? The benighted personality of Satan stands in infinite contrast to the grandeur of the eternal source of light and truth, even the Father and the Son.

Satan enticed Adam and Eve to partake of the forbidden fruit, conspired with Cain to commit murder through a secret compact, motivated the building of the Tower of Babel, and spread darkness and abominations across the globe in countless other cases. Abraham was shown the premortal realm, where he saw Jesus Christ and Lucifer as the candidates for fulfilling God's plan: "And the Lord said: Whom shall I send? And one answered like unto the Son of Man: Here am I, send me. And another answered and said: Here am I, send me. And the Lord said: I will send the first. And the second was angry, and kept not his first estate; and, at that day, many followed after him" (Abraham 3:27–28). To this day the hosts of Satan—he who would usurp the honor of God (see Moses 4:1)—rage in the

cauldron of darkness that recoils from the power of the glory of heaven.

In the visions of eternity granted to the prophet Enoch, he also beheld Satan: "And he had a great chain in his hand, and it veiled the whole face of the earth with darkness; and he looked up and laughed, and his angels rejoiced" (Moses 7:26; compare also D&C 29:36; Moses 1:19; 4:1–3). The condition of those who followed Satan caused God to weep (see Moses 7:28), much to the discomfort of Enoch—until he was told the reason why: "Behold, their sins shall be upon the heads of their fathers; Satan shall be their father, and misery shall be their doom; and the whole heavens shall weep over them, even all the workmanship of mine hands; wherefore should not the heavens weep, seeing these shall suffer?" (Moses 7:37). It is the inevitable suffering of the wicked, brought about by their own choice, that causes the heavens to weep—seeing that the divine plan of the atoning sacrifice would otherwise save God's children through the grace and truth of the Almighty and the obedience and righteousness of the faithful. Ultimately, Michael (Adam) and his armies will dispel Satan and his benighted minions forever (see D&C 88:111–116).

SAUL

(Meaning: asked.)

1. Saul was one of the early kings in the lineage descending from Esau (Edom)—see Genesis 36:37–38; 1 Chronicles 1:48 (where the name is rendered *Shaul*).

2. Saul was the first king of Israel, his reign lasting from around 1095 BC to the middle of that century. His history is recorded in the

Saul is instructed by Samuel

book of 1 Samuel, this chronicle constituting the beginning of the historical account of the kings of Israel and covering the time period from the birth of Samuel to the death of Saul and his sons. The prophet Samuel had adjured the people to relent in demanding that a king be placed over them, rehearsing before them the burdens such a ruler can impose when the people choose a worldly sovereign rather than the Lord (see 1 Samuel 8:6–18; compare Mosiah 23:7; Mosiah 29:13, 16–17, 23). But when Israel rejected the Lord as their king, insisting on having a worldly king like the neighboring cultures, the Lord caused the prophet Samuel to anoint young Saul to be king of Israel. Saul had many good qualities, including (at the beginning) a humble nature. As part of Saul's transition to leadership, the Lord gave him "another heart" (1 Samuel 10:9), and the Spirit of the Lord came upon him such that he was able to prophesy, much to the astonishment of the people who heard (see chapter 10).

However, soon after assuming the role of king in Israel, Saul began to forget the Lord and arrogate to himself the abilities of righteous judgment and priesthood authority. When Samuel delayed his arrival to offer sacrifice to the Lord, Saul took it upon himself to perform the priestly duties and was rejected of the Lord as no longer "a man after his own heart" (1 Samuel 13:14). Later, Saul disobeyed the Lord by saving the spoils from the battle with the Amalekites, thus sealing his rejection by the Lord as king over Israel: "And Samuel said unto Saul, I will not return with thee: for thou hast rejected the word of the LORD, and the LORD hath rejected thee from being king over Israel" (1 Samuel 15:26). Thereafter Saul was plagued with an evil spirit not of the Lord (see 1 Samuel 16:14–23; the Joseph Smith Translation corrects the King James Version wording "the evil spirit from God" in this passage to "the evil spirit which was not of God").

Saul was an eyewitness to the process of his own dethronement: "And Saul saw and knew that the Lord was with David. . . . And Saul was yet the more afraid of David; and Saul became David's enemy continually" (18:28–29). Saul was plagued by the spirit of jealousy and continually plotted for the death of David, but David had been chosen by the Lord and thus ultimately ascended the throne of Israel.

3. Saul was the original Jewish name of the Apostle Paul in the New Testament (see Acts 13:9).

SEED OF ABRAHAM

The expression "seed of Abraham," referring to the heirs of the promises and covenants made by the Lord to the patriarch Abraham, occurs four times in the Old Testament: In the prayer of Jehoshaphat (see 2 Chronicles 20:7); in the Psalmist's counsel to seek and remember the Lord (see Psalm 105:4–6); in the words of the blessing given by Isaiah (see Isaiah 41:8); and in the assurances of the Lord as given through Jeremiah (see Jeremiah 33:25). Compare also Romans 9:7; 11:1; 2 Corinthians 11:22; Hebrews 2:16; D&C 84:34; 103:17.

Seer

The designation *seer* is used in the Old Testament a number of times in reference to various individuals: Samuel (see 1 Samuel 9:9, 19; 1 Chronicles 9:22; 26:28; 29:29), Zadok the priest (see 2 Samuel 15:27), Gad (see 2 Samuel 24:11; 2 Chronicles 29:25), Heman (see 1 Chronicles 25:5), Iddo (see 2 Chronicles 9:29; 12:15), Hanani (see 2 Chronicles 16:7, 10; 19:2), Asaph (see 2 Chronicles 29:30), Jeduthun (see 2 Chronicles 35:15), and Amos (see Amos 7:12). Enoch was also a seer (see Moses 6:36, 38).

Seir

Seir (pronounced see'-ur) was a member of the Horite tribe and one of the so-called "dukes" of Edom living in the Seir region (see Genesis 36:20, 21; 1 Chronicles 1:38).

Sennacherib

Sennacherib (pronounced suh-nak'-uh-rib) was king of Assyria in the time frame around 705–681 BC. King Hezekiah of Judah attempted to repel the dominance of Assyria, causing Sennacherib to invade Judea and take over many cities (see 2 Kings 18:13; 2 Chronicles 32:1). Hezekiah reluctantly offered a tribute to Sennacherib (see 2 Kings 18:14–16) but defied the Assyrians when they came and besieged Jerusalem. Hezekiah sent Eliakim and other representatives to the walls of the city to hear the demands of the king, as spoken by the Assyrian chief of princes, Rab-shakeh, spoken in the Hebrew language from the midst of the hosts of the Assyrian warriors: "Thus saith the king, Let not Hezekiah deceive you: for he shall not be able to deliver you out of his hand: . . . Neither let Hezekiah make you trust in the Lord" (2 Kings 18:29–30; compare 2 Kings 19:9; Isaiah 37:8–13). When Eliakim reported this to Hezekiah, the king rent his clothes in dismay and sent Eliakim and his party to the prophet Isaiah for counsel, who responded: "Thus saith the Lord, . . . Behold, I will send a blast upon him, and he shall hear a rumour,

Enoch, a prophet and seer, teaches his people

and shall return to his own land; and I will cause him to fall by the sword in his own land" (2 Kings 19:6–7).

Then Hezekiah prayed before the Lord for the deliverance of the people, and Isaiah conveyed the promise of the Lord that the king of Assyria would "not come into this city, nor shoot an arrow there" (2 Kings 19:32; see also vv. 33–34). The dramatic outcome of the conflict fulfilled prophecy: "And it came to pass that night, that the angel of the LORD went out, and smote in the camp of the Assyrians an hundred fourscore and five thousand: and when they arose early in the morning, behold, they were all dead corpses. So Sennacherib king of Assyria departed, and went and returned, and dwelt at Nineveh" (2 Kings 19:35–36; compare 2 Chronicles 32:21–22; Isaiah 37:38). Sennacherib was later murdered by two of his sons (see 2 Kings 19:37; 2 Chronicles 32:21; Isaiah 37:38) and succeeded by another son, Esarhaddon.

SERAPHIM(S)

The word *seraphims* is used only twice in the Old Testament—both times in connection with the vision of Isaiah on the occasion of his being called as a prophet (see Isaiah 6:2, 6; compare the equivalent passages in 2 Nephi 16:2, 6, where the word is rendered as *seraphim*). Apparently these are angelic beings in the court of the Lord depicted in symbolic representation as having the capacity to fly (hence winged) and the commission to administer rites of purification (see Isaiah 6:6–8).

SETH

Seth was a son of Adam and Eve. According to the biblical account, his mother "called his name Seth: For God, said she, hath appointed me another seed instead of Abel, whom Cain slew" (Genesis 4:25; compare Moses 6:2, where it is stated that Adam named his son Seth). Seth was "in his [Adam's] own likeness, after his image" (Genesis 5:3). Seth, who lived 912 years, was the father of Enos as well as other sons and daughters (see Genesis 5:6–8; Luke 3:38; Moses 6:16). Like Abel, Seth offered an acceptable sacrifice to the Lord (see Moses 6:3). From latter-day scripture we gain a fuller understanding of Seth:

> From Adam to Seth, who was ordained by Adam at the age of sixty-nine years, and was blessed by him three years previous to his (Adam's) death, and received the promise of God by his father, that his posterity should be the chosen of the Lord, and that they should be preserved unto the end of the earth;
>
> Because he (Seth) was a perfect man, and his likeness was the express likeness of his father, insomuch that he seemed to be like unto his father in all things, and could be distinguished from him only by his age. (D&C 107:41–43; see also D&C 107:51, 53)

Seth is also mentioned as one of the noble personages viewed by President Joseph F. Smith in his vision of the spirit realm (see D&C 138:40).

SHADRACH

Shadrach (pronounced shad'-rak) was a

Daniel refuses the king's meat and wine on behalf of Shadrach, Meshach, and Abed-nego

Jewish youth captured along with Daniel and several others (including Azariah and Mishael) by the forces of the Babylonian king Nebuchadnezzar and taken to Babylon to the palace of the king on the eve of the conquest of Jerusalem around 587 BC (see Daniel 1:6–7). His real name was Hananiah, but he was given the name *Shadrach* by the prince of the eunuchs (v. 7). Daniel, Shadrach, Mishael (now called Meshach), and Azariah (now called Abed-nego) refused to eat the rich foods of the court and instead sustained themselves on "pulse" (seeds and vegetables). After ten days, the four appeared healthier than the children who had eaten the rich food, and the king discovered that they were also wiser than his own magicians and astrologers (see vv. 15, 20). When Daniel pleased the king with his power to interpret dreams, he and his three associates were given leadership positions in the realm (see 2:49).

Later, when Shadrach, Meshach, and Abed-nego refused to comply with the king's command to worship his golden idol (see 3:17–18), the enraged king caused the three to be cast into a fiery furnace. However, they were not consumed, being ministered to by one "like the Son of God" (v. 25). After this miracle, the king promoted the three young men to higher stations of prominence in the realm and decreed that no one was to speak ill of their God (see vv. 24–30).

SHALLUM

1. Shallum (pronounced shal'-um), son of Jabesh, assassinated King Zachariah of Israel and ruled in his stead for one month until he, too, was deposed and died at the hand of Menahem, son of Gadi (see 2 Kings 15:10–15).

2. Shallum was the husband of Huldah, the prophetess, during the days of King Josiah of Judah (see 2 Kings 22:14).

3. Shallum was the fourth son of King Josiah of Judah and his successor on the throne for a period of three months (see 1 Chronicles 3:15; Jeremiah 22:11). (He is called *Jehoahaz* in 2 Kings 23:30 and 2 Chronicles 36:1.)

4. Shallum is the name of various other individuals mentioned in the Old Testament (see 1 Chronicles 4:25; 6:12–13; 7:13; 9:17, 19, 31; 2 Chronicles 28:12; Ezra 2:42; 7:2; 10:24, 42; Nehemiah 3:12; 7:45; Jeremiah 32:7; 35:4).

SHALMANESER

Shalmaneser (pronounced shal'-muhn-ee'-zuhr) was king of Assyria in the time frame around 727–722 BC. He made Israel under King Hoshea a tributary domain, but when Hoshea failed to deliver and instead approached So, king of Egypt, to cultivate an alliance, Shalmaneser took dramatic action by imprisoning Hoshea and taking the ten tribes of the Northern Kingdom captive to Assyria around 722–721 BC (see 2 Kings 17:4–8; 18:9–12).

SHEBA

1. Sheba was the son of Raamah, who was the son of Cush, the son of Ham (see Genesis 10:7; 1 Chronicles 1:9).

2. Sheba was the son of Joktan, a descendant of Shem (see Genesis 10:28; 1 Chronicles 1:22).

3. Sheba was the son of Jokshan, son of Abraham and Keturah (see Genesis 25:3).

4. Sheba, the queen of—see *Queen of Sheba*.

5. Sheba, son of Bichri the Benjamite, instigated a revolt against David. The revolt was put down by Joab and consummated when a loyal woman of the city where Sheba was hiding arranged for his beheading in order to spare the besieged city from harm (see 2 Samuel 20:1–22).

SHECHEM

Shechem (pronounced shee'-kem or shee'-kuhm), son of Hamor, was a Hivite who fell in love with Dinah, daughter of Jacob, and defiled her. In response, Levi and Simeon (sons of Jacob) removed Dinah and initiated a callous campaign of vengeance against the Hivite community, killing all of the males and despoiling the city (see Genesis 34). When

Jacob learned of their actions, he was greatly distressed and gathered his people together and moved away to Bethel at the command of God (see Genesis 34:30; 35:1–5).

SHEM

(Meaning: name.) Shem is the first mentioned of Noah's three sons (see Genesis 5:32; 6:10; 1 Chronicles 1:4) but was in fact the middle child (see Moses 8:12). Shem and his wife were two of the eight individuals who embarked on the ark (see Genesis 7:13; compare Genesis 9:18, 26). The descendants of Shem are listed in the scriptural text (see Genesis 10:21–31; 11:10–27, 1 Chronicles 1:17–28) and include Abram (later named Abraham). Shem is traditionally considered to be the ancestor of the Semitic races, including the Hebrews, Phoenicians, Arabs, Aramaeans (or Syrians), Babylonians, and Assyrians.

Shem is mentioned in the Doctrine and Covenants as a "great high priest" (138:41) who is carrying on the work of salvation in the spirit world. Shem was a righteous man (see Moses 8:27; compare Genesis 9:18–27, where Shem and Japheth are commended for having better judgment than Ham on the occasion of an incident where their father was incapacitated), who is listed in the genealogy of Jesus Christ as *Sem* (see Luke 3:36).

SHEMAIAH

(Meaning: the Lord heareth.)

1. Shemaiah (pronounced shem-y'-uh) was a prophet who admonished Rehoboam, king of Judah, not to rise up against the northern tribes, though they had defied the heavy tax burden imposed by the regime of Solomon and continued by Rehoboam, his son and successor

(see 1 Kings 12:22–24; compare 2 Chronicles 11:2–4). Rehoboam heeded the counsel, but his power was greatly weakened not long thereafter as a result of an invasion by the Egyptians under Shishak, king of Egypt—something else Shemaiah had warned him about (see 1 Kings 14:25–31; 2 Chronicles 12:5–12, 15).

2. Shemaiah was the name of a great many other individuals mentioned in the Old Testament (see 1 Chronicles 3:22; 4:37; 5:4; 9:14, 16; 15:8, 11; 24:6; 26:4, 6–7; 2 Chronicles 17:8; 29:14; 31:15; 35:9; Ezra 8:13, 16; 10:21, 31; Nehemiah 3:29; 6:10; 10:8; 11:15; 12:6, 18, 34–36, 42; Jeremiah 26:20).

3. Shemaiah was a false prophet in the days of Jeremiah who attempted to usurp power and undermine the cause of the Lord at the time of the Babylonian captivity (see Jeremiah 29:24). As a lesson to all who pridefully arrogate authority to themselves without any divine commission, Shemaiah was sternly reproved by the Lord through Jeremiah (see Jeremiah 29:31–32).

SHIMEI

1. Shimei (pronounced shim'-ee-y) was the son of Gershon of the tribe of Levi (see Numbers 3:18; 1 Chronicles 6:17; referred to as *Shimi* in Exodus 6:17).

2. Shimei, son of Gera, was a Benjamite of the house of Saul who actively and aggressively opposed David during the uprising of Absalom (see 2 Samuel 16:5–8). Following the defeat and death of Absalom (18:15), Shimei came back with a host of his colleagues to demonstrate his subservient contrition before David (see 19:19–20), who magnanimously pardoned

Shimei journeys away from Jerusalem

him (see 19:21–23) but warned Solomon of the man's duplicity (see 1 Kings 2:9). When Shimei violated an oath not to journey away from Jerusalem, King Solomon ordered his execution (see 1 Kings 2:36–46).

3. Shimei was one of David's loyal supporters who opposed the attempted seizure of the throne by Adonijah, David's son (see 1 Kings 1:8; possibly the same as the Shimei of Solomon's court mentioned in 1 Kings 4:18).

4. Shimei was the name of other individuals in the Old Testament record (see 1 Chronicles 3:19; 4:26–27; 5:4; 23:7–10; 25:17; 27:27; 2 Chronicles 29:14; 31:12–13; Ezra 10:23, 33, 38; Esther 2:5; Zechariah 12:13).

SHISHAK

Shishak (pronounced shy'-shak) was the king of Egypt to whom Jeroboam fled to escape the sword of Solomon until Solomon's death (see 1 Kings 11:40), after which Jeroboam was elevated to the throne of the northern kingdom of Israel (see 1 Kings 12:20). Later, in the fifth year of the reign of Rehoboam, successor to Solomon, the Lord allowed Shishak to invade and subjugate the southern kingdom because of the lack of full devotion on the part of the princes of Israel (see 2 Chronicles 12:5–9; see also 1 Kings 14:25–28).

SIDON

Sidon (pronounced sy'-duhn) was the first-born son of Canaan, son of Ham (see Genesis 10:15; called Zidon in 1 Chronicles 1:13). Sidon (Zidon) was also the name of a Phoenician coastal city (located south of Beirut in modern Lebanon).

SIHON

Sihon (pronounced sy'-hahn) was king of the Amorites. When he refused to allow the Israelites to pass through his land and instead rose up in battle against them, Moses and his armies defeated the Amorites decisively and possessed their territory (see Numbers 21:21–35). This triumph over the enemy became an ensign of God's power of deliverance for generations (see Deuteronomy 1:4; 2:26–32; 3:2, 6; 29:7; 31:4; Joshua 2:10; 9:10; 12:2, 5; 13:10, 21, 27; Judges 11:19–21; 1 Kings 4:19; Nehemiah 9:22; Psalm 135:11; 136:19; Jeremiah 48:45).

SIMEON

(Meaning: that hears.) Simeon was the second son of Jacob by his wife Leah (see Genesis 29:33; 35:23; Exodus 1:2). Simeon and Levi inflicted drastic retribution on the Shechemites for the mistreatment of their sister Dinah (see Genesis 34; see also *Dinah*).

Simeon also figures into the dramatic encounter between Joseph of Egypt and his brothers. The brothers had sold Joseph into slavery years earlier, but now came to Egypt appealing for provisions during the famine in Canaan. Simeon was retained by Joseph (still not recognized by his brothers) as hostage collateral to guarantee the delivery of the youngest brother, Benjamin. Simeon was released when Benjamin was brought to Egypt, and all the brothers were reconciled (see Genesis 42:24, 36; 43:23).

The last pronouncement of Jacob (Israel) upon the head of Simeon and Levi recounted the cruelty against the Shechemites and promised division and scattering (see Genesis 49:5–7). The inheritance of the tribe of Simeon in the promised land is indicated in Joshua 19:1–9 and 1 Chronicles 4:24–33.

SISERA

Sisera (pronounced sis'-uh-ruh) was the captain of the army of Jabin, king of Canaan, during the time of Deborah—who commissioned Barak, the son of Abinoam, to wage battle against the encroaching Canaanites. Barak agreed to gather the forces and attack, provided Deborah would consent to accompany him. That she did, saying: "Up; for this is the day in which the LORD hath delivered Sisera into thine hand: is not the LORD gone out before thee?" (Judges 4:14). That day the Canaanites, with their much larger force, were annihilated, along with Jabin, their king (see vv. 23–24). Sisera fled to the house of Heber the Kenite (a supposed ally), whose wife Jael strategically extended hospitality to him but then slew him as he was sleeping (see vv. 18–22). Thereafter Deborah and Barak joined in singing a glorious anthem of praise to the Lord in which the memory of the notorious Sisera is repeatedly invoked (see Judges 5:20, 26, 28, 30; see also the additional references in Ezra 2:53; Nehemiah 7:55; Psalm 83:9).

SOLOMON

(Meaning: peaceable.) Solomon, son of David and Bathsheba, was the successor to David on the throne of Israel, reigning from around 1015 BC until his death around 975 BC. The story of Solomon is presented in chapters 1 through 11 of 1 Kings. He is well known for his wisdom, the temple he built, his great wealth, and his many wives and concubines.

Solomon is most revered for two things: his wisdom and his building of the Lord's temple.

THE WISDOM OF SOLOMON. We read: "And Solomon loved the Lord, walking in the statutes of David his father" (1 Kings 3:3). Consequently, Solomon received "a wise and an understanding heart" from the Lord (v. 12). "And there came of all people to hear the wisdom of Solomon, from all kings of the earth, which had heard of his wisdom" (1 Kings 4:34). The book of Proverbs was authored by Solomon and successors who imitated his craft. Proverbs is one of the eleven books of the Old Testament that belong to the Hagiographa ("sacred writings") of the Jewish canon.

Solomon was enormously prolific: "And he spake three thousand proverbs: and his songs were a thousand and five" (1 Kings 4:32). He is also considered traditionally to be the author of Ecclesiastes; however, the writing of Ecclesiastes appears to have occurred much later (in the time frame from around 300–250 BC). The proverbs of Solomon (together with the pronouncements of the "Preacher" in the book of Ecclesiastes) include a veritable garden of wisdom in the form of cogent maxims, exhortations, and poems for governing one's life. It is doubtful that Solomon authored the Song of Solomon, an allegory about God's love for Israel. The Joseph Smith Translation man-

King Solomon petitions the Lord in prayer

uscript contained the statement that "the Song of Solomon is not inspired scripture" (see Bible Dictionary, *Song of Solomon*).

There are, in general, four principal themes running through the Proverbs: 1) Trusting in God is the foundation of wisdom: "The fear of the Lord is the beginning of wisdom" (Proverbs 1:7; compare Proverbs 9:10); 2) A willingness to be entreated is the key to cultivating wisdom: "For whom the Lord loveth he correcteth; even as a father the son in whom he delighteth" (Proverbs 3:12); 3) The flowering of wisdom is to bring forth good fruit unto the Lord: "Wisdom is the principal thing; therefore get wisdom: and with all thy getting get understanding" (Proverbs 4:7); and 4) Pride leads to folly: "Pride goeth before destruction, and a haughty spirit before a fall" (Proverbs 16:18).

In the course of his own life, as it turned out, Solomon was rather better at conveying wisdom than in becoming its leading practitioner. Despite his enormous wisdom,

Solomon eventually allowed his interests to shift unwisely to behaviors that violated his sacred trust, for he married outside Israel and his heart turned to idolatry (see 1 Kings 11).

BUILDING THE TEMPLE. The Lord had promised David that his son would build a house to the Lord (see 1 Kings 5:5). Solomon followed through with this project and erected a magnificent temple complex for sacred worship. The dedicatory program (see 1 Kings 8) was replete with utterances importuning the Lord to accept His people as His own and prosper their way as long as they heeded His word and kept His commandments, looking toward the temple as a continual reminder of their covenant commitments. The temple edifice became renowned throughout the region, and rulers and potentates came from all around to admire it and bask in the opulence and wisdom of Solomon's court.

The temple was made from wood, stone, gold, and other precious materials, using meticulous craftsmanship, and included a baptismal font upheld by twelve oxen. The inner sanctuary, the Holy of Holies, housed the ark of the covenant. The construction took seven long years. When Solomon dedicated the temple to the Lord as His dwelling place, he also sought forgiveness for his people. The Lord accepted the temple and encouraged the people to keep His commandments (see 1 Kings 9:3–4).

The resurrected Savior refers to Solomon in teaching the Saints in Bountiful the essence of the Sermon on the Mount: "And why take ye thought for raiment? Consider the lilies of the field how they grow; they toil not, neither do they spin; And yet I say unto you, that even Solomon, in all his glory, was not arrayed like one of these" (3 Nephi 13:28–29; compare Matthew 6:28–29; 12:42; Luke 12:27). Solomon is mentioned several other times in the Book of Mormon. Nephi invokes the name of Solomon in one passage concerning the temple (see 2 Nephi 5:16). In his address on the need to embrace the high moral ground, Jacob also refers to Solomon in relation to his immoral practices in later life (see Jacob 1:15; 2:23, 24).

SONS OF AARON

The expression "sons of Aaron" is used fairly frequently in the Old Testament in connection with the priesthood commission given to the descendants of Aaron (for example, Leviticus 1:7; 3:13; 21:1; Numbers 10:8; 1 Chronicles 23:32; 2 Chronicles 13:9–10; 35:14). The sons of Aaron over the generations provided services associated with sacred rites of sacrifice and worship. (See also D&C 68:15–16; 84:31–34.)

SONS OF GOD

The expression *sons of God* generally refers to those who accept the gospel of Christ and heed the Spirit of God (see John 1:12; Romans 8:14; Moroni 7:26). The most celebrated reference to "sons of God" in the Old Testament is found in Job, when the Lord is speaking to Job about the gospel plan as presented in the premortal realm: "Where wast thou when I laid the foundations of the earth? . . . When the morning stars sang together, and all the sons of God shouted for joy?" (Job 38:4, 7; see also Job 1:6; 2:1). Moses 8:13 indicates, "And Noah and his sons hearkened unto the Lord, and gave heed, and they were called the sons of God."

SONS OF JACOB

The expression *sons of Jacob* is used in the Old Testament in reference to the first-generation offspring of Jacob (Israel)—the twelve men who became heads of the tribes of Israel (see Genesis 35:22–26; Genesis 49:2; 1 Kings 18:31). The expression *sons of Jacob* is also used on occasion to denote the people of Israel in general (see Psalm 77:15; Malachi 3:6; compare 3 Nephi 24:6; D&C 109:58).

SONS OF LEVI

The expression *sons of Levi* is used occasionally in the Old Testament in connection with the priesthood commission given to the descendants of Levi (Aaron being the first appointed) in connection with assisting in the work of the sacred rites of sacrifice and worship. For example: "And the priests the sons of Levi shall come near; for them the LORD thy God hath chosen to minister unto him, and to bless in the name of the LORD" (Deuteronomy 21:5; see also Deuteronomy 31:9; 1 Chronicles 23:24; Nehemiah 12:23; Ezekiel 40:46; Malachi 3:3; 3 Nephi 24:3; Hebrews 7:5). *See Levi.*

From the Doctrine and Covenants we gain additional understanding about the commission of the sons of Levi. When John the Baptist restored the Aaronic Priesthood on May 15, 1829, he declared to Joseph Smith and Oliver Cowdery, "UPON you my fellow servants, in the name of Messiah I confer the Priesthood of Aaron, which holds the keys of the ministering of angels, and of the gospel of repentance, and of baptism by immersion for the remission of sins; and this shall never be taken again from the earth, until the sons of Levi do offer again an offering unto the Lord

Sons of Levi work in the temple

in righteousness" (D&C 13:1). The expression *sons of Levi* occurs two other times in the Doctrine and Covenants—once in connection with "the sacrifices by the sons of Levi" associated with temple work (see D&C 124:39), and another time in connection with the process of purification required of those who provide leadership for temple work (see D&C 128:24; also JS–H 1:69).

SONS OF MEN

The expression *sons of men* is used pervasively in the Old Testament and other standard works to denote mortals in general.

SONS OF MOSES

The expression *sons of Moses* is used only once in the Old Testament, in connection with the two actual sons of Moses, Gershom and Eliezer (see 1 Chronicles 23:15). However, the expression *sons of Moses* is used in the Doctrine and Covenants as a general designation for worthy priesthood holders in the kingdom of God (see 84:6, 31–34).

SOOTHSAYER(S)

Soothsayer is a designation for a diviner who claims the ability to predict the future. The word *soothsayer* is used in connection with the demise of Balaam (see Joshua 13:22). The word *soothsayers* is used elsewhere in the Old Testament, always in a pejorative sense (see Isaiah 2:6; Daniel 2:27; 4:7; 5:7, 11; Micah 5:12).

SORCERER(S)

A sorcerer is one who claims the power to foretell future events, such as the sorcerers at the court of Pharaoh during the days of Moses (see Exodus 7:11) or those during the days of Jeremiah, who gave counsel in opposition to the word of the Lord (see Jeremiah 27:9). Sorcerers were active during the days of Daniel, attempting without success to interpret the dreams of Nebuchadnezzar (see Daniel 2:2). Malachi prophesies divine judgment against sorcerers and other evil-doers (see Malachi 3:5; compare 3 Nephi 24:5; also Revelation 21:8; 22:15; D&C 76:103).

SPIRIT OF GOD (SEE HOLY GHOST)

SPIRIT OF THE LORD (SEE HOLY GHOST)

STEM OF JESSE (SEE JESSE)

STRANGER

The term *stranger* can refer to an unknown person, but most generally means foreigner or outsider. It could relate to a person of Israelite extraction coming into a non-Israelite environment (such as Abraham in Canaan or the Israelites in Egypt)—or the opposite: those of non-Israelite extraction living among the Israelites. In the latter case there were protocols in the law concerning how to integrate such people in authorized and accommodating ways (see, for example, Exodus 12:19, 48–49; 20:10; Leviticus 16:29; 17:8–15; Numbers 9:14; 15:14–30; Deuteronomy 1:16; 10:19; 14:21). Although there were cautions (and even prohibitions) regarding mixing or intermarrying (to avoid adopting heathen ways), much counsel was peaceable, such as the following: "Love ye therefore the stranger: for ye were strangers in the land of Egypt" (Deuteronomy 10:19; compare Matthew 25:35).

SUCCOTH-BENOTH

Succoth-benoth (pronounced sook'-oth-be-nohth') was a female idol worshipped by Babylonian colonists who occupied Samaria following the captivity of the ten tribes by the Assyrian kings (see 2 Kings 17:30).

SUSANCHITES

The Susanchites (mentioned in Ezra 4:9) were settlers in Samaria (an area about 30 miles north of Jerusalem) who—along with eight other confederate groups—opposed the rebuilding of Jerusalem and the temple following the Babylonian conquest (see Ezra 4:11–14).

Syrians

The Syrians were a people of Semitic origin (see Genesis 10:22; 22:21) living in the ancient realm of Syria, north and northeast of Palestine, originally called "Aram," meaning highlands (see, for example, Numbers 23:7)—hence the term *Aramaeans* is a general equivalent to the term *Syrians*. Aramaic became the language of diplomatic communication in the days of Hezekiah and gradually became the language of daily life among the Jewish people, thus the native language spoken by Jesus. The Syrians (or Aramaeans) were generally rivals of Israel (see, for example, 2 Samuel 8:3–6; 1 Kings 11:23–25; 15:18; 20:34; 22; 2 Kings 6:24 to 7:20; 8:28–29). *See also Aram.*

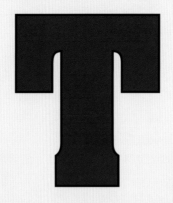

TABEAL

Tabeal (pronounced tab'-ee-uhl) was a man whose son the king of Israel (Pekah)—in league with the king of Syria (Rezin)—wanted to place on the throne of Judah during the reign of Ahaz, king of Judah (see Isaiah 7:6; compare 2 Nephi 17:6; see also 2 Kings 15:37; 16:5; 2 Chronicles 28:6). King Ahaz induced the Assyrians to advance on Damascus, causing Rezin to return to his own domain. Damascus fell and Rezin was slain (see 2 Kings 16:9). Nothing more of Tabeal or his son is known.

TAMMUZ

Tammuz (pronounced tam'-uhs), equivalent to the Greek god Adonis, was a Babylonian deity invoked in the autumn in a ceremonial lament over the seasonal decline of vegetation. In vision, the prophet Ezekiel was shown manifestations of idolatry among the people in Jerusalem, who, among other evils, participated in the process of "weeping for Tammuz"—something done by women near the gate of the Lord's house (see Ezekiel 8:14—the only specific reference to this idol in the scriptures).

TERAH

Terah (pronounced ter'-uh), the father of Abram (later Abraham—see Genesis 11:25–26), is included among those who "served other gods" (Joshua 24:2). He and his family circle (including Abram, Sarai, and Lot—son of Haran) left Ur of the Chaldees en route to Canaan, abiding for a time in Haran, where Terah eventually passed away (see Genesis 11:31–32). More detail on Terah's idolatrous practices, which endangered the life of Abraham in Ur, is given in the Pearl of Great Price (see Abraham 1:5–6, 15–20, 30; 2:5).

TIGLATH-PILESER

Tiglath-pileser (pronounced tig'-lath-puh-lee'-zuhr) was king of Assyria in the time frame from around 747 to 734 BC. When Ahaz ascended the throne in Judah, he reached out to Tiglath-pileser to counter the conspiracy of Pekah, king of Israel, and Rezin, king of Syria, against Judah (see 2 Kings 16:7). Subsequently, Tiglath-pileser put Rezin to death and carried many inhabitants of Pekah's realm—the tribe of Reuben, the tribe of Gad, and half the tribe of Manasseh—into captivity (see 2 Kings 15:29; 16:5–9; compare 1 Chronicles 5:26, where the name is spelled *Tilgath-pilneser*; also 2 Chronicles 28:20) before being succeeded by Shalmaneser.

Tirshatha

Tirshatha (pronounced tir-shay'-thah) was an administrative title of Persian origin applied to one appointed as a governor over an area, such as Zerubbabel (in relation to Judea—see Ezra 2:63; Nehemiah 7:65, 70) or Nehemiah (see Nehemiah 8:9; 10:1).

Uriah

Uriah (pronounced yoo-ry'-uh) was husband of Bathsheba and a Hittite warrior in the army of King David (see 2 Samuel 11). At the time of Israel's successful battle against the Ammonites, David remained in Jerusalem. Having observed Bathsheba from the roof of his residence, David desired her and followed through with an immoral relationship that resulted in Bathsheba's pregnancy (see vv. 2–5). He then attempted to cover up his sin by sending for Uriah to return home to his wife, Bathsheba, in hopes the child's paternity would thus not be called into question. But out of solemn duty to his military commission, Uriah demurred to go in to Bathsheba (see v. 11). Thereupon David compounded his own guilt by arranging through Joab, his commander, to send Uriah to the front lines, where his death was assured. Uriah did indeed perish (v. 21). The Lord placed a heavy judgment on David for his sins in the matter (see 2 Samuel 21:9–10; D&C 132:39). *See also David and Bathsheba.*

Uzzah

(Meaning: strength.) Uzzah (pronounced ooz'-uh) was one of the sons of Abinadab, a Levite at whose house at Kirjath-jearim, located a short distance west of Jerusalem, the ark of the covenant was kept after it was retrieved from Philistine hands (see 1 Samuel 7:1–2). David directed that the ark should be removed from the house of Abinadab and brought forth to be returned to Jerusalem (see 2 Samuel 6:1–4; 1 Chronicles 13:7). During the procedure, Uzzah, reaching out to steady the ark when the oxen's movement shook it, was smitten of the Lord for having violated the long-standing commandment against touching the ark (see 2 Samuel 6:6–7, 8–12; Numbers 4:15).

Uzziah

(Meaning: strength of the Lord.) Uzziah (pronounced uh-zy'uh), son of Amaziah, was a righteous king of Judah whose rule commenced around the turn of the eighth century B.C. at the time of Isaiah, Hosea, and Amos (see 2 Chronicles 26:1–5; compare 2 Kings 14:21–22, where he is called *Azariah*; Isaiah

1:1, 6:1; Hosea 1:1; Amos 1:1). The king accomplished much good for Israel, defeating the Philistines and the Arabians, making tributary vassals of the Ammonites, fortifying Jerusalem, making great advances in farming and cattle-raising, and devising innovative weapons of defense (see 2 Chronicles 26:6–14)—all this elevating his reputation and renown as far away as Egypt (see v. 15). Later he was stricken permanently with leprosy when he took it upon himself to administer the priestly sacramental rites in the temple (see v. 16), thus leaving his son Jotham to perform his kingly duties (see v. 21; compare 2 Kings 15:5).

Uzziah is punished for his pride

Vashti

(Meaning: beautiful.) Vashti (pronounced vash'-ty) was the wife of Ahasuerus (see Esther 1–2), king of Persia, usually identified with Xerxes, whose rule began around 486 BC. Vashti was disobedient to the commands of the king and was therefore deposed (see Esther 1:9–21; Esther 2:1–5). The king chose Esther to be his new queen (see Esther 2:17). *See Esther.*

ZACHARIAH

(Meaning: the Lord hath remembered.)

1. Zachariah (pronounced zack'-uh-ry'-uh) succeeded his father Jeroboam as king of Israel after an interregnum period of a few years (see 2 Kings 14:29). He reigned six months in wickedness, following the pattern of his father, before he was deposed and killed by Shallum, son of Jabesh (see 15:8–12). Zachariah's reign fulfilled the word of the Lord unto Jehu, Zachariah's progenitor, since Jehu had been told his descendants would be kings over Israel for four more generations (see 10:30; 15:12). Preceded by Jehoahaz, Jehoash, and Jeroboam, Zachariah was the last of the kings in the line of Jehu.

2. Zachariah was the father of Abi, who was the mother of Hezekiah (see 2 Kings 18:2; compare 2 Chronicles 29:1, where the names are given as *Abijah* and *Zechariah*).

ZADOK

(Meaning: righteous.)

1. Zadok (pronounced zay'-dock) was a leading priest at the time of David (see 2 Samuel 8:17; 1 Chronicles 16:39) and a descendant in the line of priests stemming from Eleazar, son of Aaron (1 Chronicles 6:4–8; 24:3). The other leading priest during this time was Abiathar, of the line of descent from Ithamar, brother of Eleazar, through Eli (see 1 Samuel 23:6, 9; 30:7). Along with Abiathar, Zadok took the ark to Jerusalem according to the command of David, newly anointed king of Israel (see 1 Chronicles 15:11–12; 2 Samuel 15:24–36). When Adonijah, fourth son of David, rose up

Zadok anoints Solomon king

185

and aspired to become king in the place of his aging father, Abiathar supported him as successor to the king, rather than Solomon (see 1 Kings 1:7).

In contrast, Zadok remained faithful to the cause of David, who had named Solomon as his successor. When Adonijah claimed the throne (sometime in the period 1026–1015 BC) and engaged in a banquet of celebration with his confederates (see 1 Kings 1:17–18). David intervened (see vv. 11–37), ordering the immediate installation of Solomon: "And Zadok the priest took an horn of oil out of the Tabernacle, and anointed Solomon. And they blew the trumpet; and all the people said, God save king Solomon" (1:39). After Adonijah and his banquet guests had fled in horror, Solomon, the new king, was left to decide on their fate. In due course, Adonijah was put to death as a schemer; Abiathar was stripped of his priestly authority and exiled, putting an end to the priestly service of the line descending from Eli (see 1 Kings 2:26–27; compare 1 Samuel 2:31–35); and Zadok was made chief priest (see 1 Kings 2:34–35; 1 Chronicles 29:22; Ezekiel 40:46; 43:19; 44:15; 48:11—the references in 1 Chronicles 6:12; 9:11; and Nehemiah 11:11 likely also refer to this Zadok).

2. Zadok was the father of Jerusha (or Jerushah), mother of King Jotham of Judah (see 2 Kings 15:33; 2 Chronicles 27:1).

3. Zadok was one of David's mighty men (see 1 Chronicles 12:28).

4. Zadok, the son of Baana, helped repair the walls of Jerusalem after the return from the Babylonian captivity (see Nehemiah 3:4).

5. Zadok, the son of Immer, also helped repair the walls of Jerusalem after the return from the Babylonian captivity (see Nehemiah 3:29).

6. Zadok was mentioned as a scribe at the time of Nehemiah (see Nehemiah 13:13).

ZAMZUMMIMS (SEE ANAK/ANAKIM(S) AND EMIMS)

ZAPHNATH-PAANEAH

Zaphnath-paaneah (pronounced perhaps zaf'-nath-pah-ah-nee'-uh) was a name given to Joseph by the pharaoh (see Genesis 41:45). The meaning of the name is uncertain.

ZAREPHATH, WIDOW OF (SEE ELIJAH)

ZEBULUN

Zebulun (pronounced zeb'-yuh-lun) was a son born to Leah and Jacob (see Genesis 30:20; 35:23). The blessing pronounced on him by Jacob is found in Genesis 49:13. See also Moses' blessing on his tribe (see Deuteronomy 33:18) and the allocation of his tribe's inheritance (see Joshua 19:10–16, 27, 34). The tribe of Zebulon was generally steady and valiant in supporting the cause of the Lord over the years as in assisting (along with Naphtali) in achieving the victory against the Canaanites during the days of Deborah and Barak (see Judges 4:6, 10; 5:14, 18), contributing one of the judges in Israel (named Elon—see Judges 12:11–12), assisting Gideon in defeating the Midianites (see Judges 6:35), contributing considerable strength to the forces of David (see 1 Chronicles 12:33), and being among the minorities supporting King Hezekiah when he restored the practice of the Passover in Jerusalem (see 2 Chronicles 30:10–18).

ZECHARIAH

1. Zechariah (pronounced zeck'-uh-ry'-uh), son of Berechiah, the son of Iddo, prophesied in the days of Darius I (in the time frame around 520–518 BC—see Nehemiah 12:4, 16; Zechariah 1:1, 7; 7:1, 8). He was a contemporary of the prophet Haggai (see Ezra 5:1; 6:14). The book of Zechariah was written shortly after the return of Judah from exile in Babylon under the authority of Cyrus.

The book of Zechariah beautifully unfolds the vision of the Lord's plan of salvation for His people, symbolically using (as did Isaiah) contemporary events to capture the scope and grandeur of the ultimate restoration and sublimation of Israel's faithful at the Second Coming. In broad contours, the book deals with visions concerning the future of the chosen people of the Lord (chapters 1–8) and additional prophecies concerning the unfolding of the Lord's plan for defeating the wicked and sustaining and redeeming the righteous in the final days (chapters 9–14).

2. Zechariah was the son (or perhaps grandson) of Jehoiada, the high priest who was instrumental in the overthrow of wicked Queen Athaliah, daughter of Ahab (king of Israel in the days of Elijah) and successor to her son Ahaziah, king of Judah.

Queen Athaliah's successor, King Joash (or Jehoash), worked with Jehoiada diligently to repair and restore the house of the Lord (see 2 Chronicles 24:1–14). However, after the death of Jehoiada, the king submitted to the demands of the princes of the land to turn away from the house of the Lord and return to idolatry (see vv. 18–19). Zechariah then took courageous action, and called the people to repentance (see v. 20). At the command of the king, the people stoned Zechariah to death (see vv. 21–22).

Just as Zechariah prophesied, because the people had forsaken the Lord, He forsook them (see v. 20): the Syrians invaded Judea before the end of the year and destroyed all the princes of the realm, taking a great spoil from the people and leaving Joash in a diseased state. He was subsequently slain in his bed by his own servants, who were distressed over the killing of the righteous, such as Zechariah. The king was then buried in Jerusalem but denied burial in the sepulchre of the kings (see 2 Chronicles 24:24–27).

3. Zechariah was a prophet during the days of Uzziah, king of Judah: "And he [Uzziah] sought God in the days of Zechariah, who had understanding in the visions of God: and as long as he sought the Lord, God made him to prosper" (2 Chronicles 26:5).

4. Zechariah was the father of Abijah, who was the mother of Hezekiah (see 2 Chronicles 29:1; compare 2 Kings 18:2, where the names are given as *Abi* and *Zachariah*).

5. Zechariah was mentioned once by the prophet Isaiah: "And I took unto me faithful witnesses to record, Uriah the priest, and Zechariah the son of Jeberechiah" (Isaiah 8:2; compare 2 Nephi 18:2). Nothing more of this Zechariah is given in the scriptures. The prophet of the same name—author of the book of Zechariah—was active in the time frame 520–518 BC, long after the tenure of the prophet Isaiah (740–701 BC).

6. Zechariah is the name of many other individuals in the Old Testament (see 1 Chronicles 5:7; 9:21, 37; 15:18, 20, 24; 16:5; 24:20; 26:2,11, 14; 27:21; 2 Chronicles 17:7; 20:14; 21:2; 29:13; 34:12; 35:8; Ezra 8:3, 11,

16; 10:26; Nehemiah 8:4; 11:4, 5, 12; 12:16, 35, 41).

ZEDEKIAH

(Meaning: the Lord is righteousness.) Zedekiah (pronounced zed'-uh-ky'-uh), originally named Mattaniah (see 2 Kings 24:17), was the last king of Judah. He was "one and twenty years old when he began to reign, and reigned eleven years in Jerusalem" (2 Chronicles 36:11). Nephi informs us that it was during the first year of Zedekiah's rule that Lehi was called to warn the people of Jerusalem about the impending judgments of God about to befall them (see 2 Nephi 1:4). Zedekiah's tenure ended with the Babylonian conquest of Jerusalem around 587 BC (see Jeremiah 52:10–11; compare 2 Kings 25:7). The implication is that all the sons of

The Babylonian conquest of Jerusalem

Zedekiah perished; however, the Book of Mormon makes clear that Zedekiah's youngest son, Mulek, survived the ordeal and was guided by the Lord to the promised land, where he established a colony and founded a new nation (see Helaman 8:21). When the Nephite leader Mosiah I was commanded of the Lord to flee from the land south (the land of Lehi, also called the land of Nephi) sometime in the period 279–130 BC, he and his loyal followers were guided northward to Zarahemla, where the Mulekites had eventually settled (see Omni 1:12–16). Thereafter the Mulekites and the Nephites were united as one nation.

ZEPHANIAH

(Meaning: the Lord hides.)

1. Zephaniah (pronounced zef'-uh-ny'-uh) was a prophet of the Lord during the reign of Josiah, king of Judah (around 640–608 BC), hence contemporary with Jeremiah and Daniel (as well as Lehi). The purpose of the book of Zephaniah is to proclaim severe judgments against the unrighteous and to confirm hope and joy for the righteous at the Second Coming. In broad contours, the book covers the judgments of the Lord that are to be poured out upon an unrighteous Judah, just as upon the entire world in the last days (chapter 1), the Lord's counsel to His people to avoid the destruction decreed against their enemies (chapter 2), and a panoramic view of the affairs of the righteous and the wicked at the Second Coming (chapter 3).

2. Zephaniah, son of Maaseiah (see Jeremiah 21:1), was the second priest, next in rank to the high priest, during the reign of Zedekiah (Jeremiah 21:1; 29:25, 29; 37:3). When Jerusalem was captured by the forces of

Nebuchadnezzar, Zephaniah was taken away and slain (see Jeremiah 52:24, 27; 2 Kings 25:18, 21).

3. Zephaniah was listed among the sons of Levi during the time of David (see 1 Chronicles 6:36).

4. Zephaniah was mentioned as the father of Josiah and Hen in the context of the vision seen by Zechariah concerning the "BRANCH," who is Christ (see Zechariah 6:10, 12).

ZERUBBABEL

(Meaning of the Assyrian name: born in Babylon.) Zerubbabel (pronounced zuh-roob'-uh-buhl)—grandson of Jehoiachin, king of Judah, and son of Pedaiah (see 1 Chronicles 3:16–19)—was appointed governor over Judea by the Persian authorities when Cyrus issued his decree in 537 BC allowing the captive Jewish people to return to Palestine (see Ezra 1:8, where Zerubbabel is called by the Persian name *Sheshbazzar, prince of Judah*). Zerubbabel rebuilt the altar and the temple in Jerusalem (see Ezra 3:2, 8; 4:2–3; 5:2), aided by the prophets Haggai (see Haggai 1:1–15; 2:1–23) and Zechariah (see Zechariah 4:6–10)—despite much opposition from the local tribes, including the Samaritans (see *Samaritans*). Scholar Sydney B. Sperry indicates the nature of the rebuilt temple:

> The plan of Solomon's temple was followed in general, but due to the poverty of the people, not on such a lavish scale. Many of the vessels used in the former temple were restored. (Ezra 1:7–11.) The Holy of Holies was empty, for the Ark of the Covenant disappeared when Nebuchadnezzar's forces invaded Palestine.
>
> This temple, called after Zerubbabel, and sometimes known as the Second Temple, was completed in the sixth year of Darius, 515 B.C. (Ezra 3:8; Ezra 6:15.) (Sidney B. Sperry, "Ancient Temples and Their Functions," *Ensign*, Jan. 1972, 67)

ZION

The name *Zion* appears many times in the Old Testament—mostly as a term indicating the place where the Lord's people dwell. However, in certain passages in Isaiah, the word takes on the nature of an appellation for the people themselves: "And I have put my words in thy mouth, and I have covered thee in the shadow of mine hand, that I may plant the heavens, and lay the foundations of the earth, and say unto Zion, Thou art my people" (Isaiah 51:16; see also 52:1–2, 6–7).

Zion consists of a people unified in the discipleship of the Redeemer, like unto the people of Enoch: "And the Lord called his people ZION, because they were of one heart and one mind, and dwelt in righteousness; and there was no poor among them" (Moses 7:18). Using the word *Zion* as a name for the people of the Lord is reinforced in latter-day scripture, as in the following passage from the Doctrine and Covenants: "Therefore, verily, thus saith the Lord, let Zion rejoice, for this is Zion—THE PURE IN HEART; therefore, let Zion rejoice, while all the wicked shall mourn" (97:21; compare 100:16).

ZIPPORAH

Zipporah (pronounced zih-pohr'-uh) was the wife of Moses and the daughter of Jethro (or Reuel), priest of Midian (see Exodus 2:21; 4:25; 18:2). She was the mother of the two sons of Moses, Gershom and Eliezer. Of her life we know very little, except that she intervened when the Lord was angry with Moses for failing to circumcise his son as commanded. As the Lord was about to fall upon Moses, Zipporah accomplished the circumcision herself and Moses was spared, humbly repenting before the Lord (see JST Exodus 4:24–27, in the Appendix of the Church's edition of the Bible).

IMPORTANT COMPARATIVE DATES
RELATING TO THE OLD TESTAMENT
AND PEARL OF GREAT PRICE

TRAD. DATING*	REVISED DATING**	EVENT	SCRIPTURAL REFERENCES THAT INCLUDE TIME FRAMES	SYNCHRONISMS FROM OTHER CULTURES
4000	—	Fall of Adam		
3870	—	Birth of Seth	Gen. 5:3–5	
3765	—	Birth of Enos	Gen. 5:6–8	
3675	—	Birth of Cainan	Gen. 5:9–11	
3605	—	Birth of Mahalaleel	Gen. 5:12–14	
3540	—	Birth of Jared	Gen. 5:15–17	
3478	—	Birth of Enoch	Gen. 5:18–20	
3313	—	Birth of Methusalah	Gen. 5:27	
	3150			Beginning of Hieroglyphic writing about this time; development of the calendar
3126	—	Birth of Lamech	Gen. 5:25	
3070	—	Death of Adam	Gen. 5:5; 2:17; 2 Pet. 3:8	
2958	—	Death of Seth	Gen. 5:8	
2957	—	Enoch translated	Gen. 5:23–24; Heb. 11:5–6	
2944	—	Birth of Noah	Gen. 5:28–31	
2860	—	Death of Enos	Gen. 5:11	
2778	—	Death of Cainan	Gen. 5:14	
2765	—	Death of Jared	Gen. 5:20	
2710	—	Death of Mahalaleel	Gen. 5:17	
	2600			The period of the pyramids of Egypt (ca. 2600–2500)
2442	—	Birth of Shem	Gen. 5:32; 11:10	
2349	—	Death of Lamech	Gen. 5:31	
2344	—	Death of Methuselah	Gen. 5:26–27; 7:6	
2344– 2343	2340– 2300	The Flood	Gen. 5:26–27; 7:6	
2343	—	Birth of Arphaxad, son of Shem	Gen. 11:10–11	
2307	—	Birth of Salah, son of Arphaxad	Gen. 11:12–13	
2277	—	Birth of Eber, son of Salah	Gen. 11:14–15	
2243	—	Birth of Peleg, son of Eber	Gen. 11:16; 10:25	

*Approximate dates B.C. from Biblical references
** Approximate dates B.C. from secular references

2243– 2004	—	"... in his [Peleg's] days the earth was divided"	Gen. 10:25; 10:32; Deut. 32:8; Acts 17:26
2213	—	Birth of Reu, son of Peleg	Gen. 11:18–19
2181	—	Birth of Serug, son of Reu	Gen. 11:20–21
2151	—	Birth of Nahor, son of Serug	Gen. 11:22–23
2122	—	Birth of Terah, son of Nahor	Gen. 11:24–25
2052	—	Birth of Abram, son of Terah	Gen. 11:26
2042	—	Sarai is born (Abram's future wife)	Gen. 17:17
2004	—	Death of Peleg	Gen. 11:19
2004	2004	Tower of Babel	Gen. 11:1; 9
2003	—	Death of Nahor	Gen. 11:25
1997	—	Death of Noah	Gen. 9:28–29
1994	—	Departure of Abram and Lot from Haran	Gen. 12:1–5
1974	—	Death of Reu	Gen. 11:21
	1968?	Abram settles in Hebron; ministry of Melchizedek in this time frame; Abram pays tithes to Melchizedek	JST, Gen. 14:25–40
1967	—	Marriage of Abram and Hagar	Gen. 16:3–4
1966	—	Birth of Ishmael, son of Abram	Gen. 16:16
1953	—	God's covenant with Abram (Abraham)	Gen. 17:25
1952	—	Birth of Isaac, son of Abraham	Gen. 17:17
1951	—	Death of Serug	Gen. 11:23
1947	—	Ishmael and Hagar are cast out	Gen. 21:14
1917	—	Death of Terah	Gen. 11:32
1915	—	Death of Sarah	Gen. 23:1–2
1912	—	Marriage of Isaac and Rebekah	Gen. 25:20
1904	—	Death of Arphaxad (son of Shem, grandson of Noah)	Gen. 11:13
1892	—	Birth of Jacob and Esau, sons of Isaac	Gen. 25:26

1877	—	Death of Abraham	Gen. 25:7
1874	—	Death of Salah	Gen. 11:14–15
1852	—	Marriage of Esau and Judith	Gen. 26:34
1842	—	Death of Shem	Gen. 11:11
1829	—	Death of Ishmael	Gen. 25:17
1816	—	Jacob asks for Rachel's hand	Gen. 29:18–21
1813	—	Death of Eber	Gen. 11:16–17
1809	—	Jacob is given Leah instead of Rachel (for whom he must work seven more years)	Gen. 29:25–30
1808	—	Birth of Reuben, son of Jacob and Leah	Gen. 29:32
1807	—	Birth of Simeon, son of Jacob and Leah	Gen. 29:33
1806	—	Birth of Levi, son of Jacob and Leah	Gen. 29:34
1805	—	Birth of Judah, son of Jacob and Leah	Gen. 29:35
1802	—	Marriage of Jacob and Rachel	—
1801	—	Birth of Joseph, son of Jacob and Rachel	Gen. 30:25–34
1796	—	Jacob completes tasks for Laban and leaves	Gen. 31:41
1795	—	Jacob's name changed to Israel	Gen. 32:28
1788	—	Around this time Benjamin is born to Jacob and Rachel; Rachel dies	Gen. 35:17–20
1784	—	Israel makes the coat of many colors for Joseph, who is sold into Egypt by his brothers	Gen. 37:2
1783	—	Joseph begins working for Potiphar	Gen. 39:1–6
1774	—	Joseph is made ruler over the house of Potiphar	Gen. 39:7–10
1773	—	Joseph is imprisoned on the basis of false accusations	Gen. 40:5
1772	—	Death of Isaac	Gen. 35:27–28; 41:46

1771	—	Joseph interprets the dream of Pharaoh	
1770	—	Joseph made ruler over all of Egypt, next to Pharaoh	Gen. 41:39–40
1762	—	Jacob moves to Egypt	Gen. 45:6–11; 47:9, 28
1671	—	Death of Joseph	Gen. 50:26
1669	—	Death of Levi	Ex. 6:16
1630	—	Birth of Aaron	Ex. 7:7
1627	—	Birth of Moses	Gen. 15:12–16
1587	—	Birth of Joshua	Joshua 14:7
1547	1547	The Exodus (when Moses was 80 years old)	Ex. 7:7, Gen. 15:16
1507	—	Death (translation) of Moses; end of the Wandering; Joshua takes Israel into the promised land	Deut. 34:7–9; Numbers 32:13
1506	—	Beginning of the wars with the nations of Palestine	
1502	—	Fifth year of the wars; period of rest begins	Joshua 14:10, 15
1501	—	Joshua begins his tenure as judge only	
1477	—	Death of Joshua	Judges 2:8
1468	—	Commencement of the period of the judges, beginning with Othniel	Judges 3:9–11
1429	—	Death of Othniel	Judges 3:11
1387	—	Tenure of Ehud as judge begins (Shamgar also acts as deliverer)	Judges 3:15, 31
1331	—	Death of Ehud	
1310	—	Tenure of Deborah as judge and prophetess	Judges 4:4
1271	—	Death of Deborah	Judges 5:31
1263	—	Tenure of Gideon as judge	Judges 6:11–16
1224	—	Gideon (Jerubbaal) refuses to be king of Israel	Judges 8:22, 28
1223	—	Birth of Abimelech, son of Gideon	Judges 8:31–33

	1190			Period of the legendary Trojan War
1157	—	Jephthah made captain of Israel's armies	Judges 11:1–11	
1152	—	Death of Jephthah	Judges 12:7	
1126	—	Tenure of Eli as judge occurs around this time; Samson acts as deliverer during this period as well	Judges 13–16	
1125	—	Birth of Samuel around this time; Samuel is soon placed in service to Eli	1 Sam. 2:18, 26	
1107	—	Samuel recognized as a prophet by the people	1 Sam. 3:20	
1096	1095	Birth of David occurs around this time; reign of Saul over the next period		Tiglath-pilesar I is king of Assyria around this time
1066	—	Death of Samuel and Saul. David made king over the house of Judah. David retrieves the ark out of Kirjathjearim.	2 Sam. 2:4; 1 Chron. 13:5–6	
	1063	David annointed by Samuel		
	1055	David made king in Hebron		
	1047	David made king in Jerusalem		
	1047	Ministry of the prophets Nathan and Gad		
1026	1015	Death of David. Ascension of Solomon	1 Kings 2:12	
1022	1012	Solomon commences building the temple	1 Kings 6:37–38	Hiram is king of Tyre in this time frame
1015	991	Temple completed and dedicated	1 Kings 6:38; 8:1–2, 65–66; 2 Chron. 7:9–10	

986	975	Commencement of reign of 22-year Jeroboam of Israel; revolt of the Ten Tribes from Rehoboam	1 Kings 14:20–21	Shishak is king of Egypt in this time frame
985	975	Commencement of 17-year reign of Rehoboam of Judah		
969	932	Commencement of 3-year reign of Abijah (Abijam) of Judah	1 Kings 15:1; 2 Chron. 13:21	
967	929	Commencement of 41-year reign of Asa of Judah	1 Kings 15:9	
965	927	Commencement of 2-year reign of Nadab of Israel	1 Kings 15:25	
964	925	Commencement of 24-year reign of Baasha of Israel	1 Kings 15:28, 33	
941	901	Commencement of 2-year reign of Elah of Israel	1 Kings 16:8	
936	897	Commencement of 12-year reign of Omri of Israel	1 Kings 16:23	
929	875	Commencement of 22-year reign of Ahab of Israel	Joshua 6:26; 1 Kings 16:29	
926	873	Commencement of 35-year reign of Jehoshaphat of Judah; beginning of ministry of the prophet Elijah; rebuilding of Jericho	1 Kings 22:41–42	
909	853	Commencement of 8-year reign of Ahaziah of Israel	1 Kings 22:51	
908	851	Commencement of 12-year reign of Jehoram of Israel; beginning of ministry of the prophet Elisha if the revised dating is correct	2 Kings 3:1	

904	848	Commencement of 8-year reign of Jehoram (Joram) of Judah	2 Kings 8:16	
898	844	Commencement of 8-year reign of Ahaziah of Judah	2 Kings 9:29	
897	843	Commencement of 28-year reign of Jehu of Israel	2 Kings 8:25–26	
897	843	Commencement of 6-year reign of Athaliah Queen of Judah	2 Kings 11:1–3; 2 Chron. 22:10–12	
891	837	Commencement of 40-year reign of Joash of Judah; the time of the prophecies of Joel	2 Kings 11:4; 12:1	
869	—	Commencement of 17-year reign of Jehoahaz of Israel	2 Kings 13:1	
855	798	Commencement of 16-year reign of Jehoash of Israel	2 Kings 14:1; 13:10	It is thought that the Greek poet Homer flourished sometime in the period 800 to 700
854	—	Commencement of 29-year reign of Amaziah of Israel	2 Kings 14:1; 2 Chron. 24:25; 25:1	
840	790	Commencement of reign of Jeroboam II of Israel	2 Kings 15:1	
	790–749	Ministry of Jonah occurred during this period		
825	—	Commencement of 52-year reign of Azariah of Israel	2 Kings 14:21	
794	—	Commencement of period of interregnum	2 Kings 15:8–17	
788	749	Commencement of brief reign of Zachariah of Israel	2 Kings 15:8	
787	748	Commencement of brief reign of Shallum of Israel, followed by 10-year reign of Menahem of Israel	2 Kings 15:13, 17	

776	—	Commencement of 2-year reign of Pekahiah of Israel	2 Kings 15:23	First Olympic games held in Greece (776)
774	—	Commencement of 20-year reign of Pekah of Israel	2 Kings 15:27	
773	740	Commencement of 25-year reign of Jotham of Israel	2 Kings 15:32–33	
758	734	Commencement of 16-year reign of Ahaz of Judah		
757	733	Commencement of 9-year reign of Hoshea of Israel	2 Kings 17:1	
750–740	—	It is probably in this general time frame that the prophet Hosea and the prophet Amos commenced their ministry	Book of Hosea; Book of Amos	Legendary founding of Rome around 750 by Romulus and Remus
755	728	Commencement of 29-year reign of Hezekiah of Judah	2 Kings 18:1; 2 Chron. 29:1	
740	—	Commencement of 39-year ministry of Isaiah (740–701)		
	728–699	The time frame for the ministry of the prophet Micah	Book of Micah	
721	722	End of the Northern Kingdom	2 Kings 18:9–10	Conquest of Israel by Shalmanesar of Assyria
693	697	Commencement of the 55-year reign of Manasseh of Judah	2 Kings 21:1	
	670			The Republic founded in Athens about this time
639	642	Commencement of 2-year reign of Amon of Judah; ministry of Nahum might well be around this time	2 Kings 21:17–19	
638	640	Commencement of 31-year reign of Josiah of Judah	2 Kings 21:23–26; 22:1–2	
639–608	640	Time frame for the ministry of the prophet Zephaniah	Book of Zephaniah	

626	628	Commencement of 23-year ministry of the prophet Jeremiah	Jer. 25:1–4	
625	—	Commencement of the Babylonian Empire		Nabopolassar defeats the Assyrians; Babylonian Empire launched
621	—	Law of Moses discovered in the temple	2 Kings 22:3; 23:22	
612	606	End of Assyrian Empire		Nabopolassar and Cyazares destroy Nineveh, effectively ending Assyrian Empire
608	609	Commencement of short reign of Jehoahaz of Judah	2 Kings 23:31–33	Nebuchadnezzar fights Assyrians; King Josiah killed
607	609	Commencement of 11-year reign of Eliakim (Jehoiakim) of Judah	2 Kings 23:34–37	
605	—	Ascension year of Nebuchadnezzar	Daniel 1:1; 2 Kings 24:12	Nebuchadnezzar comes into power
604	—	Many Jews taken captive to Babylon, including Daniel, during this time period		Nebuchadnezzar defeats Pharaoh Necho in the battle of Carchemish and then reigns 43 years as King of Babylon
604–600	—	During this period the prophet Daniel commences his ministry	Book of Daniel	
600	598	Perhaps the time frame for the ministry of the prophet Habakkuk	Book of Habakkuk	
597	598	Commencement of reign of Zedekiah of Judah (following brief reign of Jehoiachin, who is taken captive); commencement of the ministry of Lehi and also of his son Nephi	2 Kings 24:18; 1 Ne. 1:4; 5:12–13; Hel. 8:21	
592–593	—	Ministry of Ezekiel begins and lasts until 570	Ezekiel 1:1–2	
589	—	Siege of Jerusalem	2 Kings 25:1	Nebuchadnezzar lays siege to Jerusalem

587	—	Destruction of Jerusalem, including the temple	Jer. 44:30; 52:12–13; 2 Kings 25:8–10	Nebuchadnezzar destroys the city and takes many captive to Babylon
587	609?	Probably also the time frame for the ministry of the prophet Obadiah		
587–585	—	Jeremiah writes the Lamentations	Book of Lamentations	
562	—	Death of Nebuchadnezzar		
561	561	Release of Jehoiachin from prison by the Babylonians		Evil-merodach king of Babylon
	555			Belshazzar as co-regent of Babylon with Nabonidus
538	559	Babylon defeated	Jer. 27:6–7; Ezra 1:1; Isa. 44:26–28; 45:1–5	Cyrus (Darius) the Persian defeats Babylon and reigns 9 years
537	—	Decree of Cyrus (Darius) to allow the Jews to return to their land and rebuild the temple	Ezra 2:36; 3:12; 1 Chron. 24:11; 2 Chron. 31:15; Neh. 7:7; 12:1, 7, 10, 26	The Greek philosopher and mathematician Pythagoras flourished around this time
	536	Joshua as high priest		
	525			Birth of Greek playwright Aeschylus (525–456)
519–520	—	Time frame for the ministry of the prophet Haggai and the prophet Zechariah	Haggai 2:10–18; Zech. 1:12–17	
485	496			Birth of Greek playwright Sophocles (496?–406)
	486	Commencement of reign of Xerxes	Esther 1:1	Accession of Xerxes, King of Persia (ruled 21 years: 486–465)
479	—	Service of Esther takes place around this time	Book of Esther	
	470?–399			Life span of Socrates, Greek philosopher
463	—	Commencement of reign of Artaxerxes, son of Xerxes	Ezra 7:1	Accession of Artaxerxes, King of Persia (ruled 39 years)
	460?–400?			Life span of Greek historian Thucydides, chronicler of the Peloponnesian War

459	—	Repatriation of many of the captive Jews		
457	458	Ezra receives the order to rebuild the city and set up a government	Dan. 9:26, 25–27	
444	—	Ministry of Nehemiah on behalf of the Jews occurred around this time; he was appointed governor of Judaea	Neh. 2:1; 5:14	Parthenon in Athens completed around this time
	432	Nehemiah's second mission to Jerusalem		
430	432	Ministry of the prophet Malachi takes place		
	431–404			Peloponnesian War 431–404
	427			Birth of Plato (427?–347?)
	424			Accession of Darius II
	359			Accession of Philip, king of Macedon
	332			Alexander in Syria and Egypt
	330			Darius III slain; end of Persian hegemony
	323			Death of Alexander the Great

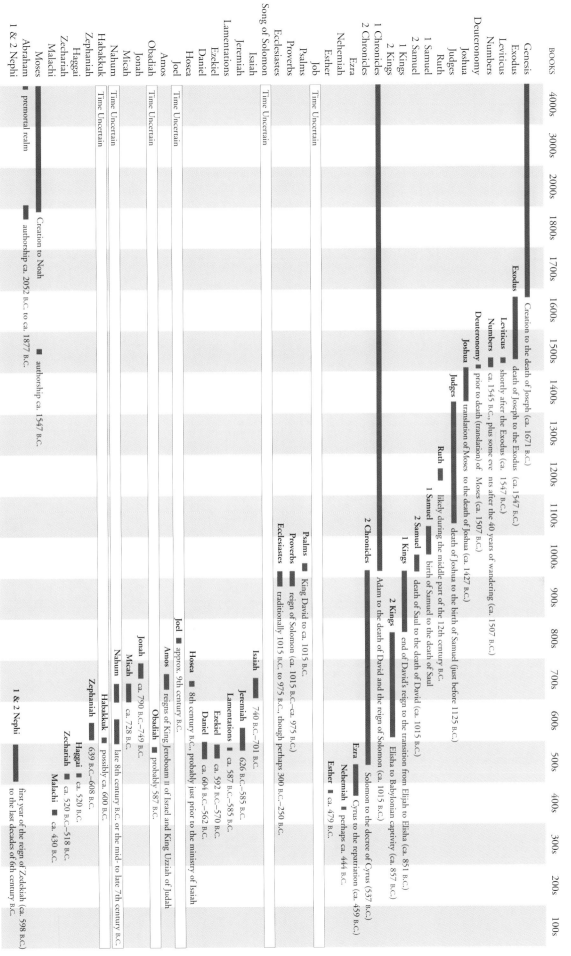

CHRONOLOGY OF THE BOOKS OF THE OLD TESTAMENT AND PEARL OF GREAT PRICE

BOOKS																																						

Genesis — Creation to the death of Joseph (ca. 1671 B.C.)

Exodus — death of Joseph to the Exodus (ca. 1547 B.C.)

Leviticus — shortly after the Exodus (ca. 1547 B.C.)

Numbers — ca. 1545 B.C., plus some events after the 40 years of wandering (ca. 1507 B.C.)

Deuteronomy — prior to death (translation) of Moses (ca. 1507 B.C.)

Joshua — translation of Moses to the death of Joshua (ca. 1427 B.C.)

Judges — death of Joshua to the birth of Samuel (just before 1125 B.C.)

Ruth — likely during the middle part of the 12th century B.C.

1 Samuel — birth of Samuel to the death of Saul

2 Samuel — death of Saul to the death of David (ca. 1015 B.C.)

1 Kings — end of David's reign to the transition from Elijah to Elisha (ca. 851 B.C.)

2 Kings — Elisha to Babylonian captivity (ca. 857 B.C.)

1 Chronicles — Adam to the death of David and the reign of Solomon (ca. 1015 B.C.)

2 Chronicles — Solomon to the decree of Cyrus (537 B.C.)

Ezra — Cyrus to the reparriation (ca. 459 B.C.)

Nehemiah — perhaps ca. 444 B.C.

Esther — ca. 479 B.C.

Job — Time Uncertain

Psalms — King David to ca. 1015 B.C.

Proverbs — reign of Solomon (ca. 1015 B.C.–ca. 975 B.C.)

Ecclesiastes — traditionally 1015 B.C. to 975 B.C., though perhaps 300 B.C.–250 B.C.

Song of Solomon — Time Uncertain

Isaiah — 740 B.C.–701 B.C.

Jeremiah — 626 B.C.–585 B.C.

Lamentations — ca. 587 B.C.–585 B.C.

Ezekiel — ca. 592 B.C.–570 B.C.

Daniel — ca. 604 B.C.–562 B.C.

Hosea — 8th century B.C., probably just prior to the ministry of Isaiah

Joel — approx. 9th century B.C.

Amos — reigns of King Jeroboam II of Israel and King Uzziah of Judah

Obadiah — probably 587 B.C.

Jonah — ca. 790 B.C.–749 B.C.

Micah — ca. 728 B.C.

Nahum — late 8th century B.C. or the mid- to late 7th century B.C.

Habakkuk — possibly ca. 600 B.C.

Zephaniah — 639 B.C.–608 B.C.

Haggai — ca. 520 B.C.

Zechariah — ca. 520 B.C.–518 B.C.

Malachi — ca. 430 B.C.

Abraham — premortal realm; authorship ca. 2052 B.C. to ca. 1877 B.C.

Moses — Creation to Noah; authorship ca. 1547 B.C.

1 & 2 Nephi — first year of the reign of Zedekiah (ca. 598 B.C.) to the last decades of 6th century B.C.

ART CREDITS

Page 175   *King Solomon Petitioning the Lord in Prayer* © Robert T. Barrett.

Page 177   *An Atonement Sacrifice Is Presented to the Priests* © Robert T. Barrett.

Page 183   *Uzziah's Pride and Punishment* by A.M. Boon © Intellectual Reserve, Inc. Courtesy of the Church History Museum.

Page 185   *Solomon Is Anointed King* by Julius Schnorr von Carolsfeld, *Treasury of Bible Illustrations*, Dover Publications.

Page 188   *Jerusalem Is Despoiled* by Julius Schnorr von Carolsfeld, *Treasury of Bible Illustrations*, Dover Publications.